THE BLACK LIGHTS

Inside the World of Professional Boxing

THOMAS HAUSER

A FIRESIDE BOOK
Published by Simon & Schuster
New York   London   Toronto   Sydney   Tokyo   Singapore

Fireside
Simon & Schuster Building
Rockefeller Center
1230 Avenue of the Americas
New York, New York 10020

First Fireside Edition 1991
Published by arrangement with the author.

FIRESIDE and colophon are registered trademarks
of Simon & Schuster Inc.

Manufactured in the United States of America

1   3   5   7   9   10   8   6   4   2   Pbk.

Library of Congress Cataloging in Publication Data
Hauser, Thomas.
The black lights: inside the world of professional boxing/
Thomas Hauser.—1st Fireside ed.
p.   cm.
Reprint. First published: New York: McGraw-Hill, © 1986.
"A Fireside book."
1. Boxing.   2. Professional sports.   I. Title.
GV1133.H34   1991
796.8'3—dc20   90-28284
CIP
ISBN 0-671-69393-X Pbk.

*For Ed Nordlinger and Bonnie Levine,
two very special people*

They say when you get hit and hurt bad you see black lights—the black lights of unconsciousness. But I don't know nothing about that. I've had twenty-eight fights and twenty-eight wins. I ain't never been stopped.

—Muhammad Ali, 1967

On November 3, 1984, Billy Costello fought to defend his World Boxing Council superlightweight championship. This is a book about that fight and about the sport and business of professional boxing.

PART

1

To understand boxing, you have to understand tradition and what it takes to get inside a ring. You have to learn about promoters and television and what goes on inside a fighter's head from the time his career begins until the day it ends. You have to grasp the reality of smashed faces and pain, and understand how they can be part of something courageous, exciting, and beautiful. I know, I've been there. I co-managed Gerry Cooney and made ten million dollars with him. If he'd beaten Larry Holmes it would have changed the face of sports in America. I signed Howard Davis to a contract out of the Olympics, and got him more money than anyone could have dreamed. I managed Wilford Scypion, and was in his corner the night he battered Willie Classen. I lived through it with Wilford when Classen died. And after everything, I can look you square in the eye and tell you boxing is beautiful—the purest sport in the world. You can knock promoters; you can knock trainers, managers, even fighters. But don't knock boxing. It's the best sport there is, and anyone who's ever been involved will tell you it's an honor to be associated with boxing.

—Mike Jones,
Manager

Boxing people are a special breed, denizens of a strange world that few outsiders see and even fewer understand. It's a dark world that takes what's most savage in man and pushes it center stage against a backdrop of exploitation and pain. But beyond the spectacle of violent confrontation, boxing offers courage and beauty, loyalty and strength. Its adherents live in a world of flattened noses, scarred faces, beautifully muscled bodies, and the will to overcome insurmountable odds. Many people who watch a professional fight are physically revulsed. They never want to go back again. But for others, boxing is a narcotic—the most pervasive of drugs—and once hooked, they never get it out of their system.

Mike Jones is hooked on boxing. Born in Brooklyn, fifty years old, he stands six feet tall, one hundred eighty pounds. His long, curly brown hair is receding in front. Depending on the mood of the moment, his expression alternates between a warm smile and slightly disgruntled look. A fight manager by trade, Mike is as decent as the business allows. In an environment where most people have only allies, he has friends. To his fighters, he's a professional who guides them with cunning and care. To promoters, he's a man who doesn't walk out on a deal once it's been made. To the television networks and print media, he's a salesman, but a salesman they trust. He never takes an average interest in anything he does. Whatever he undertakes is done with intensity, or not at all. He's fortunate in that his livelihood involves what he loves to do. "It's not the money," he's said more than once. "I can't prove that because I've been financially successful, but boxing means more to me than dollars and cents. It's my way of life. How many people get to make their fantasies come true?"

Mike Jones's fantasies are rooted in simple instincts and a time long ago. Man's first weapons were his fists. Self-preservation is nature's first law. From these axioms boxing has evolved— not like other sports, but from personal combat ungoverned by rules, which is not a sport at all. The ancient Greeks were the first to make boxing a "sport," and for the most part their combatants were free men. The Romans forced gladiatorial slaves into combat wearing cesti weighted with iron spikes on their hands. Then boxing as entertainment disappeared, and for well over a millennium was largely unknown. Not until the 1600s did it surface again, this time in England, the "cradle of modern pugilism."

In England as elsewhere men had long settled grudges with their hands. In the late seventeenth century some with superior talent began touring the countryside, engaging in contests for side bets. Soon these matches, which consisted largely of wrestling and throwing an opponent to the ground, became staples at county fairs. The fighters themselves were anonymous; the audience cared little or not at all for the men involved. Thereafter, the sport evolved. By 1900 there were world champions in eight divisions, and succeeding generations of champions came to trace their lineage like members of British royalty. But instead of identifying with the House of Windsor or House of Tudor, the ancestors were members of different weight lines. And as the years progressed there grew into legend a group of fighters regarded as gods.

Jack Dempsey, one of the early gods, reigned as heavyweight champion of the world during the "Golden Age" of Babe Ruth, Bill Tilden, and Red Grange. After winning the title in 1919, he became the greatest drawing card in the history of sports. On September 23, 1926, over 120,000 people jammed Sesquicentennial Stadium in Philadelphia to watch him defend his crown against Gene Tunney. One year later, their rematch drew live gate receipts of $2,658,660—a record that stood for fifty years. Joe Louis was perhaps the greatest fighter in the heavyweight line. His fists were weapons that seemed to fire automatically. Fighting Joe Louis in his prime was like staying in the casino too long. Eventually, you knew, you were going to lose. Rocky Marciano compiled a record as heavyweight champion that stands unsurpassed in any weight division—49 fights, 43 knockouts, 49 wins. After a man fought Marciano he was never quite the same. All Marciano seemed to want to do was punch in the ring. He moved forward, arms pounding, hands coming from every angle, anxious to make contact with any part of an opponent's body. And always he had one simple idea in mind—to trade punches and test who could take and give more pain.

But boxing's gods weren't limited to one size. Benny Leonard, who reigned as world lightweight champion from 1917 through 1923, lost three fights by the age of sixteen, and then only two more in a career that spanned 210 bouts over twenty-one years. Willie Pep, world featherweight champion for seven years, invented moves that other fighters studied and have employed ever since. Pep won his first 62 fights, lost a ten-round decision, then went through 73 more bouts before losing again. Archie Moore began his career in 1935 with a second-round knockout of Piano Mover Jones in Hot Springs, Arkansas. Denied the chance to fight for a world title until 1952, he captured the light-heavyweight crown at age 39 and held onto it for ten years. When Moore retired, nine months shy of his fiftieth birthday, it was with 199 wins and a record 145 knockouts in the ring.

Old champions are often cherished by men who were young when they were. They bring back memories of things past and simpler times, like the most beautiful girl at a long-ago high-school prom. But boxing's mythic fighters offer more than memories: they raised their sport to a level of myth and artistry known in few endeavors. Witness the career of Sugar Ray Robinson.

Robinson's first professional fight was a second-round knockout of Joe Escheverria in Madison Square Garden on October 4, 1940. His last was a ten-round decision in Pittsburgh on November 10, 1965. In 201 fights spanning 25 years—a career that began before Pearl Harbor and ended at the height of the war in Vietnam—Sugar Ray Robinson was knocked out only once, by Joey Maxim when he challenged for the world lightheavyweight title and collapsed from heat prostration after dominating Maxim for thirteen rounds. From 1943 through 1951, Robinson had 91 consecutive bouts without a loss. In his first 131 professional fights he was beaten once—on a ten-round decision by Jake LaMotta. He beat LaMotta five times.

There's no such thing as perfection in boxing, but Sugar Ray Robinson as a welterweight in his prime came very close. "I'd like to be remembered as one of the greatest fighters of all time," is a refrain one often hears from young fighters. "I can't be remembered as *the* greatest because that was Sugar Ray Robinson." "Pound for pound," Joe Louis once said, "Ray Robinson was the greatest fighter to ever enter the ring. He was the best fighter who ever lived."

"Do you think you can hurt him?" Robinson was asked once of an opponent before a fight.

"I can hurt anybody. The question is, can I hurt him enough?"

"Are you worried about the referee?"

Robinson held up his fists. "I got my referees right here."

At the end of his career, "the greatest fighter who ever lived" was asked what he liked least about boxing.

"Getting hit," he answered.

Recently, aging badly and suffering from what is believed to be Alzheimer's disease, Robinson commented on his status as the greatest fighter of all time: "It's the most wonderful feeling in the world. I can't say any more. I loved boxing, and every time I hear someone say 'pound for pound' . . ." His voice trailed off, then picked up again. "It's the most wonderful feeling in the world."

But what kind of world is it? When two men are paid to step into a ring together, inflict corporal damage, and beat one another senseless, what does it mean?

Boxing is known as "the sweet science" and "the manly art of self-defense," but essentially it is an attacking sport. A fighter punches to hurt and disable his opponent. Gloves are worn to protect the fists, not the brain. It's the most violent activity condoned by man except for certain phases of law enforcement and war. Some fights are such patent mismatches that the crowd isn't paying to watch a competitive battle; it's paying to watch someone get beaten up. This thirst for blood is widespread, and has led many to suggest that boxing is a skill, not a sport at all.

"The sport dignified by the name of boxing," it has been written, "is not a sport, but a vicious man-destroying racket that seduces healthy kids with the promise of glory, squeezes blood money out of them, and then callously tosses them aside." As for fans, one observer declared, "They crowd into boxing halls and stadiums to feast their eyes on bruises and swollen lips; on the spectacle of some boxer having his senses, strength and the power to remain upright bashed out of him. If these people were honest, they would admit that boxing as boxing does not attract them at all. They would speak of it as a dull, unentertaining sight, a waste of time. Then, supposing the frankness lasted, they would go on to say that what they really want is smashing punches that sap consciousness. Boxing as a skill or an art would never draw them to watch or induce them to pay admission. Fighting is what they want to see."

There can be no doubt that boxing is a cruel sport; violent ballet in freestyle; a primitive form of social Darwinism. But looking beyond the blood and violence one sees more—something that has made boxing the only sport practiced and cheered the world over, something that tells us much about human potential and about ourselves.

Man is obsessed with victory. Winning is the foundation of sports mythology. Boxing simply carries these truths one step further. Rather than employing a simple test of winning and losing, it is conquest and destruction, pure competition, man against man. Like other sports it requires skill. More than other sports it demands courage. Boxers know the dangers of their trade, and accept them as part of the challenge. They climb into a ring, virtually naked, fully exposed, to face an awful, terrifying, exhilarating moment of truth when all they have to work with and protect themselves are their hands.

"How come you like boxing so much?" is the question asked of Eddie Brown, middleweight contender in W. C. Heinz's novel *The Professional*. And Brown answers, "Because I find so much in it. The basic law of man. The truth of life. It's a fight, man against man, and if you're going to defeat another man, defeat him completely. Don't starve him to death like they do 'in the fine, clean competitive world of commerce. Leave him lying there, senseless on the floor."

Boxing is a microcosm of life. It excites people. It's ingrown.

When two children fight in the school playground, other children gather, watch, and cheer one or the other on. The sport, like life, is "sudden death." A fighter can lose at any time; yet no matter how far behind he can maintain hope of winning until the very end.

Boxing is the epitome of aggression, but aggression is central to all competitive sports. Bobby Fischer, the greatest chess player of modern times, once remarked, "Chess is like war. The object is to crush the other man's mind. I like to see them squirm." Injury? Automobile racers are killed. Hockey players lose their teeth, and are cut to ribbons.

The reality of life is that we live in a violent world. Boxers and boxing fans let their violence out in a far more socially acceptable manner than nations that build nuclear weapons capable of destroying the planet we live on many times over.

The sport will endure.

Most fighters come from tough places; small beginnings where life is hard.

Billy Costello was born in Kingston, New York, on April 10, 1956. His father was a professional gambler—pool, dice, anything that paid, but mostly cards. His mother, a nurses' aid, took primary responsibility for raising seven children in a house that has since been torn down.

"Growing up in Kingston was all right," Billy remembers, "but there were times it was hard. My father's white and my mother is Asian Indian. People were always calling me a half-breed and zebra. A lot of black guys were mad at me because, even though I looked black, I joined the Boy Scouts and had friendships with white kids too. To get ahead, it seemed I always had to try harder than other people. Everyone was always telling me, 'Billy, you can't do this' and 'Billy, you can't do that.' But all that ever did was make me more determined than before."

Somehow for Billy Costello the right lessons took hold. "I'd watch my father play pool," he recalls. "My father could sit in a chair and shoot pool. He could play with a broomstick instead of a cue, and win that way too. Lots of people watch a pool hustler, and all they see is a bum. But what I saw was, to play pool and outhustle the other hustlers, he had to practice seven, eight hours a day. That's hard. I'm not a gambler. I don't play pool. I don't shoot craps. I play poker for dimes, nothing more.

But watching my father, I learned if you don't want something bad enough to do it right, don't do it at all."

As Billy Costello made his way through adolescence the learning process continued. "I wasn't a very good student," he admits, "but I always knew it was important for me to graduate from school. In sports I had natural talent for baseball, and figured maybe someday I'd make it in the pros. Drugs?" He shakes his head, then goes on. "The worst thing that ever happened to me was with drugs in ninth grade. I'd never tried any of that stuff before, but one day, during lunch period in the school cafeteria, one of my friends had this little orange pill. He said, 'Man, this little pill will fuck up your mind,' and I laughed at him. 'That little thing? Bullshit!' So he gave me the pill. I took it and didn't feel nothing; went to my next class, which was music with a Chinese teacher named Mr. Soong. So Mr. Soong was playing on the piano, Mozart or something, and I started hearing weird sounds—bang, whap, zoom! I said to myself, 'Oh boy, this shit is taking off on me.' I told Mr. Soong I didn't feel good, and asked to go to the nurse's office. He let me go, and on the way I stopped in the bathroom, looked in the mirror, and everything was wobbling like Twilight Zone. Then I went to the nurse, really scared. I walked into her office, and saw a lamb sitting behind the desk. Then the lamb changed into the nurse, and I told her I didn't feel good. All she said was I should go in the back room and lie down. So I lay down, and all the time I'm thinking, 'Why did I do this shit?' Meanwhile, I'm hot; I'm cold; I'm happy; I'm sad. At three o'clock the nurse told me it was time to go home, so I walked down the hall and it was a thousand miles long. I was wobbling, and everybody was staring at me. I got on the school bus, and started touching everybody to make sure they were real. It was like I was in a picture, reaching out from the glass behind the frame. I felt spiders crawling on me—worms, bugs, everything. There was no way I could face my father like that, so when the bus left me off I walked around until midnight before I went home. Let me tell you, it's weird that a little thing smaller than a pebble can make you lose your mind. But if you ask me about drugs—acid, cocaine, all that stuff—I can do without it. I've learned."

At sixteen Billy began to date Jane Kirk, an attractive auburn-haired girl one year his junior. Later they would be married, but not until Jane had graduated from college and Billy was a professional fighter with ten wins and no losses at age 24. "It was hard to form an opinion about him at first," Jane remembers. "He was kind of awkward and very shy. Sometimes we had trouble talking to one another. And let's be honest—Kingston's a small place and there was lots of prejudice. I'm white, and people looked on Billy as black. It was hard."

Meanwhile Billy's accomplishments as a baseball player continued to grow. There was talk of a professional career and scouts coming to Kingston High School to see what he could do. Any athlete's career is a matter of speculation, and regarding young athletes, the maxims of uncertainty hold particularly true. But before Billy Costello's talents on the baseball field could be fairly tested, his life took a shattering downward turn.

"There were five of us," he recalls. "Four friends and me. I don't know why we did it. It was just something the five of us decided to do. Duane and Cory worked cash registers in a supermarket. We had this plan where Ronnie, Raymond, and I would go into the store wearing masks, and Duane and Cory would give us the money. The store was open until midnight; we came in about eight at night. Ronnie had a paper bag over his head; Raymond and I were wearing monster masks. No one else was there. We went over to the cash registers like we'd planned, laughing, and said, 'Give us the money.' Then this old lady came in, and suddenly it wasn't funny no more. Ronnie pulled out a gun—I swear, I never knew he had it—pointed it at the lady, and told her to shut up. Then we took the money and ran. Altogether we got about seven thousand dollars. Duane was the first to get caught. He started to feel guilty, and turned himself in. Then the police found Ronnie's gun in a hedge behind the store, and traced the fingerprints to his record as a youth offender. After that it was just a matter of time, so I turned myself in. That's how I wound up in jail. My parents left me there for three days to teach me a lesson. I nearly went crazy. All I can say is, I'd never done nothing bad like that before, and I ain't gonna do nothing like that again."

When word of Billy's arrest leaked out, his high school baseball coach kicked him off the team. Now, suddenly, Billy Costello was a frightened young man, stripped of his future, facing jail. Several friends asked the coach to reinstate him. The coach re-

11

fused. Major-league scouts were no longer interested. There was no place to turn.

Then the judicial process worked its will. Because Billy Costello had never before been in trouble with the law, he would be sentenced to probation as a youthful offender, with one condition—that he participate in a Police Athletic League program. "They had some boxing equipment at the gym," Billy remembers, "and I figured, why not try it? One day on the heavy bag, and it was like God saying to me, this is what you're supposed to do."

But what is it that fighters do? What's a fighter?

"The average person," says Sugar Ray Leonard, "has very little understanding of what goes on in boxing. They think back to when they were kids or whenever it was they saw two people fighting for the first time—a real fight with people trying to hurt each other. Maybe they saw someone get his mouth cut up, or a broken nose. That's what people think of when they watch boxing. But there's a difference between being the toughest kid on the street and knowing how to fight. A lot of guys are undefeated in street fights and big losers in the ring. That," concludes Leonard, "is because boxing is more than a sport. It's a skill."

Who are the people who become boxers? First and foremost they are physically gifted young men. Boxing is largely a test of will, and between two fighters of comparable skill, the man with the greater will most often prevails. But sometimes a fighter's skill—his conditioning, experience, intelligence, and physical attributes—is so superior that he can win without his will being seriously tested. And in any event, to be a quality fighter one must be endowed with physical assets far beyond those of ordinary men.

The average sports fan believes that, with maximum effort and proper training from an early age, he could have become a professional athlete. He could have played golf in the United States Open or tennis at Wimbledon, baseball in the major leagues, or a comparable sport with professional skill. Polls show that over one-half of all American men believe this to be true, yet this perception of what it takes to be an athlete is ludicrously wrong. The average American couldn't hit a major-league fastball because he doesn't have the reflexes to meet it or the innate power, no matter how fully developed, in his wrists and arms. No matter how hard he trained he'd lack the combination of agility, timing, and power that propels John McEnroe in tennis, the speed and endurance that mark long-distance runners like Alberto Salazar. Boxing requires all of these physical attributes and then some. However, many young men are athletically gifted, and relatively few turn to boxing. Thus the question of what impels people to become fighters requires further examination.

Boxing today, and boxing always, belongs to the poor. It begins in ghettos, where life is cheap and physical well-being is at risk in the food people eat and the absence of proper medical care in their daily lives. It breeds in an environment where residents carry knives and guns for protection, and fists are perceived as the least potent of weapons. "For me, for most fighters, it began on the streets," says Michael Spinks, who won a gold medal at the Montreal Olympics and later became lightheavyweight champion of the world. "I had to know how to hurt somebody in order to protect myself, to get them to leave me alone."

How can Michael Spinks make a living from hurting someone? "Put yourself in the position of a woman who's just been raped," he answers. "Could that woman hit and hurt her attacker?" A lot of fighters have been raped by society, many brutalized physically and psychologically in their own homes. Life for them has seldom been fair. Eventually they leave school, as graduates or dropouts, and good jobs aren't there. To make money they can run numbers, sell drugs, work forty hours a week for minimum wage or, if physically gifted, become fighters.

"Finding fighting was the best thing that ever happened to me," says former heavyweight champion Floyd Patterson. "I didn't care about other sports. I disliked school. I ran away from home a lot, and spent most of my time hiding in a subway tunnel. Then one day I went to a gym and saw people hitting the speed bag. It looked so pretty, and the sound was so good. For the first time in my life, I had something to do."

"If I didn't box," says former lightheavyweight champion Eddie Mustafa Muhammad, "I would have been a bank robber. At times that's what I wanted to be. I didn't want to sell dope. I wanted to be the best, so I wanted to be a bank robber."

Poverty wears most people down, but it spurs others on with powerful incentive and anger. In a perfect world boxing might not exist. But the world is not perfect, and in the eyes of many, thousands of young men are better off because of boxing.

Jimmy Glenn operates the Times Square Boxing Club on 42nd Street just east of Seventh Avenue in Manhattan. He's one of many trainers who've spent their lives teaching boxing to youngsters. "I believe in boxing," says Glenn. "A tough kid goes into a gym and finds out he can't lick everyone. All of a sudden he isn't so tough anymore. Then he starts to admit his shortcomings, and tries to improve in other areas as well. After a while that young man has a sense of responsibility and confidence he never had before. But don't take my word for it," Glenn continues. "Walk into any gym. You'll get more respect, see more hard work and discipline coming from youngsters than you would anywhere else in the world. Young men who have fought the system all their lives go into a gym, and all of a sudden they're willing to live and abide by the rules."

Ray Arcel, who has trained a score of world champions in his 85 years, concurs. "Too many people don't take pride in what they do," says Arcel. "They do just enough to get by, maybe to hold onto their jobs, and that's all. A fighter can't be like that. Boxing, if it's done right, takes kids from poor backgrounds at a trouble-prone age, and gives them the belief that they can make something of themselves if they're disciplined and work hard. You don't even have to have been a champion or made much money for boxing to have helped. It's enough that for thousands of kids boxing has instilled a sense of self-respect and averted them from a drug-ridden life of antisocial behavior and crime. The important part of boxing is not that youngsters realize their dreams, but that they can dream. Every day in the gym they're somebody special. They're a fighter."

Perhaps because of their origins, there is little pretense in fighters. Most professional athletes are spoiled. Fawned over in high school, heavily recruited by colleges, they've been stars at every turn. There are very few pampered fighters, and it's remarkable how willing boxers are to talk with strangers, give out their home address and talk honestly and openly about their lives. Their creed is simple. In the ring, the best man wins. What a man has done outside the ring doesn't matter.

Sonny Liston was a mugger, a cop-beater, an armed robber, and a strong-arm man for the St. Louis mob. "Boxing," Jimmy

Cannon once wrote, "gave Liston the opportunity to meet big-time hoodlums instead of small ones." Yet Liston reigned as boxing's heavyweight champion. Muhammad Ali, who dethroned Liston, was stripped of his title by political authorities in 1967 after refusing induction into the Army. But grassroots boxing people continued to recognize Ali as the only true heavyweight champion until his defeat by Joe Frazier over fifteen brutal rounds at Madison Square Garden in 1971. Several of boxing's greatest champions, including one reigning world title holder, have been gay. Still they were fully accepted by the boxing community. It's what you do in the ring that counts. Indeed, as if to prove that maxim, many of boxing's greatest fighters shed their identity when they stepped into the ring and adopted totally new names. Thus, Walker Smith became Sugar Ray Robinson, Joseph Barrow became Joe Louis, and Beryl Rosofsky became Barney Ross. Thomas Barbella, Benjamin Leiner, Giuseppe Beradinelli, Arnold Cream, and Archibald Wright became Rocky Graziano, Benny Leonard, Joey Maxim, Jersey Joe Walcott, and Archie Moore. All were men with little hope. Boxing opened up a new world.

"Why do I box?" asks Larry Holmes, who has reigned for seven years as heavyweight champion of the world. "It's the money. After a while people said I had enough money, but there's never enough. Why do lawyers and business executives work seven days a week when they already got twenty million dollars? You always want more. You know what boxing has done for me?" Holmes continues. "Right now I got a roll of hundred-dollar bills in my pocket with a gold money clip around them. When I was a truck driver I used to carry ten dollars in singles wrapped in a rubber band."

Fighters are mercenaries, soldiers of fortune. Boxing isn't a form of idealism or a way to advance their people. It's their job. "When you're fighting," Jack Dempsey once said, "you're fighting for one thing—to get money. When I was a young fellow I was knocked down plenty. I wanted to stay down. I couldn't. I had to collect that two dollars for winning, or go hungry. I had one fight when I was knocked down eleven times before I got up to win. I had to get up. I was a hungry fighter. When you haven't eaten for two days, you'll understand."

"He's a nice boy," Rocky Marciano's manager, Al Weill, said of his fighter, shortly before Marciano won the heavyweight crown. "The dollar is his god. He's a poor Italian boy from a poor Italian family, and he appreciates the buck more than almost anybody. He only got two halfway decent purses, and it was like a tiger tasting blood."

So it's the money, but that's not all. It's something more. Four-round preliminary fighters on the way to the gym look back and see kids on the street tagging along, offering to help carry their bag. A fighter comes home, and a bunch of neighborhood children are sitting on the stoop. They look at him and say, "Wow, he's a fighter."

"Being a fighter makes me feel big," says former middleweight champion Vito Antuofermo. "You go to a dance with a nice girl, she's the prettiest girl there, and you feel proud. When I got in the ring for my first fight, I listened to the crowd. It was the first time in my life I ever heard people cheering for me."

"For most of my life," says Marvin Hagler, one of the premier fighters of the 1980s, "nobody listened to what I had to say. Now, wherever I am, everyone pushes and shoves, trying to get close so they can hear me."

Money, adoration—both are part of what spurs boxers on. But there are times when neither is sufficient to pull a fighter through. In the end, then, the greatest motivating factor might be simply that good fighters like to fight. It's what they do best. It's what they want to do.

"We're all endowed with certain God-given talents," Sugar Ray Leonard once told an audience at Harvard University. "Mine happens to be punching people in the head." The remark was made in jest, but it was also true. Leonard liked being in the ring because he was good.

Joe Frazier is the prime example of a champion who was good, in part because he loved to fight, and loved to fight because he was good. "When I get in the ring," Frazier once said, "it's to fight, not fool around. And my opponent better understand that when he's fighting me, he's fighting." Frazier fought in a way that can't be motivated by money—nonstop, with an intensity approaching orgasm for three minutes of every round. Muhammad Ali said of Joe Frazier, "He will fight way beyond exhaustion and still come on. Whatever the price, he'll pay it. You can knock him down a dozen times and he'll come again."

Joe Frazier's eyes still gleam when he talks about fighting.

He lived for the moment when his opponent was in trouble, and he could let loose with all that he had as though punching the heavy bag. "Being a fighter made a good living for me and my family," Frazier says, "but that wasn't all. I loved fighting. I loved the competitiveness, the one-on-one. I loved to stand on my own. People don't understand what an honor it is to be a fighter. It gave me the opportunity to prove myself, to stand up and say, 'I'm the best. I matter. I am.' "

Boxing is one of the few professions that give people from the underclass an opportunity to earn large sums of money and be heroes in their native land. It offers a young man hope, and the possibility that he will someday possess a world title once held by a god like Joe Louis or Sugar Ray Robinson. There is a unique importance to the heroes of old because they stand for the proposition that greatness in boxing is not a mirage. But in reality most fighters never become champions. The vast majority never even advance to the status of "main event" fighters. And along the way a price is paid—by some, for good value in return; for others, not so good. The price is high.

Being a fighter is more than a job; it's a way of life. Everything a fighter does affects his profession—what he eats, what he drinks, how he sleeps, what he does at night. Yet unless a fighter is considered a valuable "prospect," there's no one to push and prod him on. Thus the trade requires extraordinary self-motivation.

"It takes ten years to develop a quality ten-round fighter," says Angelo Dundee, who guided Muhammad Ali to the heavyweight crown. "And during those years a fighter has to work at it one hundred percent of the time. That means very early in his career a young man has to decide whether he's interested in boxing as a sport or as his livelihood. And if it's for his livelihood, he'd better understand what it means to train and train right."

Hard physical labor in training is the first prerequisite of boxing. A fighter can't be good unless he's in good condition. It's as simple as that. A fighter must harden his body and develop muscles, particularly in his neck and abdomen, strong enough to withstand punches, yet supple and flexible enough to allow him to bob, weave, and bend. The process takes years. Human bodies aren't machines. They must be brought along slowly in order to absorb blows, avoid blows, and retaliate with speed and power.

"Take the average person walking down the street," Dundee continues. "One punch in the neck from a fighter will tear his head off. Even things that look simple are tough. Everyone knows a fighter is supposed to keep his hands up. Try it! Don't even throw punches. Just walk around with your fists clenched at eye level for three minutes and see how tired your arms get."

There are no shortcuts to becoming a quality fighter. A boxer takes out of training what he puts into it. If he hits the heavy bag hard in training for three minutes a round, he'll be able to punch hard for three minutes a round during a fight. If he plays pitty-pat with the heavy bag, he'll get arm weary when the chips are down. Wasted talent is the oldest story in boxing. A fighter who coasts in training betrays his dreams and his future.

Still, hard physical labor is only part of the price paid by professional boxers. For many, a more difficult aspect of their trade is developing the ability to master themselves. No athlete spends emotionally like a fighter. His life is one intimidating situation after another, and to succeed he must be emotionally disciplined in the ring. That means learning to curb anger, making the right mental moves at the right time, and above all conquering fear.

Fear is an intriguing topic of conversation with fighters. Society demands that its heroes be free of fear. Most people are embarrassed by it. They don't like to think of themselves as being frightened. By and large fighters admit to "nervousness" and "butterflies"; rarely do they talk in terms of "fear." But there are very few times in life when a man really goes it alone, and in the ring is one of them. It's a strange feeling to see another man moving toward you, eyes fixed on destruction. At times like that the ring seems very small.

One of boxing's foremost authorities on the subject of fear is Cus D'Amato, the legendary trainer of Jose Torres and Floyd Patterson. A diminutive, outspoken man who has worked with young fighters for most of his 77 years, D'Amato often looks back on his own experiences to put the subject of fear in context.

"I remember the first time I got involved in what I call a waiting fight," D'Amato reminisces. "In the neighborhood in which I lived, which was a pretty tough neighborhood, you got involved in fights all the time. Whenever you got angry, you fought or you lost respect. Under those conditions you didn't think about being frightened. You replaced fear with anger. But it's different when you have the experience of waiting, an experience I had once. I lived in an Italian neighborhood, and a few blocks away there was an Irish neighborhood. I never used to have trouble with the Irish; I got along with everybody. But then the neighborhoods had some trouble, and both sides said, 'You bring a guy and we'll bring a guy, and they'll fight it out. Instead of both gangs fighting, we'll have two guys representing the neighborhoods.' I was sixteen," D'Amato continues, "and the Italian guys chose me. I wasn't mad at the Irish, I wasn't mad at anybody. But three days ahead of time I knew I had to fight this big Irish guy at nine o'clock on Saturday night. So comes the night of the fight, I didn't want to fight because this guy never did anything to me, but I got no choice. All the Italian guys and I go over to the street between the neighborhoods, and wait under a big street light. We got there, maybe five minutes to nine, with eighty or ninety guys, and the Irish must have had a hundred but their fighter hadn't shown yet. I sat down on the curb, and I was thinking to myself, 'How the hell did I get into this mess?' To tell the truth, I was scared. All my life, when I got mad I'd fought. I was fighting grown men when I was fourteen, but now I'm saying, 'Jesus Christ, what's the matter with me? I got to be crazy to do this. The next time some guys try to get me to fight, I'll fight them first; I got nothing against these Irish fellows.' " D'Amato's eyes grow larger, his face more animated, as his tale progresses. "Anyway, I'm sitting there, really sweating. I reached up, felt the sweat on my forehead, and figured it was blood, but it was only sweat. Nine o'clock comes and the Irish guy isn't there. Quarter after nine, the Irish guy isn't there. Nine-thirty, I'm still waiting, and all the time the waiting is getting worse because this guy is gonna be there, and I'm gonna have to fight him. Finally, at ten o'clock, one of his buddies comes and says the Irish guy is scared. He ain't showing. It was the happiest moment of my life."

Fighters are the most exposed athletes in the world. During a fight, the crowd observes every twitch and movement. Still, spectators rarely see fear in a quality fighter. "That," says D'Amato, "is because the fighter has mastered his emotions to the extent that he can conceal and control them." But whatever a fighter says, the fear is there. It never goes away. He just learns to live with it. "And the truth is," D'Amato continues, "fear is an asset to a fighter. It makes him move faster, be quicker and more alert. Heroes and cowards feel exactly the same fear. Heroes just react to it differently. On the morning of a fight, a boxer wakes up and says, 'How can I fight? I didn't sleep at all last night.' What he has to realize is, the other guy didn't sleep either. Later, as the fighter walks toward the ring, his feet want to walk in the opposite direction. He's asking himself how he got into this mess. He climbs the stairs into the ring, and it's like going to the guillotine. Maybe he looks at the other fighter, and sees by the way he's loosening up that his opponent is experienced, strong, very confident. Then when the opponent takes off his robe, he's got big bulging muscles. What the fighter has to realize," concludes D'Amato, "is that he's got exactly the same effect on his opponent, only he doesn't know it. And when the bell rings, instead of facing a monster built up by the imagination, he's simply up against another fighter."

There's something special about men who climb into the ring to face one another. Improved medical care has eliminated some of the outward scars. "Cauliflower ears," caused by blood seeping between ear cartilage, used to be common in fighters. Now where the condition exists blood is drained from the ear with a hypodermic needle. "I had my ears drained after the first Duran fight," Sugar Ray Leonard remembers. "Otherwise, I wouldn't be doing all those 7-Up commercials on TV."

Still, the human body wasn't built for the purpose of absorbing punishment, and boxing is a contact sport. It's axiomatic that fighters are going to get hit. Flattened noses, scar tissue around the eyes, and other signs of a boxer's trade are commonplace. A lot of fighters breathe through the mouth when their career is over. Their nose is too clogged to take in air. Few fighters have any hard cartilage left in their nose, the result of too many jabs down the middle of the face. The hard cartilage has softened to the point where the fighter can simply push on his nose with a finger and it flattens out. "I look at fights," says former lightweight champ Ray Mancini. "Someone gets hit, and I say, 'Jesus, what a shot.' Then I say to myself, 'Wait a minute, I get hit all the time like that.' "

Most fighters voice contempt for pain. Almost without exception they state that they're more afraid of losing than of being hurt; that during a fight an opponent's punches are less damaging physically than psychologically. "You can't stop to think about getting hit," says Thomas Hearns, who blasted Roberto Duran into retirement in consolidating the world junior-middleweight championship in 1984. "It's something that happens, and then you go on." Still, there's a unique quality to men who can get hit in the face time after time and keep coming. Reactions differ.

"Getting hit hard," says Larry Holmes, "doesn't really hurt. It's more like someone taking your picture. You see a flash, and then suddenly everything is groggy; but you recover."

"It's scary," says heavyweight Leroy Diggs, who served for years as Holmes's sparring partner. "All of a sudden you're in a moment of blackness, and there's a guy right there as big and strong as you are, only he can see. It's like you're in a room at night with all the lights out and someone's hitting you, only he can see and you can't."

Some fighters' reaction to getting hit is anger. "I want to hit back," says former junior-middleweight champion Davey Moore. "What goes through my mind is I definitely want to kill him. That's the only thing on my mind—get even, kill." Emile Griffith, who held two world titles, remembers, "When I was hit and hurt, I'd say, 'Please, Lord, just let me get over this one.' "

All fighters get hit. All they can do is hope not to get hit too hard, too often, or with two hard shots in a row. Over time they get used to the experience, and grow to accept it. After a while it's not the same nauseating eye-watering feeling it was at the start. Still, "it goes down on tape," says former heavyweight champ Joe Walcott, "and you play it back at funny times, when you're dreaming or just walking down the street."

The punches that land mount up during a fight. Hard punches can temporarily disable a fighter, enabling his opponent to inflict exponential damage. Fighters generally weaken as a fight goes on. Sometimes both combatants come out of a battle unscathed. Often even a knockout victim quickly recovers.

"So I got beat up in the ring a few times," says former heavyweight contender Chuck Wepner. "It was a few minutes of punishment, and then they paid me." In 1975, Wepner challenged Muhammad Ali for the heavyweight crown. Badly overmatched, he was knocked out in the fifteenth round. A young actor named Sylvester Stallone saw the fight, was moved by Wepner's courage, and sat down to write a screenplay called *Rocky*. But Wepner's attitude belies the dangers of the ring. And winners can get beaten up just as badly as losers.

On October 1, 1975, Muhammad Ali retained his title by knocking out Joe Frazier in "the thriller in Manila" in the fourteenth round. Physically, neither fighter was ever the same. Years before, Carmen Basilio retained his world welterweight crown by knocking out Tony DeMarco. Describing a critical moment in the fight, Basilio said, "I got hit with a left hook. People don't realize how you're affected when you're hit with a left hook on the point of the chin. What happens is, it pulls your jawbone out of your socket from the right side and jams it into the left side. The nerve there paralyzed the whole left side of my body."

Even one fight, if it's a war, can destroy a fighter, particularly if the fighter is over thirty. Sometimes, after a particularly bad physical defeat a fighter becomes gunshy. Rarely is he the same again. Abe Simon, a heavyweight contender who was knocked out twice in title bouts by Joe Louis, once said, "My particular physical and glandular structure was such that I never felt any pain from punches in the ring. With all honesty, I can say that no fighter ever hurt me, and that includes both fights with Joe Louis. But I can't say that Louis inflicted no damage. There's a whole lot of difference between pain and damage. The bruises from punches are like icebergs. You see only a small part of the damage on the surface."

Getting punched in the head is an integral part of boxing. The basic idea is to inflict as much damage as possible on an opponent. Often the effects of a fight evaporate within days. Sometimes they linger or last forever. In extreme cases the result is death.

Benny Paret, Duk Koo Kim, Johnny Owen, Kiko Bejines . . . To boxing fans the names are familiar. Each died of injuries sustained in a championship fight seen on television, live or taped, around the world. They are among the hundreds of fatalities that have resulted from boxing.

Sonny Liston, who reigned as heavyweight champion until dethroned by Muhammad Ali, once offered a description of how brain damage occurs. "All the brains are in a sort of cup," Liston explained. "And after you get hit a few times, it shakes them out of the cup. When they give you smelling salts, it puts them back in the cup. When the brains get shook up and run together, you get punch-drunk."

Liston must be forgiven for the simplicity of his explanation. He was a man without formal education, who had assiduously avoided school and couldn't read or write. But he understood what many people in boxing seem unable or unwilling to grasp—getting hit in the head thousands of times in training and in fights can cause brain damage.

Boxing is ironically a marvelous showcase for the brain. Skilled fighting requires balance, coordination, speed, reflexes, power, instinct, discipline, memory, and creative thought. These assets enable a professional fighter to deliver blows with force exceeding one thousand pounds, blows that snap an opponent's head back and twist it violently from side to side. The brain is a jellylike mass suspended inside the skull in cerebrospinal fluid. A hard blow shakes and shocks the brain, sending it careening off the inside of the skull. When this happens, blood vessels stretch and sometimes snap. In extreme cases, damaged brain tissue begins to swell.

The human brain is a complex creation. Nothing does it more harm than punching the head in which it resides. When a boxer is struck repeatedly, peticchial hemorrhages (small bleeding spots) and other lesions form in the brain. Cuts to the face and body heal. Brain tissue does not; it is not regenerative, and once destroyed is gone forever. "Boxers' encephalopathy" is the scientific term for what others call "punch-drunk." Early symptoms include unsteadiness of gait, slight memory loss, and mental confusion. As the condition advances, hand tremors, nodding of the head, and slurred speech occur. In severe cases, marked mental deterioration, backward swaying of the body, and the facial characteristics of Parkinson's syndrome are evident.

Most studies indicate that where chronic brain damage is

concerned, repetitive subconcussive blows such as those sustained regularly in training are more damaging than one-time knockouts. However, it is the devastating knockout that most often causes death. Such a blow can cause blood vessels to snap, and when that happens the brain begins to bleed. Since there is no room inside the skull for anything except the brain and surrounding cerebrospinal fluid, the pressure of the added blood compresses the brain, causing unconciousness, coma, and sometimes death.

On December 5, 1984, meeting at its annual convention in Hawaii, the House of Delegates of the American Medical Association adopted a resolution calling for the abolition of amateur and professional boxing. After the vote, speaking for the delegates, AMA President Dr. Joseph Boyle said, "It has been increasingly evident from scientific investigation that there is both acute and long-term brain injury to people who are involved in boxing. Evaluation of that evidence indicates that people are seriously disabled even after short exposure to boxing. I believe that physicians all over the country should participate in a public dialogue which would ultimately lead to persuading legislators and the public that this is indeed a very dangerous sport and that it ought to be outlawed."

Dr. George Lundberg, editor of the *Journal of the American Medical Association,* concurred: "Life is very complicated. We need all the brain we can get. And to take large numbers of already-disadvantaged youths and cause them to sustain chronic brain damage which will be lifelong is an obvious moral, medical, economic and social issue."

Reaction from the boxing community to the AMA's proposed ban was swift. "Look at auto racing," counterattacked former *Ring Magazine* editor Bert Sugar. "Its underlying rationale—that you should drive your car at two hundred miles an hour—is completely antithetical to safety. Race drivers get killed in far greater percentages than boxers, but General Motors and STP are behind the sport so nobody complains. Look at pro football," Sugar continued. "How many times have you turned on the television, seen someone carried off the field on a stretcher, and heard the announcer say, 'Boy, he took a good lick,' or 'so-and-so really got his bell rung on that one.' If a fighter gets knocked out, in most states he can't fight for weeks, sometimes months. Quarterbacks get knocked woozy and are back on the field five minutes later."

More than one member of the fight community sought to counter the AMA's stand by taking refuge in the words of A. J. Liebling: "If a boxer ever went as batty as Nijinsky, all the wowsers in the world would be screaming 'punch-drunk.' Well, who hit Nijinsky?" Said another observer, "Katharine Hepburn has Parkinson's disease. I don't recall her ever getting knocked around in the ring." Others noted that many fighters have lived well into their eighties with no ill effects from their trade.

The truth of the matter is that there are genuine risks attached to boxing. Over the years hundreds of healthy young men have died as participants. It's inherent in the sport that some people will take a beating and others worse. The issue is whether those risks are acceptable in relation to what is gained. But to discount the blood and death factor in boxing is to refuse to recognize the courage it takes for a man to step into the ring.

And what of the fighters? What do they think of the dangers that accompany their trade? "If something bad's gonna happen, it's gonna happen," says heavyweight champion Larry Holmes. "You're going out to fight, not play volleyball."

"I'd love it if someone guaranteed there'd never be another death in boxing," adds Michael Spinks. "But you know sometimes something is gonna happen."

One listens, and wonders whether in their hearts fighters understand that it could happen to them. Probably they do. It's impossible to be a boxer without reflecting every day on what you're doing and why you do it. The job requires a man to move toward a beaten, battered foe whose hands are down, whose eyes are rolling and, if the referee allows, smash his face again. "There's nothing personal about it," Rocky Marciano once said. "What it comes down to is, it's the other guy or you. Anybody in there with me is there to get me, and I'm there to get him."

Professional fighters, then, don't think in terms of causing injury. Rather, they operate like surgeons, who cut through flesh as though it were paper. A surgeon who thinks in terms of cutting up people could never do his job. His mind would rebel at the idea of slicing up human beings with a scalpel.

"I don't look at it as beating up another person," says Billy

Costello. "I look at it as bringing up something from inside myself, something I've worked at for ten years. I'm not trying to hurt anybody. I just say to myself, 'This is my job; it's me or him.' "

Could something bad happen to Billy Costello in the ring? He pauses for a moment.

"Yeah, I guess so."

3

Fifty years ago there were hundreds of small fight clubs in the United States, and many fighters went directly from street battles to the pros. Then in the 1950s television and the increased popularity of other sports killed the clubs, and fighters began to emerge almost exclusively from the ranks of amateurs.

Amateurs receive no pay, and box under the sponsorship of various youth organizations. Not until a fighter turns pro does he compete for money. Early in his professional career he'll engage in four-round preliminary bouts. Then as skills increase he moves to six-, eight-, and finally ten-rounders against more experienced foes. The ultimate goal of every fighter is to become a world champion, yet most fighters never fight for a world title, and even the best are seldom in position to reach for the brass ring more than once. Among lesser fighters, not only are titles absent, unemployment is high. There simply aren't enough fight clubs and fights to go around, and most boxers find themselves competing for purses of one or two hundred dollars.

Like all fighters, Billy Costello faced a difficult upward climb. The Kingston Police Athletic League offered only rudimentary instruction, and soon he began working out on his own in a small garage behind Joe LaLima's barbershop about a mile from home. "Joe and my father were friends," Billy remembers, "on account of a certain poker game and crap shoot that Joe ran back then. Once I got interested in boxing, he set up some equipment, and every day I'd go there after school."

Graduating from Kingston High School in 1975, Billy took a job as a meat cutter in Ulster County, and continued training. Then came the opportunity that shaped his life. Eleven amateurs from New York City journeyed upstate for a fund-raising exhibition with their trainer, Mike Rosario. Rosario had grown up on the streets of New York, and fought professionally, compiling a record of twenty-seven and five. After retiring from boxing, he worked as a storeroom clerk at Roosevelt Hospital, while he and his wife Negra operated a gym for underprivileged youngsters in their spare time. Among those youngsters were the amateurs he'd brought to Kingston, and one of them—Ronald Cuffe—needed an opponent. Someone suggested that a local boy named Billy Costello might want to go a few rounds.

"Cuffe was an experienced fighter," Rosario recalls. "He was a Golden Gloves semifinalist, very talented. Before the fight I could see that Billy was nervous—a yellow streak, I figured—so I told Ronald to go easy."

"It was like I wanted to fight him," Billy remembers, "but I didn't want to at the same time."

The bell for round one rang, and Billy came out throwing wild punches. One landed, knocking Cuffe out before the fight was two minutes old. A week later, Billy Costello moved into the New York City housing project that Mike Rosario and his family called home. For the next two years, Mike and Negra slept in one bedroom; Billy and their two sons in the other. The education of a fighter had begun.

Man's fists are wondrous weapons.

Any man will use his hands when under attack.

These maxims are at the heart of boxing, but there is a third maxim of equal importance: To be successful, a man must be able to use his fists well. He must juxtapose rhythm and flow with scientific action; be aggressive yet always ready to evade an opponent's blows. His movement in the ring must be instinctive, throwing punches the very moment, and sometimes before, an opening appears. He must learn to take blows with no outward sign of distress, and control his passions without losing them. In a sense it's like playing goalie in hockey, having two pucks (fists) flying inward every moment, and being called on to shoot the puck (throw punches) as well. "You don't think," Sugar Ray Robinson once said. "It's all instinct. If you stop to think, you're gone."

Yet no man starts out as a finely tuned precision weapon. In Joe Louis's first amateur fight, which he lost, he was knocked down seven times. Later, Louis looked back on the experience and observed, "There's no such thing as a natural fighter. A natural dancer has to practice hard. A natural painter has to paint all the time. Even a natural fool has to work at it."

For Billy Costello, practice began in Mike Rosario's gym. Fighters lose because they make mistakes. When they make mistakes, they get hit. Thus like all good trainers Rosario began by emphasizing defense and the world of centimeters in which boxers live. Straight punches are slipped by moving the head to the side. Bobbing the head is a defense against hooks. Some punches are parried, pushed off course by a defender's gloves. Others are blocked; high punches to the outside, body blows downward. The lessons were learned through negative reinforcement. In a boxer's world, mistakes are paid for on the spot.

Then came offense. For right-handed fighters there are four basic punches. The left jab—boxing's basic weapon—begins with the left leg moving forward and left arm thrust out. At the moment of impact, the fist is squeezed and rotated laces downward for maximum effect. The straight right. The left hook. Uppercuts with either hand. Most people use only one hand effectively. Fighters must be able to use two.

Month after month the education of Billy Costello continued. A fighter must be a moving target. If he doesn't move, if he fails to vary his moves, he'll get hit. Next came feints, simulated attacks that entice an opponent to move to one spot while a second attack is being planned. Combinations followed. Like a pool player who uses a single shot to sink one ball and set up another, a fighter learns to throw punches in succession, each punch creating an opening for the next. Counterpunching. Any time a fighter throws a punch, it creates an opening for his opponent. Counterpunching is the art of exploiting those openings, taking advantage of an adversary who brings his hands back too slowly or keeps them too low after taking the offensive.

But physical skills were only part of what Billy Costello had to learn. The psychological lessons were equally important. It's very difficult to maintain discipline in the ring when an opponent is trying to knock your head off, yet fighters must act with a patient, almost detached, emotional attitude. Loss of temper in the ring results in a fighter getting hit. A momentary break in concentration carries with it the potential for a devastating knockout blow.

Always there was more to assimilate. Man's most fundamental instinct is the avoidance of pain, yet a fighter must risk pain and sometimes accept it in order to hit his opponent. When hurt he must respond like a professional, protecting the unhurt areas of his body as well as the hurt ones. And most important, no matter how badly hurt, a fighter must protect his head. When stunned, he must hold, move, clinch, run, do anything, but protect the head at all times.

Fighters learn to take punches by taking punches. The best combat training for fighting hurt is to be hurt in the gym. Over time Billy Costello's lessons were learned. As the months passed he picked up small tricks of survival in the ring. He developed the ability to anticipate an opponent's punches a split second before they were thrown by watching shoulder movements and his opponent's eyes. But beyond all training, beyond all practice and science, it was growing clear that Billy Costello had something no fighter can learn. He had *the punch.*

In boxing, form and speed combine to produce power. Punches are most effective when they travel in a straight line. To a degree, punching technique can be improved by teaching a boxer to shift his weight and deliver blows with the force of his body rather than just his arms. But if a fighter isn't born with a great punch, he doesn't have it.

Jack Kearns, who managed Jack Dempsey and Joey Maxim to world titles, once opined, "Maxim is as good a fighter as Dempsey, except he can't hit." To that, Rocky Marciano added, "It doesn't do any good to hit a guy if you don't hurt him." Joe Louis once said the first time he realized he could hurt an opponent was "something like people getting religion." The punch is boxing's great equalizer, and Billy Costello had it. "God just gave me a better punch than he gave most people," he told a friend in a moment of reflection. "I can't explain it. I'm just happy it's there."

THE BLACK LIGHTS

* * *

For three years, Billy Costello worked his way up through the ranks of amateurs with Mike Rosario at his side. Then, on the night of Friday, March 10, 1978, he stepped into the ring at Madison Square Garden to face Raymond Johnson for the Golden Gloves, 135-pound open crown. Nineteen seconds into the second round, he stunned Johnson with a straight right hand, and followed with a left hook that left Johnson dazed on the canvas for a count of ten and ten minutes more.

In the delirium that followed, Billy made his way to the dressing room, showered, dressed, and returned to ringside to watch the rest of the Golden Gloves card. As he took his seat, a man in his mid-forties with long, curly brown hair approached and extended his right hand: "My name is Mike Jones. When you're ready to turn pro, give me a call."

"He looked honest," Billy remembers. "He talked honest. He didn't pressure me, just gave me his card. A year later, when I decided to turn pro, I needed a manager. I remembered I'd liked him, so I decided to give Mike Jones a call."

In many ways, professional boxing starts with managers. Fighters come and go, but managers stay on, some of them seemingly forever. Like gamblers, they feed on eternal hope. Except for the few who've been financially successful, they scrape and claw, waiting for the next fighter to pin their hopes on. They work nights in restaurants and bars, believing in their hearts that someday they'll be in the gym, they'll look up, and the next Sugar Ray Robinson or Joe Louis will be coming through the door. That's what a manager lives for.

Mike Jones was born in Brooklyn on March 30, 1935. He grew up on Bedford Avenue between Y and Z Streets when the area was called "Jew-town." If you walked too far out of the neighborhood, you had to fight your way home. "The only fight I ever really lost," Mike recalls, "was in basic training in the Army. I stood up for my rights against a guy who knew how to fight, and I've got scars today to prove it. I lost. No doubt about it. We went at it for twenty minutes, and things had reached a point where I was backed up against a tree, and everything was kind of hazy. Then someone stepped in and stopped it, but I never went down; and it wasn't any picnic for the other guy either."

Jones got out of the Army in 1957, and went to work selling ladies' shoes in Paramus, New Jersey. After a while he got bored, and decided to try real estate. "I got a job selling residential properties for J. I. Kislak, one of the largest brokers in New Jersey," he remembers. "I was good. I've always had the ability to make money. Maybe because I wasn't a college graduate, I work harder; I don't have a degree to fall back on. One year, at the company's annual convention, Mr. Kislak announced that I was the only salesman in the history of the company to sell one house on Christmas Eve and another on New Year's Day. Then, after about two years, I went to work for a real-estate office in Queens because the money was better. My first week on the job I sold two houses. One of them had been on the market for three years. After that the other salesmen in the office hated me."

In 1960 Jones married Estelle Shulder, whom he'd met on a blind date arranged by his mother. Twenty-five years later they're still married, with three children. In 1966 he entered into a real-estate partnership with Lenny Leo, who remained his closest friend until passing away from a heart attack eighteen years later. In 1969 he founded his own company, buying, rehabilitating, and selling one- and two-family homes. "I did well there too," Mike recalls. "In a couple of years I had twelve people working for me. Then I went into partnerships on two more offices. I enjoyed real estate, I really did. But I had this fantasy. You see, every night before I went to sleep I'd fight for the middleweight championship of the world. Thousands of times, I'd done it. I still do. The place is Madison Square Garden. Nowadays the opponent is Marvin Hagler, although I've done battle with Ray Robinson, Carlos Monzon, and many others before. And every night I'd fall asleep at the bell for round one, so even in my fantasies the thrill of victory and agony of defeat eluded me. After a while, as near as possible I wanted to make that fantasy come true."

The first step was to find a partner. In 1970 Mike had met Dennis Rappaport, a fellow real-estate broker, at a poker game on Long Island. Rappaport was a fast-talking salesman with a penchant for gold jewelry and modish clothes. At various times he had marketed locks and security devices, sold chinchillas, and run a karate school in Greenwich Village. More to the point, he shared Mike Jones's love of boxing, and the two men started going to fights together, talking boxing until four and five A.M. Then in 1976 they decided to manage a fighter.

A manager is a fighter's business representative. His job is to handle business details, negotiate fight contracts, and get his fighter the most money possible in the safest environment available in the shortest period of time. Generally a manager takes 30 percent of his fighter's earnings, although the figure varies.

Managers aren't particularly popular in the lexicon of boxing. "Never have so few taken so much from so many" is one frequently heard refrain. "The fight manager wouldn't fight to defend his own mother," is another. Fighters who are continually matched against superior fighters are known to have "brave managers." An often-voiced fighter's lament is, "Why do I have to give thirty percent of my money to a manager? I'm the one fighting. The manager ain't getting hit."

There are good managers in boxing, but like diamonds, they're rare and hard to find. Talking with some of the best provides a composite view of their job. Jim Jacobs, who co-managed Wilfred Benitez and Edwin Rosario to world titles, says, "The cardinal rule of managing is never put your fighter in a match you don't think he can win. And if you put him in a match that figures to be a war, you'd better be sure it will significantly advance his career or pay him a lot of money."

Dave Wolf, who guided Ray Mancini to international renown, observes, "A good manager does everything himself. That's the only way he can protect his fighter. You check the ring ropes. You check the other fighter's bandages. You check what the other corner is using on their man. You do it yourself. You can't rely on athletic commission officials or anyone else to do the job."

Emanuel Steward shepherded Thomas Hearns, Hilmer Kenty, and Milton McCrory from the streets of Detroit to championship status. Now Steward declares, "My job is to outwit people. Every fight requires that I be in there looking for an edge. And if I can find an opponent who gives the appearance of being formidable while posing no threat whatsoever to my fighter, that's fine."

Eddie Futch, best known for his handling of Joe Frazier, Ken Norton, and Bob Foster, adds, "I never take on a fighter I don't like. If I find myself with a fighter I dislike, I get rid of him no matter how much profit is in it. I've seen managers who subconsciously hate one of their fighters and enjoy seeing him beat. You've got to love your fighter. Otherwise it's dangerous. You'll send him out and get him mangled or killed."

Without exception, quality managers know that boxing is a sport where one or two losses can kill a fighter's career at any time. "I've managed guys through thirty or forty wins without a loss," says Mickey Duff, the preeminent manager and promoter in Great Britain. "I've done it with ordinary fighters because I found worse opponents, and that was the way it seemed right to do things at the time. But sooner or later you're faced with a moment of truth when your guy has to fight a real fight. That's when you realize it's a lot more exciting and a lot easier to be successful when you're managing a quality fighter. It's the difference between managing Frank Sinatra and some guy who sings at weddings and bar mitzvahs."

But the fact of the matter is that there are very few Frank Sinatras and very few great fighters. Managing boxers is an unlikely way to get rich. "You probably think I'm a little crazy," Mike Jones says. "I mean, it's a little off the wall to give up the good life to go into boxing. Regardless, Dennis and I decided to become managers, and two quality fighters were available at the time." One of those fighters was Eddie Gregory, then a middleweight, who trained at Gleason's Gym in Manhattan. The other was Ronnie Harris, a former Olympic gold-medal winner who lived in Canton, Ohio. Jones and Rappaport flew Harris to New York, put the two fighters in the ring together, and Harris dominated all five rounds. So they signed him. That was when they learned they had a fighter who was undefeated in seventeen fights, but no one would fight him. Other managers wouldn't put their fighters in the ring with a talented tough lefthander. Promoters wouldn't pay money for an efficient but dull black fighter.

"Dennis was fabulous during that period," Mike remembers. "We've had our disagreements over the years, but then he was magnificent. First, he dreamed up the idea of telling everyone that Harris was Jewish, and suing the New York State Athletic Commission to allow Ronnie to fight wearing a yarmulke. After a while we dropped the idea because the safety pins necessary to hold a yarmulke in place might have injured somebody, but Ronnie got lots of publicity out of it. Then, because we still couldn't get a fight, Dennis dressed a guy up in a gorilla costume, brought him to Madison Square Garden on a chain, and started shouting, 'I found someone who'll fight Ronnie Harris.' The Garden didn't think it was funny. Security guards charged in from all over the place, but it worked. While Dennis was running around with the gorilla, I got a telephone call from Teddy Brenner, who was the matchmaker for Madison Square Garden."

"Jones! Do you want a fight for Ronnie Harris?"

"Yes."

"Then get your crazy partner with the gorilla out of here, and you can fight Sugar Ray Seales."

"How much?"

"Twenty-five hundred."

"You gotta do a little better than that."

"Jones, I'm gonna say it once more, and you're going to say either yes or no. Twenty-five hundred."

"Yes."

On March 2, 1977, Harris won a ten-round decision over Sugar Ray Seales at Madison Square Garden. Thereafter "The Wacko Twins," as Jones and Rappaport had become known, guided their fighter to a 26 and 0 record and an August 5, 1978, title shot against world middleweight champion Hugo Corro of Argentina.

"The Corro fight was in Buenos Aires," Mike remembers, "and the arena was jammed to the rafters with screaming Argentinians. Everywhere we looked there were soldiers with rifles. Once the fight was over and Ronnie had lost, they were very nice to us. I had the distinct feeling they wouldn't have been so nice if Ronnie had won."

The loss was a setback. But there was still ample reason for the "Wacko Twins" to feel proud. Newcomers to boxing are tested with every form of chicanery and intimidation imaginable, but despite this they had led their first fighter to a shot at the world middleweight crown. Now their sea legs were stronger, and, more important, a second fighter had been signed.

"Anyone who knew anything about boxing knew about Howard Davis," Mike says, looking back on that time. En route to a gold medal at the 1976 Olympics in Montreal, Davis had compiled an amateur record of 120 and 5, with four Golden Gloves titles and an amateur world crown. Before the Olympics the two erstwhile real-estate brokers had contacted Davis's father, and soon after Montreal a contract was signed.

Davis's first professional fight was a six-round decision over Jose Resto in January 1977 that was televised on NBC. Then Jones and Rappaport struck a bargain with CBS that was unprecedented. CBS was granted the right to televise Davis's next fifteen fights. In return the fighter's camp was to be paid on the following scale: $40,000 each for three six-rounders; $50,000 each for six eight-rounders; and $185,000 each for six ten-rounders. Davis was allowed to select his opponents, with the network having limited veto power. Including a $50,000 signing bonus, the package came to $1,580,000 for television rights alone. Davis was also entitled to receive whatever "live gate" promoters paid him. By contrast, after Muhammad Ali won a gold medal at the 1960 Olympics in Rome, the total purses from his first fifteen professional fights came to $59,723, a per fight average of $3,982. And Davis's deal was sweetened after his sixth fight, when it was decided that he was ready for ten-rounders. At that time the purses for fights seven through nine were raised to $100,000 each, lifting the total contract value to $1,730,000.

In boxing circles, the "Wacko Twins" were now renamed "The Gold Dust Twins," but artistically there were problems. Howard Davis had classic skills, but lacked what many insiders called "heart." While remaining undefeated against a succession of carefully chosen opponents, he lacked the daring necessary to become a great fighter. Too often he was staggered or floored by punches from ordinary opponents. "Howard Davis's chin isn't a question mark," commented one observer. "It's a problem." Eventually Davis challenged for the world lightweight crown held by James Watt of Scotland, and lost a unanimous fifteen-round decision. Still, even as he wrestled with the nuances of Howard Davis's chin, Mike Jones had found another fighter and was readying for a rollercoaster ride of incredible proportions.

The fighter was Gerry Cooney, son of a construction worker who had boxed in the service during World War II and decided that his four sons should know how to fight. Tony Cooney set up a heavy bag in the basement of his Huntington, Long Island, home, and one of his sons grew to be six feet five inches tall, 225 pounds.

"Dennis and I had seen Gerry fight in the Golden Gloves," Mike recalls. "His amateur record was 55 and 2, and he'd won two New York City Golden Gloves titles. When he began talking to prospective managers—a big white heavyweight who could punch—we stood on line. Fortunately we got along, and after several meetings with his family and lawyer we signed him for a package that provided living expenses and the promise he could train full time."

Very few managers "make" their fighters—take a kid who's an amateur, teach him about boxing, and bring him carefully along. But that was what Jones and Rappaport did with Gerry Cooney. The contract they'd signed in late 1976 called for the fighter to receive an interest-free advance of $200 a week against future earnings. The investment paid off.

In 1977 Cooney had seven fights and won them all. In 1978 he fought eight times with eight victories. Seven fights and seven victories followed in 1979. Eighteen of Cooney's first twenty-two wins were by knockout. His power was such that Gil Clancy, trainer and manager of former heavyweight champ George Foreman, observed, "When you go in the ring with Cooney, he puts marks on you. If you're in there with him for three minutes, you look like you've been in there three hours."

All managers hype their fighters. It's part of the game. But with Gerry Cooney the hype reached unprecedented proportions. Cooney was good. Cooney had charisma. Cooney was a devastating puncher. And Cooney was white. More precisely, suburban middle-class, Irish Catholic white.

Boxing, more than any other sport, thrives on ethnic confrontation, and there are relatively few quality white fighters around. The most common ethnic confrontation in boxing today is Hispanic versus black. Suddenly in Gerry Cooney, boxing had a "white hope"—the first white man since Rocky Marciano to hold out the promise of preeminence in the ring.

Yet even as "Cooney hysteria" was reaching its peak, Mike Jones was looking for something more. He wanted to manage another fighter, this one without Dennis Rappaport. Not a superstar, just a fighter of his own. And when the opportunity came, he reached out to Billy Costello.

"My wife Stella and I were at the Golden Gloves," Mike remembers. "And this fellow won by a stunning knockout. 'You should sign him,' my wife said. And I told her, 'Nah, he's awkward; he's too old; probably he's got a manager lined up already.'

Twenty minutes later, who comes back to ringside and sits down behind us but Billy Costello. So I gave him my card."

Jones's smile vanishes, and his face takes on a slightly pensive look. "But the early years were tough for Billy. Compared to Gerry Cooney and Howard Davis, he was like a middle child who gets hand-me-downs and learns early that life is hard. People kept telling me that of all my fighters Billy was the one least likely to become a champion. The sporting press almost completely ignored him. His purses were small. Still, Billy had one very important thing going for him. He was always willing to pay the price. Billy Costello was the most dedicated fighter I'd ever had."

5

In 1979 Billy Costello and Mike Jones signed the standard New York State Athletic Commission "Boxer-Manager Contract." Mike agreed to use his best efforts to provide adequate training and secure "reasonably remunerative boxing contests against opponents of similar qualifications and skill" for the fighter. Billy, in turn, agreed to "render boxing services, including training, sparring, and boxing in exhibitions and contests at such times and places as designated by the manager." Sixty percent of the money collected was to go to Billy, thirty percent to Mike. The other ten percent would go to Billy's trainer.

The trainer was an important factor in Billy's decision to sign with Mike. Few people realize how crucial a trainer is. He's the man who teaches a fighter how to fight, yet many professional boxers don't even have a trainer. Former middleweight champion Vito Antuofermo, who immigrated to the United States from Italy at age fifteen, exemplifies their plight. "Before I fought for the title," Antuofermo remembers, "I never had anybody real to train me. All I had were guys who hung around the gym and told me instead of taught me. Then when I was leaving the gym they'd say to watch what I ate, slap me on the back, and tell me 'good luck.' "

During his amateur career Billy Costello had been guided by Mike Rosario, but Rosario had a full-time job and dozens of other fighters to teach. As a professional, Billy wanted a full-time professional trainer. Mike Jones promised him Victor Valle.

Valle was born in San Juan, Puerto Rico, on October 6, 1917, one of thirteen children of Santiago and Celestina Valle. Six died in infancy; two more in their teens. "I come from plain, tough, hardworking people," Valle reminisces. "We weren't rich, but my father always paid his debts and didn't owe nothing to nobody." When Victor was eight, his father contracted pneumonia. "At that time," he continues, "medicine wasn't so advanced as today. Sick people were kept at home to die. That's the way it was with my father. There wasn't nothing we could do."

One afternoon Santiago Valle called each of his sons to his bedside, blessed them, and kissed them on the forehead. Then he died. "My sister Carmen was already living in the United States," Victor remembers, "so when my father died she sent for the family. We moved into Harlem, which was a Jewish neighborhood, and it was a beautiful life. New York didn't have drugs the way it does now. You could sleep on the roof when it was hot at night. There was plenty of jobs, even for the children part-time."

Then the Depression struck. Victor was twelve years old. "Those were hard times," he says. "My mother kept us eating by sewing all night on an old pedal machine, and every morning I'd find her asleep over her sewing. So I did what I had to do. I'd always played at fighting. In the backyards of Harlem there were sandbags tied to fire escapes, and all the kids used to work out the way kids today play ball—for fun. I got good. Starting in 1929 my brother, Liberty, took me block to block to fight for money. Each place we stopped, people would pass the hat, and when we got a couple of dollars in it I'd fight the toughest kid around, winner take all. Every fight lasted until somebody quit. Once I had a fight that lasted over an hour, but I won."

At age seventeen Valle turned professional, compiling a record of 46 and 1 over the next four years, losing only to future lightweight champion Sammy Angott. In many ways he was blessed as a fighter—strong, quick, adept at feinting and slipping an opponent's blows. "Boxing gets in your blood," he says. "It's a germ, and I loved it." Then at age twenty-one he broke his right hand for the third time, and was forced to retire. "It was a bad time," he remembers. "A man is born for certain things, and I was born to be in boxing. I work boxing; I eat boxing; sometimes in the privacy of my bed with my wife, she asks what I'm thinking, and I'm thinking boxing. I loved to box, and suddenly I couldn't do it no more. For a while I was in despair, but even as a boy I'd known someday I wanted to be a trainer. In the gym when I was fighting I'd always watched the trainers with their fighters. So when my hand went bad I decided to share the knowledge I had with other fighters."

In 1938, at age twenty-one, Victor Valle began the career he has pursued for almost fifty years—training boxers. The job carries with it considerable responsibility, and few men do it well. Trainers need an instinct for teaching and an understanding of fighting. They must be motivators, confidants, and surrogate fathers. At their best they are artists.

The prototype of a boxing trainer is Ray Arcel, who trained, developed, or worked the corner for twenty world champions, including Barney Ross, Ezzard Charles, and Roberto Duran. "In the old days," Arcel reminisces, "trainers were teachers and the gym was a school. The last thing I'd do when my kids left the gym each day was ask, 'What did you learn today?' Now, most trainers don't know how to teach, and fighters don't really learn their trade."

Still, the components of a good trainer have remained largely unchanged over time. Eddie Futch, one of today's best, says, "A trainer must understand conditioning and the art of boxing. But more important, he must know the strengths and limitations, both mental and physical, of his fighter. No matter how much effort a fighter puts in, there are some things he simply won't be able to do. A good trainer won't try to teach a fighter more than he can learn."

Angelo Dundee, a trainer who ranks with Futch, agrees. "The most important prerequisite for a trainer," says Dundee, "is to know his subject. All fighters are different. No boxer ever fights entirely by the book. It's a changeover every time you take on a new man. So what you have to realize is you can't train a fighter to be like someone else. The best fighters don't try to be like Ali or Ray Leonard. They try to be themselves."

It is often felt that a fighter makes the trainer, rather than the other way around. "I'm the greatest trainer who ever lived,"

George Gainsford once boasted. "I trained Sugar Ray Robinson when he was young." And the response was, "George, you've had hundreds of fighters. Why aren't they all as good as Sugar Ray?"

"Sure, you hear comments like that," Dundee answers. "Lots of guys tell me they could have trained Ali and he would have been a champion anyway. Maybe that's so. I'm not the only trainer in the world, and Muhammad Ali was a great natural talent. I just know the job was done, and I'll let the job speak for itself."

The demands of being a good trainer are endless. "There's so much to boxing," says Teddy Atlas, one of the better young trainers in the business today. "I've never seen a trainer, fighter, manager, anyone, who couldn't learn something more. Sometimes I'll see an amateur who's had four or five fights do something. I'll like it, take it, improve it, and add it on to one of my fighters."

Then there's the aspect of regularity. "The first two qualities a good trainer needs," says Gil Clancy, "are punctuality and reliability, for him and his fighter. Whenever I had a fighter, whether it was Emile Griffith, Jerry Quarry, anybody, I stressed regularity. The fighter would do his roadwork at the same time every day, have his breakfast at the same time every day, go to the gym the same time every day, and go to bed the same time every day."

And last there are the intangibles.

"A trainer must know boxing," says Victor Valle. "He must be able to communicate. But there's two very important things more. First, a trainer must demand respect, because if the fighter don't respect him, there will be no interest in what the trainer is teaching. Sometimes fighters get like a mule and don't listen to nobody. That's when you tell them, 'If you don't listen to me, you don't need me; goodbye.' And second, a trainer must show the fighter that he cares. That's not a machine out there. You don't stick a tape in a fighter and send him to box like some kind of computer toy. You got to show your fighter some love. That's how I feel about my fighters. Someday I'll have to leave boxing, and when that happens I'll be very sad. But leaving will be better because my fighters will know I gave them some love."

* * *

The union of Victor Valle and Mike Jones came about in late 1976. Mike and Dennis Rappaport had just signed Gerry Cooney, and the heavyweight needed a trainer. Cooney was interested in Cus D'Amato, who had guided Floyd Patterson to the heavyweight crown, but D'Amato wanted more say in managing the fighter than Mike and Dennis were willing to cede. Thus, Cooney's people turned to Valle.

"I'd seen Victor work out with fighters at Gleason's Gym," Mike remembers. "And I'd liked what I'd seen. He was the only trainer there who actually got in the ring and showed his fighters what to do. His reputation was good, he'd had a world champion in Afredo Escalera; so Dennis and I asked if he wanted to train Gerry. Naturally we thought Victor would jump up and down like crazy. Instead he looked at us and said, 'Gerry Cooney, I know the boy, and that's a lot of work. First I'd like to have a meeting with him.' "

Soon after, Victor and Gerry met at a restaurant in Manhattan, where Valle outlined what he would expect of the fighter—sacrifice, discipline, abstinence, and hard work. The next day Cooney began the daily commute from Long Island to work with Valle at Gleason's Gym. "He was a good learner," the trainer remembers, "but there were problems. His punches were too long, and his footwork wasn't nothing to brag about. His defense was bad, and he was a little soft. But he worked hard, and his left hook was the best I'd seen."

For two and a half years Valle labored with Gerry Cooney, teaching him mental as well as physical toughness. Then at a point when Cooney was 17 and 0, Billy Costello came on board.

"Billy was raw when I first saw him," says Victor. "And he had a big disadvantage because he hadn't started boxing until nineteen, and a lot of things that fighters do as second nature, he was just starting to learn. But he was a good boy, a very hard worker, with tremendous power in both hands."

Painstakingly, the polishing of Billy Costello began. First defense. Then the left jab. A fighter's jab is like pots and pans to a cook. If he doesn't have one, the restaurant is closed. A good jab keeps an opponent off balance, forces him to assume a defensive posture, and creates openings for other blows. It's not something a fighter should flick out in the general direction of his opponent's face. It's a punch intended to inflict pain, thrown like a spear or battering ram. But throwing the jab is like opening a door, and once the door is open an opponent can walk through it too. Every time a fighter throws the jab, he puts himself in danger. His left arm is extended, he's completely exposed, and he can be hit hard if his opponent times the jab properly and fires a counterright in return.

"Victor and I became very close," Billy remembers, looking back on their early days together. "He knew what made me tick, how to make me get started and go. It got so, during a round in the gym, sparring or whatever, the only voice I heard was Victor's. He gave me confidence. He taught me most of what I know. Fighting is like being a lion tamer in a cage and you got all those lions in with you. Victor made me realize that when I was fighting there was just one lion, and I could beat him."

There's a special bond between a fighter and the trainer who brings him to adulthood. Trust and belief in his trainer can motivate a fighter, and between Billy and Victor the chemistry was good. Soon Billy moved to a small apartment on 57th Street in Manhattan, and his bond with Victor grew even stronger.

They were an odd couple. Billy Costello was five foot eight, 140 pounds. His body looked like a Michelangelo sculpture, with clearly defined muscles bulging beneath olive-brown skin. His short curly black hair was always cropped close. A gold-rimmed tooth and penetrating brown eyes marked a visage that in the ring seemed unusually grim. Victor was two inches shorter, and looked like a giant elf or a diminutive Babe Ruth. His round face was topped by wavy gray hair, and his once-lean body had grown rotund. On one level the two men related as father and son, but always they spoke of themselves as equals. Neither worked for the other. They were a team.

"Training Billy was a joy," Victor remembers. "He wasn't what I call a natural fighter. His punches didn't flow like they do with Leonard or Ali. He couldn't go in the ring and invent things on his own. But Billy understood how to listen and work. He never took shortcuts in learning his trade."

In boxing, a fighter pays in the ring for every mistake he's ever made—mistakes in conditioning, mistakes in training, every lazy moment he's ever had. Maybe he gets by for a while without working hard. He might win a few fights, like a child in school who doesn't study and looks over someone else's shoulder to copy answers during an exam. But sooner or later there comes a test when the next seat is empty, and a person is on his own. That's what happens to a fighter in the ring when he has a tough fight and all his lazy work habits of the past catch up with him. That's when he gets cut around the eyes and knocked down, and if he has guts he gets back up. But it's too late. He hasn't trained properly, and he's beaten badly. Billy Costello understood that. He wasn't boxing like it was a game to him. It was his future, his family's future, his livelihood.

"I don't build castles in the air for my fighters," says Victor Valle. "I tell them the truth, the facts of life. Billy understood that to be a success he was gonna have to do things he'd never done, and accept things he had never accepted before. That's the price a man pays if he wants to be a fighter."

By mid-1979 Billy Costello was ready for his first professional fight, and it was here that he began to reap tangible benefits from having Mike Jones as his manager. A fighter's early fights are the minor leagues of his career. Theoretically each bout should be a competitive match, a major test graded "pass-fail" with a 50 percent fail rate. In practice, however, up-and-coming prospects are matched with opponents who are little more than learning devices, fighters who shouldn't be in the same ring with them.

"For Billy's early fights," Mike remembers, "we wanted guys who were in front of him; not runners; guys he could hit. And not punchers; anything can happen when the opponent can punch. Each fight was designed to present a different set of circumstances, problems Billy could solve in winning the fight."

Thus it was that Billy Costello's early opponents were a mixture of has-beens and never-weres. Aging club fighters with expanding stomachs; fighters of all ages with the mistakes of their trade marked on their faces; human cannon fodder thrown into the ring for $100 or $200 a night. Yet always there was danger. It's one thing for a fighter to execute in the gym, and quite another to perform properly when facing an attacker whose livelihood is at stake. Any fight can end at any moment, and any loss stains a fighter's record forever. A baseball player can go hitless at bat, and come back the next day to redeem himself. A pitcher can get knocked out of the box in the first inning, and return three days later to even the score. But a fighter can't have an off-day. He can't say "it's not my day" and walk away flat. If he loses, it might take two or three years to get his career back to where it was before he lost—or it might never get there.

On August 22, 1979, Billy Costello made his professional debut against Angel Ortiz in the Felt Forum at Madison Square Garden. "In some ways," he remembers, "it was like the first day of school. The bell for round one rang, and I was psyched. I went out too fast and was left hook crazy early in the fight. Then I dropped him twice and won a four-round decision."

September 12, 1979, Jose Gonzalez: "I felt him out in the first round and said to myself, 'Oh shit, this guy is slicker than the last one; he knows something about boxing.' Then in the third round he got careless, and I knocked him out."

October 12, 1979, Dave Bolden: "A real tough mother. I knocked him down a couple of times, and each time he got up throwing punches. I was glad to get out of that one with a decision."

October 19, 1979, John Jones: "He was a stiff. In clinches he kept saying, 'Hey man, take it easy.' I didn't know if he was scared or trying to con me. In the second round I hit him hard, and he quit."

October 26, 1979, George Casher: "This was in the big Madison Square Garden on the undercard of Wilfredo Gomez and Nicky Perez. Casher was a real pro. I won a four-round decision."

The victory over Casher was Billy Costello's third win in two weeks and his fifth in a little more than two months. Everything was running smoothly. Then, the day after Thanksgiving, tragedy struck.

Two weeks earlier Mike Jones had signed on as co-manager of Wilford Scypion, a Texas middleweight with a 12 and 0 record. Now Scypion was in New York, matched at Madison Square Garden against a fighter named Wille Classen. In April, Classen had been suspended indefinitely by the New York State Athletic Commission after taking a bad beating in a Felt Forum fight. However, instead of undergoing the required neurological tests before fighting again, he accepted an October bout in London and was knocked down three times before the fight was stopped. Returning to New York, Classen falsely reported that his latest loss had been due to cuts rather than punishing blows to the head, and after neurological tests he was cleared for the Scypion bout. Scypion administered a brutal beating, knocking his foe unconscious in the early seconds of the tenth round. Classen never regained consciousness, and died several days later.

"Yeah, it bothered me," Billy says. "It made me realize that something bad can happen on any night. Probably I was a little nervous, so for my next fight Mike and Victor gave me a real stiff. The guy's name was Marvin Edwards. At the prefight weigh-in he was giving me all kinds of shit. 'Don't call me Marvin; call me Marvin The Shark Edwards; gonna kick your ass, man.' I knocked him out in the first round."

Then came another, more trying, test. On February 13, 1980, Billy entered the ring against Kato Ali for his first scheduled six-round fight. Moving from four to six rounds carries with it new demands on several levels. A fighter must be in better condition to go the extra distance, and more important, he's likely to be facing a more talented foe. "I'd gotten the flu four days before the fight," Billy remembers. "But I had to fight him. I needed the money. He knocked me down twice; once in the first round, once in the fifth; each time from an overhand right. Two guys had knocked me down in the amateurs, but these were my first knockdowns as a pro. I remember thinking when I got decked, 'Use your brain.' I couldn't say, 'Don't hit me with that punch again until after I go back to the corner and get some advice from Victor.' I felt good about myself, not breaking down that fight, maintaining my composure. I won a decision, and two months later when I fought Ali again, I knew he only had one punch, the overhand right. I waited for it, and when he threw it I nailed him with a left hook to the body for a third-round knockout."

Once again Billy Costello was back on track, and the victories kept coming.

May 4, 1980, Richie Garland: "He was a quality fighter who weighed about twelve pounds more than me and had never been knocked out. I stopped him in five."

May 14, 1980, Rich Sienna: "This was the first southpaw I'd faced as a pro. I wasn't going to press the issue and get hit with something I didn't understand, so I lay back and won a decision in six."

September 17, 1980, Paul Moore: "He could fight, but he threw out a long, slow, lazy jab and I nailed him with a right before he brought it back for a first-round knockout. I remember the fight because it was the day after Jane and I got married."

October 2, 1980, Jose Green: "He was tough until I hit him with body shots. It was a KO in five."

October 24, 1980, Orlando Montalvo: "This was my first eight-rounder. All fight long he was cursing, calling me names. And he fought dirty. Right before the final bell I dropped him. The bell saved him, but I won the decision easy."

January 21, 1981, Charlie Thomas: "The record book says I knocked him out in the second round. But to be honest, him I don't remember."

At this point, Mike Jones and Victor Valle were starting to get excited. Billy Costello was 14 and 0 with eight knockouts. He was determined and he was good. The time had come for his first main event—ten rounds against Marvin Jenkins on March 18, 1981, at the Westchester County Center in White Plains, New York. "Jenkins was a good boxer," Billy remembers. "He had the best jab I'd faced that far, and he thumbed me in the eye a couple of times besides. Going ten rounds is as much psychological as physical. You have to pace yourself, and be ready mentally. It was a good fight, and I won a decision."

April 24, 1981, Trevor Evelyn: "He was tough, but I knocked him out in the fifth."

July 18, 1981, Rosendo Ramirez: "This was on the undercard of Michael Spinks against Eddie Mustafa Muhammad, and the big crowd made me nervous. I hurt him and knocked him through the ropes in the sixth round, but the ropes broke and it took ten minutes to fix them. That gave him a rest and he survived, but I won an eight-round decision."

December 5, 1981, Chico Rosa: "He was nothing. I knocked him out with a body shot at thirty-nine seconds of the first round."

February 17, 1982, Raul Hernandez: "Very tough; a Cuban living in Miami. I boxed him early, then broke him down with body shots and left hooks, and knocked him out in the sixth."

Body shots, left hooks, *the punch*. Billy had it. Still, as his career progressed, he was to learn that as a fighter steps up in class, his opponents don't fall with the first good punch. Sometimes the first good punch doesn't even hurt them.

April 14, 1982, Bob Harvey: "This was the toughest guy I'd ever faced until I got up to championship caliber. I hit him with everything, and he just kept coming. He didn't flinch. He didn't turn red. He just kept coming, and I was saying to myself, 'Fuck, man, this guy must have bricks in his chin.' It was a good lesson for me. I won the decision, but it made me realize that no matter how hard I hit, when the competition got better, it wouldn't be enough. I'd have to box."

May 23, 1982, Felix Favella: "Favella was another southpaw, but he didn't have nothing. I hit him with a three-punch combination in the third round, and it was goodnight. That made my record 21 and 0, but no one seemed to notice much. By then everyone was going crazy over Gerry Cooney."

"Crazy" is an understatement. In 1980 Cooney had beaten Jimmy Young to a bloody pulp in four rounds, and crushed Ron Lyle's ribs in less than three minutes. Then in 1981 he'd punched Ken Norton senseless in 54 seconds, leaving the former heavyweight champion unconscious, mouth agape, his eyes wide open and unfocused. Hysteria followed. Cooney graced the cover of *Time* magazine and, twice, the cover of *Sports Illustrated*. *The New York Times* touted him as "potentially the highest paid athlete ever." Billy was relegated to Cooney's shadow.

"We have a concept of how Gerry will be marketed," Dennis Rappaport told the media. "Gerry's not going to be just a spokesman for a company, and then, when his recognition factor may not be as great, be discarded. We're going to take small or medium-sized companies, get an equity position plus a guarantee against a percentage of gross sales. I saw estimates that said he could be worth fifty million dollars. That's absurdly low. I could give you a figure that would sound like a telephone number with a direct dialing prefix, and three years from now even that might seem minuscule. How about one billion dollars? The first billion-dollar athlete in the world. It's possible."

A billion dollars! And Billy Costello, who was laboring for

three- and four-digit purses, felt lost in the shuffle. What could he expect from Victor Valle, when Victor was training a man with the potential to make him millions of dollars? How much attention would Mike Jones give a little-known fighter from Kingston, when he was co-manager of the most financially profitable prospect in sports history? Gerry Cooney stood on the verge of rewriting every financial rule ever written. But there was one prerequisite: For it all to happen he had to wrest the heavyweight championship of the world from Larry Holmes. The fight was signed, then postponed when Cooney pulled a muscle in his left shoulder. Signed again. The sports world waited.

"There's going to be a love affair between the rest of the world and Gerry Cooney," Rappaport predicted. "There will be America, apple pie, Wheaties, and Gerry Cooney."

The fight took place on June 11, 1982. As testimony to Cooney's drawing power, his camp demanded and received unprecedented parity with Holmes on everything from purse dollars to free tickets at ringside. The bout, shown live on theater TV, was the richest in heavyweight history. Its appeal was such that every single seat was sold out at all 78 closed-circuit locations in the New York-New Jersey-Connecticut area. Cooney's purse came to over nine million dollars.

Larry Holmes knocked Gerry Cooney out in the thirteenth round.

And suddenly Mike Jones's world was redrawn. Howard Davis was about to depart in a bitter contractual dispute that would linger for years. Soon Wilford Scypion would be knocked out in a bid to dethrone middleweight champ Marvin Hagler. And it would be more than two years before Cooney, who had been physically and psychologically devastated by Holmes, fought again.

"It's a terribly frustrating experience," Mike would say later, "for a manager to watch his fighter in the ring. To know that your own hopes and dreams are on the line, and yet to be unable to do anything about it. And then, if your fighter loses, you feel guilty about feeling sorry for yourself because you know that whatever you might have lost, your fighter has lost more. That's how Victor and I both felt about Gerry's defeat. We cried for Gerry far more than we cried for ourselves."

On October 8, 1982, four months after Gerry Cooney lost to Larry Holmes, Billy Costello returned to Kingston to fight as a professional in his home town for the first time. The opponent was Dominic Fox. "In the second round," Billy remembers, "I hit him with a right hand over a jab, then a left hook. He fell like a ton of bricks." One month later, on November 7, Costello received his first national television exposure in a ten-round bout against former United States Boxing Association champion Willie Rodriguez. The bout was crucial because it marked the first time Billy had faced a world-class opponent. "I was nervous again," he remembers. "Rodriguez was a veteran and slick as hell. Whenever I hurt him, he'd slide and make me miss. I had more firepower than he did, but he took me to school a few times; knocked me down in the ninth round."

The decision was unanimous: 6–3–1, 6–3–1, 6–4 for Costello.

Next came Carl Crowley, April 15, 1983: "He was a nice guy; gave me a pair of baby shoes for my daughter, who was about to be born. I hit him with a body shot, and knocked him out in the third round."

September 30, 1983, Clemente Rojas: "He was tough; another one of those Cuban guys fighting out of Miami. Three times I knocked him down, and each time he got up. Finally in the fifth round they stopped it."

December 21, 1983, Mike Essett: "Just a survivor. I didn't really even hit him good. He just quit in the fourth round. Christmas was coming, and I guess he needed the money. We both did."

A lot of trains leave the same station at the same time, but they don't all ride the same track or get to the same destination. Billy Costello was now undefeated in 26 fights. "He'd come a long way," Victor Valle remembers. "He'd turned himself into a world-class fighter."

Still, in boxing as in the rest of life, a man is judged both by the scope of his ambitions and the extent to which he fulfills them. And Billy Costello's ambition was quite simple. He wanted to be a world champion. That had been his goal from the first day he'd stepped into a ring, and it remained the only way he could make enough money to provide adequately for his wife and newborn child.

"I had a philosophy with Billy," Mike Jones remembers. "We'd talk, and I'd tell him I didn't want him to fight for the world title; I wanted him to *win* the damn thing." Now Billy Costello was ready to win. But the road to the title lay through a thorn-filled thicket of competing powers; through world sanctioning bodies, American television networks, and a man named Don King.

PART

2

Don King is a liar and a thief, the greediest bastard I've ever known. This guy wants all the money and all the fighters. He talks about fairness and equality, but he wants everything for himself, and doesn't want to give anything to anybody. I spent years hoping Don would change. He didn't and he won't. It's like, you can take a tiger and paint him yellow with spots, but sooner or later the paint wears off and the stripes come back again. The man's greatest asset is that he was born black, because the fighters are black. He knows them. He knows how to rile them, how to sweet-talk them. He'll say and do whatever it takes to win them over. And all the while the man's so insecure he goes around wearing his hair like a fucking idiot so people will recognize him. If I was a fighter and needed a promotor, who would I take? Don King. The man is the best. Don King delivers.

—Rich Giachetti,
former manager and trainer
of Larry Holmes

6

Fifty years ago the legendary publisher and boxing scholar Nat Fleisher warned, "The most insidious and dangerous enemies of boxing have not been foes from without, but the terrible breakers-down on the inside. The most serious threats to boxing always have come from within."

Much has changed in the world at large since Fleisher's admonition, but the business of boxing remains largely unchanged. It is the red-light district of professional sports, an arena marked by greed and corruption, rife with shifting alliances and private wars; a world where promises take funny bounces, and one is best advised to heed the referee's warning—"protect yourself at all times."

New arrivals to the boxing business learn the rules of the game, and then either play by those rules or get out. Honesty is not tolerated to the point of being brave or foolish. Sometimes the chicanery has a Runyanesque ring. Early in his career Rocky Marciano fought his brother, who was using an assumed name. Each man pulled his punches, and it was a payday for both of them. But other deceptions have been more dangerous. Fighters with nine or ten losses in a row are given phony records and put into bouts they have no chance of surviving. Young men with medical infirmities are cleared by corrupt officials to fight, with often tragic results. "Anything seems to go in a business in which larceny is sometimes mistaken for charm, and cheating for cleverness," writes Michael Katz of *The New York Times*.

"People who should be in jail are looked upon as characters instead of the scum they really are." The almighty dollar takes the place of ethics, and the bottom line is all that counts. No matter how crooked a man is, if he has the connections, everyone beats a path to his door.

Only the ring is square. Outside the ring, a sport of courage turns to a business of exploitation. "When you come up from the street," says Butch Lewis, who rose to prominence as the promotor of Leon and Michael Spinks, "you're supposed to be able to go on a man's word. You don't have written contracts on the streets. You have handshakes, and that's what fighters go by. Then they get fucked."

In sum, the Marquis of Queensberry Rules apply only to what goes on inside the ring. "Outside the ring," the late Paddy Flood observed, boxing brings out the worst in people. If you put all the promoters, trainers and managers in a room for a week, there'd be nothing left but bones."

Boxing today is where American business was in the age of the robber barons—monopolistic without effective antitrust control, growing spectacularly in terms of revenue, yet with widespread unconscionable worker exploitation. Television brings an enormous amount of money into the fold, but very little of that money trickles down. Rather, the bulk of boxing's revenue is divided among noncombatants, and the fighters—who have no union and none of the other protections normally accorded professional athletes—are left with poor wages, inadequate medical care, and no pension beyond a pocketful of memories when their career is done. Frequently even fighters who make it to the top find themselves penniless and in debt. A man who earns millions of dollars in the ring is not necessarily a good banker. Many fighters who are able to protect themselves with their fists have none of the tools necessary to manage their financial affairs.

In theory, boxing in the United States is regulated at the state and local levels. At present 43 states and the District of Columbia have some form of athletic commission to govern the sport. In two states regulation is at the county or city level. Five states have no public regulation at all. The result is a frightening mishmash of rules and regulations with widely divergent safeguards and standards. Some jurisdictions require two physicians and emergency medical equipment to be present at every fight. Others don't even require a boxer to take a physical examination before he steps into the ring. Some states suspend a boxer for up to ninety days after a severe beating; others allow a fighter to be knocked out two days in a row. Commission record keeping is erratic. No one knows how many licensed boxers there are in the United States, although best estimates place the number at around five thousand. Many states don't even have a complete set of rules and regulations gathered together in one place for official use. Often no mechanism exists for verifying a fighter's record. Testifying before Congress in support of a bill that would have established a federal advisory panel on professional boxing, Bert Sugar declared, "The various state athletic commissions do not share information; in many cases, they do not even talk to each other. Let a fighter fight in State A on Tuesday, and no other state will find out about it for weeks, perhaps ever. There is no central control. Were these state commissions manufacturers of widgets or distributors of toilet seats, they would have a national association. Not so with boxing."

Even scoring differs from state to state. In New York the fighter who wins the most rounds is declared the victor. In Nevada the winner of each round is given ten points, the loser nine or less, and whoever has the most points at the end of the fight wins. Other states use a "five point must" or different form of point system. Fight financial figures are seldom released. In some states a fighter's contract with the promoter is a matter of public record, so the media can find out how much the fighter's camp has earned; but the fighter never learns the extent to which the promoter has profited. All it takes to be licensed as a manager in most jurisdictions is $50 or $100. Practical experience and a knowledge of boxing aren't required. No state adequately regulates the gyms in which fighters train. A man suspended from the ring for thirty days after being badly beaten can get knocked out in sparring every day. A fighter banned for life because of brain damage can still find work as a sparring partner in someone's gym.

Any fighter who is knocked out and fights soon afterward becomes a candidate for death. Yet consider the following:

- The state of Oklahoma allowed a middleweight named Benny Harjo to fight, knowing that Harjo had a pacemaker to regulate his heart. The fight took place on August 5, 1983. Harjo was knocked out in the first round.

- In 1981 an Ohio lightheavyweight named Darnell Hayes lost twenty fights and was knocked out fourteen times. In one month he was knocked out in three different states and the province of Ontario.

- Another Ohio lightheavyweight, Obie Garnett, was knocked out in the first round in each of his first nine fights. A fellow boxer, Sylvester Wilder, lost 36 fights in a row.

- Former United States Olympic gold-medal winner Sugar Ray Seales fought for two years while he was blind in one eye and vision-impaired in the other. "I knew the eye charts pretty well," Seales says, "so I could fake it. In the last few years I would say I never took a prefight physical that lasted longer than three minutes."

- During a prefight physical, New Jersey heavyweight Randy Neumann asked why the examining doctor was putting a blood-pressure cuff around Neumann's arm while the fighter still had his winter overcoat on. "Look," the doctor told him, "it's getting late. If you're stupid enough to get in there and fight, I'm not going to stop you."

Some states make a genuine effort to properly regulate boxing. But protecting boxers in one state is as meaningless as killing all the gypsy moths in one person's front yard. There are 49 infested neighbors. And with television accounting for an ever-greater share of boxing revenues, a fight's "live gate" becomes less and less important. Thus a promoter who encounters difficulties in complying with the regulations of one state will simply move his business to another.

In this regard, a look at New Jersey is instructive. In 1976 eleven professional boxing cards were held in the state. Then legalized gambling was enacted for Atlantic City, and the sport took hold. Boxing is a marketing tool for the gambling industry. Casinos are willing to pay large sums of money for fights, even taking a loss on promotions because they know any deficit will be made back at the gaming tables. By 1984 there were almost two hundred fight cards annually in New Jersey. The price? On March 1 of that year the State Commission of Investigation released a 72-page report that revealed the following:

The expansion of the boxing industry in New Jersey has precipitated increasingly serious problems caused by inadequate and inappropriate regulation. Boxing contests no longer can be conducted in this state without breaking the law. The Office of the State Athletic Commissioner is demonstrably unable to cope with its regulatory obligations or keep pace with the workload. Its licensing procedures are slipshod, erratic and antiquated, and its auditing controls over receipts and disbursements are almost nonexistent. More important, the industry's monitors are failing to properly safeguard the physical welfare of boxers. In this as in other areas, both the law and related regulations affecting the industry are being flouted. Boxers of questionable physical and professional qualifications are being allowed to fight; stronger boxers are being matched with inexperienced opponents; and the policing of the matches by ringside officials is becoming increasingly irresponsible. Regulatory laxity is enlarging the sport's always threatening potential for death and injury.

Testimony by Robert W. Lee, Chairman of the New Jersey State Athletic Commission, was equally distressing:

Q.   What kind of an attempt is made to confirm the identity of a person who applies to be a boxer in New Jersey?

Lee: Well, when a fighter sits down at a table and he represents that he's John Brown, we ask if they bring pictures. Sometimes they do and sometimes they don't. We ask for licenses or registrations. These guys are loose. They don't even walk around with any identification.

Q.   You mean a driver's license?

Lee: Driver's license. You have no idea how loose they are, but we try to get them to bring something. Sometimes they do and sometimes they don't. Now, if we feel satisfied that this is fighter A or fighter B, then we'll go ahead and license that fighter to fight that night.

Q.   From the answer you just gave us, am I correct in concluding that it's possible for a person to show up in New Jersey, apply for a license, get a license, and get into a ring without ever showing any positive form of identification.

Lee: That is possible.

Q.   Now I take it from what we've talked about that the [minimum and maximum] age regulation is not complied with. Is that correct?

Lee: In its entirety, no, you're right.

Q.   Positive proof of age, documentary proof is not required?

Lee: It is not required.

Q.   Looking at C-94 [the fighter's license application form], is there any effort to verify the accuracy of the answers to those questions.

Lee: No. We accept what they put down.

Q.   What about the guy who comes in, tells you he comes from Ohio, that he's licensed in Ohio, and he arrives on the day of the fight and you're not able to contact the Ohio Commission. It's a Saturday, say. Do you automatically refuse to let him fight?

Lee: No. If we—some of it's done on gut instinct. If you have the feeling that this guy is telling you the truth and he's physically fit, you go ahead and let him fight.

New Jersey is now the boxing capital of the United States, and the contrast between the business of boxing and that of other sports is clear. Mickey Mantle and Willie Mays were barred for years from serving as batting instructors for major-league baseball teams because they performed promotional work for casinos. Professional football players are suspended if they bet on games. By contrast, boxing conducts literally thousands of fights, and showcases its prestige championship events in Las

Vegas and Atlantic City. Yet even as the inadequacy of state regulation is realized, one learns of a sub rosa government run not by state administrators, but by a handful of promoters, television executives, and other, sometimes shadowy, figures. These are the people who control boxing. They have the true power. And much of that power can be traced to the rise and fall of the most charismatic figure in boxing history—Muhammad Ali.

In the eyes of many, boxing's modern era began in 1964. That was when a young man named Cassius Clay knocked out Sonny Liston in the seventh round, and a new age dawned.

One mark of a great fighter is the ability to win a title when he's young and hold onto it until he's old. Muhammad Ali stood triumphant in ring center for a long time. He first burst upon the American consciousness as a 178-pound gold-medal winner at the 1960 Olympics in Rome. Dwight D. Eisenhower was President of the United States. The Bay of Pigs, manned space flights, Vietnam, and Watts were yet to come. In some states, black men and women were still forbidden to check into white hotels. Yet when a Russian reporter asked Cassius Clay how it felt to win a gold medal for his country when there were restaurants in America in which he wasn't allowed, the 18-year-old hero looked his inquisitor in the eye, and told him, "Russian, we got qualified people working on that problem."

Then came the career that made Muhammad Ali the best-known athlete of all time. One by one, ring opponents fell before him, and the world was captivated by his good looks, wit, energy, and charm. In a way he was childlike, almost innocent in the impetuosity of his words and deeds; outrageous, but "it ain't bragging if you can back it up," he told us all.

Boxing in 1964 was at its nadir. The small clubs were dying. The heavyweight crown was worn by Sonny Liston, a hardened criminal who radiated hostility and scorn. "If Sonny liked you," Cus D'Amato said, "he could be very friendly. The trouble was, he didn't like many people." D'Amato knew all too well of Liston's power. Twice he had watched his own fighter, Floyd Patterson, destroyed by Liston in the first round. And by some accounts Patterson had gotten off lightly. In an earlier bout Liston had knocked out Wayne Bethea, also in the first round. And when Bethea's handlers removed the mouthpiece from the unconscious victim's mouth, they found three teeth embedded in the rubber.

"A prizefight is like a cowboy movie," Liston gloated. "There has to be a good guy and a bad guy. People pays their money to see me lose. Only, in my cowboy movie, the bad guy always wins." Not against Cassius Clay, though. On a warm night in Miami Beach, the young challenger from Louisville stepped into the ring against the indestructible Liston. The champion stood waiting, eyes glowering like the leader of a Satanic cult, intent on the destruction of his brash young foe. And Clay destroyed him. The tyrant was dead. Long live the new king.

It was February 25, 1964—three months after the assassination of John F. Kennedy, sixteen days after the Beatles first appeared on the Ed Sullivan Show. What a time it was . . . and what times followed. "No black boxer," Wilfrid Sheed wrote of Ali, "ever had a better shot at full colorblind acceptance by the white community. None had less of the ghetto or the cottonfield about him." But Ali chose to trace his roots not to Joe Louis, beloved by all, but to Jack Johnson. Jack Johnson—once the most hated man in America because he was black, a winner, and he flaunted it all. In 1908 Johnson had challenged Tommy Burns for the heavyweight crown. On the eve of that fight, writing for the *New York Herald,* Jack London told the world, "Burns is a white man and so am I. Naturally, I want the white man to win." But Johnson won and continued to win, successfully defending his title for seven years. And each time white America hated him more.

Ultimately, in 1915, Johnson was defeated by Jess Willard. Not until 1937 when Joe Louis challenged James Braddock was a black man again allowed to fight for the heavyweight crown. And like Johnson, Louis became more than a fighter—he was a symbol, black America's preeminent hero. Then on June 22, 1938, he risked his title against Germany's Max Schmeling—the only man ever to have beaten him—and white America adopted Joe Louis as its hero too. The Louis-Schmeling fight was deemed the clearest confrontation between good and evil in the history of sports. And on that night Joe Louis was the greatest fighter who ever lived. Schmeling fell in the first round. "We'll win," Joe Louis told a World War II benefit rally at Madison Square Garden several years later, "because we're on God's side." Jimmy

Cannon summed up Joe Louis best in a remark that seems trite now, but was revelatory of its time: "Joe Louis is a credit to his race—the human race." And now in 1964, here was Cassius Clay—who white America wanted as its hero—changing his name to Muhammad Ali, refusing to be cast in the Joe Louis mold. Instead he thrust himself out as a symbol of religious and political discontent. So good in the ring that often his fights appeared as performances rather than contests. So good it seemed he might never lose.

Ali mastered two things, and did them to perfection—the jab and a fast right hand. Many fighters hit harder than Ali, but Ali's punches always kept coming, and with each punch his opponent got a little weaker, lost a little more coordination, and finally fell. "People talk about Joe Louis," Emanuel Steward later observed, "but Muhammad Ali was the greatest heavyweight of all. Look at Louis against Billy Conn. Louis couldn't deal with footwork. And even if Louis had hit Ali, no man ever had the punch to keep Ali down."

"Sometimes we make great fighters out to be more than they really are," says Bill Gallo, who's been with the *New York Daily News* since 1941. "Joe Louis was a brilliant fighter, the epitome of a heavyweight, but he had no personality. Outside the ring, Jack Dempsey was a nice tough simple guy; that's all. But Ali was extraordinary. He was boxing's premier fighter and its best actor as well."

Some people loved Ali, and some hated him. But everyone alive knew he was there. Twenty-nine times he went into the ring as a professional knowing he'd win, and twenty-nine times he won. Then at the height of the war in Vietnam he refused induction into the United States Army, uttering the simplest, most concise antiwar sentiment of his era: "I ain't got no quarrel with them Vietcong." And for his beliefs he was exiled from boxing at the peak of his powers.

Part two of "the Ali legend" followed. After 43 months of forced retirement he returned to defeat Jerry Quarry and Oscar Bonavena. But in his absence the lords of boxing had anointed a new champion. On March 8, 1971, Muhammad Ali entered the ring at Madison Square Garden against Joe Frazier to reclaim his crown.

Championship fights between great fighters are few and far

between. Fights with great fighters and great action are an even rarer phenomenon. Muhammad Ali and Joe Frazier fought three of the greatest fights ever seen. The first belonged to Frazier. Ali was a master at psychologically breaking an opponent down. It was part of his fight plan, a weapon as potent as a straight right or jab. By the time an opponent stepped into the ring with Ali, the master's psychological weapons had already been drawn. At times he seemed able to project an aura of confidence through the air that disabled an opponent before the fight even began. Frazier removed the psychological edge from Ali's arsenal. He was too pure a fighter to be swayed by ring antics or words. One of the scariest things in the world for a fighter is when he hits his opponent with hard clean punches and the opponent keeps coming. Suddenly the fighter starts to think that maybe he's facing an overpowering foe without the weapons to stop him. Frazier kept coming for fifteen brutal rounds. And Frazier won.

A fighter can never be considered truly great until he's beaten another great fighter. Men in the ring are measured not by bouts that are easy, but by the ones that are hard. Twice more Muhammad Ali faced Joe Frazier, and it was a measure of his greatness that both times he succeeded where before he had failed. In their final confrontation in Manila on October 1, 1975, Frazier led in the middle rounds. He wasn't just beating Ali, he was beating him up; and still Ali turned the tide to win. "The closest thing to death I know of," Ali said of the fight after knocking out Frazier in the fourteenth round. Yet a fate in some ways worse than death lay in store.

The downfall of a great fighter is always sad to behold. Every champion knows that as much as he loves his title, someday he'll have to give it up. Still, fighters never seem to quit on top. There's always a trainer or manager with a financial interest to urge them on. It's hard to walk away from the sport when there's money around.

"I saw openings I couldn't use," said Joe Louis after his 1947 fight against Jersey Joe Walcott when his career was on the downhill side. "A man gets old, he don't take advantage of those things as fast as he used to." Still, Louis fought on. A fighter can be told again and again to retire, but the only thing he'll listen to is another man's fists—and sometimes he doesn't even hear them.

Barney Ross always said that he'd retire if he took a bad beating. On May 31, 1938, he did, losing his welterweight crown to Henry Armstrong on a unanimous decision. True to his word, Ross never fought again. Rocky Marciano left the ring in 1956, in full possession of his faculties and his crown. But by and large the gods of boxing stay on too long.

"A fighter," A. J. Liebling once wrote, "is reluctant to accept evidence of his disintegration. Between fights, he is brisk, active and lusty, since he is still a young man. He therefore refuses to believe his first couple of bad fights and blames them on negligence. He has not, he thinks, taken the opposition seriously enough. Then he may lose one or two that he will blame on bad decisions." The excuses go on. Nobody notices how old a fighter gets when he's a bum. But a champion is always on center stage, and soon the world comes to see him not as the ring great he once was, but as a hollow shell—Joe Louis lurching wildly against Rocky Marciano, Sugar Ray Robinson losing to Mick Leahy and Memo Ayon.

After Frazier in Manila, the Ali road show continued, but too many pieces were gone. Each hard fight takes something out of a fighter that can never be put back. It was Ali's gift that he seemed able to absorb unlimited punishment and each time be reborn, but the gift was a mirage. More and more his reflexes slowed; too many times he fought to exhaustion in order to win. What he had more than anyone was a deep-seeded inner belief in himself. He was the best, in part because he believed it to be so. But it was the inability to let go of that belief that, in the end, destroyed him. Like Peter Pan, he seemed forever young, but he was in a sport where men grow old before their time.

"His mind," John Schulian wrote of Ali, "no longer sends messages to his muscles as fast as it used to. The words that tumble out of his mouth ceaselessly are beginning to trip over one another." Still, Ali fought on. The world was his stage. In the past he had done battle in London, Dublin, Frankfurt, Munich, Zurich, Manila, Tokyo, Kinshasha, Jakarta, and Kuala Lumpur. Now, in the twilight of his career, he refused to step down. The damage to his mind mounted, not only from competitive fights but from ferocious beatings sustained while sparring in the gym. Against Larry Holmes, the dream came to an end. For $8 million Ali was beaten into submission over ten brutal, ugly rounds. William Nack of *Sports Illustrated* described the aftermath at Caesar's Palace in Las Vegas, where the fight had been held:

A kind of bedlam had descended over the casino. Around the craps tables, even at the $100 minimum tables, prospective players stood six deep, filling the carpeted aisles waiting for openings. They gathered about the roulette and the blackjack tables, even at the wheel of fortune. All eight of the baccarat tables were full, twenty big spenders betting the $8,000 limit on every hand. And in the background, people stood cheek by jowl at the rattling, coin-spitting slot machines. Ali and Holmes had done their job.

In most gyms today fading posters cover the walls. Some bear pictures of local fighters; usually one or two announce forthcoming bouts in nearby arenas. Almost always there is a poster of Ali. "Joe Louis was my idol" were the words heard from an earlier generation. Now, among black and white fighters alike, the idol is Ali. For 21 years he graced the ring, at his best elevating the sport of boxing to artistry and myth. Over time he fought 270 rounds of heavyweight championship competition, far more than any other man.

"I'd like to write my own epitaph," Muhammad Ali once said. "To understand my life, go into the desert. Look around and you'll see nothing but sand, and each grain is for one year the earth has been. I want to take eighty grains for eighty years of my life, and paint them colors. Then I'll drop them in one spot in the desert for the whole universe to see until the wind comes and blows them away, mixing them up with the other grains of sand."

But there's another epitaph that could be written for Ali: "what might have been." Many observers are fond of asking what might have happened if Ali hadn't been deprived of his crucial middle years. Certainly there would have been more great victories; but inevitably one is forced to admit that the end would have been the same. The man simply would not have stepped down of his own free will. More poignant to consider, then, is what might have been if Ali had *never* been allowed to fight again, if the same regressive powers that stripped him of his crown and forced him from the ring in 1967 had prevailed. Under those circumstances the world would have been deprived of Ali-Frazier and Ali-Foreman. But Muhammad Ali today would be healthy and strong, the gleaming symbol of an unbeatable, unconquered fighter.

Such is speculation. For fighters the good times never last long enough, winter comes too soon. But there are other inhabitants of the boxing world for whom life can be profitable and long. These are the promoters, and the two biggest of modern times, and perhaps all time, are Bob Arum and Don King. In many ways, King and Arum are as different as two men can be. Arum—Harvard educated, Jewish, outwardly quiet and shy. King—a survivor of the streets, black, a graduate of jail. Both are intensely hated by their enemies. And for both the cornerstone of power was Muhammad Ali.

The promotion of boxing matches appears simple. On its surface, all the job seems to require is matching two fighters whose public appeal and skill result in an exciting bout that maximizes profits. However, to be successful a promoter needs a working relationship with fighters, managers, television executives, the press, and world sanctioning bodies. Also, since promotion is a business, a promoter must be able to count. Too many promoters operate without a realistic fix on income and expenditures.

Like managers—maybe more so—promoters are treated harshly by boxing scholars. "Honesty is not a criterion for membership in the promoter's lodge," writes John Schulian of the *Chicago Sun-Times.* "It may even be grounds for expulsion." Mark Kram, formerly of *Sports Illustrated,* opines, "Boxing promoters have seldom been easy on the eyes or ears. There has always been a flaccid pulpy quality to their presence, and often it seems that, if one tried to reach out and grab whatever it is they represent, there would be only air or at best a gummy substance. They view words like loyalty, character and honor as cave animals might look upon sunlight."

In general, promoters make money from three sources, the

first of which is a fight's live gate. Traditionally a promoter would rent an arena and sell tickets himself; although now, and particularly for big fights, action is often set in casinos that pay the promoter a "site fee" and give tickets away to high-rolling customers. Second, promoters receive revenue from the sale of domestic and foreign television rights. This is the major source of boxing revenue, and will remain so for the foreseeable future. Last come incidental items such as the sale of advertising on ring posts, video casettes, and fight programs.

Like fighters, promoters find big money hard to come by. The only way to get rich is through championship fights. But while boxing has had over a hundred champions in various weight divisions since the rise of Ali, two promoters have dominated the sport.

Bob Arum, 53 years old, son of an Orthodox Jewish accountant, grew up in New York City and graduated from Harvard Law School in 1956. Plump, five feet eight inches tall, he speaks with a slight lisp, and gives the appearance of a shy man who doesn't like parties and is most comfortable when left alone.

Arum's introduction to boxing came in 1962. After a stint on Wall Street, he was working for the Tax Section of the United States Attorney's Office in the Southern District of New York. Floyd Patterson was about to defend his title against Sonny Liston, and reacting to rumors of financial chicanery, the Internal Revenue Service asked the Tax Section to impound all revenue from the fight's closed-circuit television outlets. Arum had never seen a professional fight, but he could count, and the dollars involved left him very impressed. Three years later he resigned from government service to join the law firm of Phillips, Nizer, Benjamin, Krim and Ballon. By then Muhammad Ali had won the heavyweight crown, and the Louisville syndicate that backed him was breaking up. Arum stepped into the void. Through pro football's Jim Brown he managed an introduction to Ali, and soon after formed a company called Main Bout Incorporated to promote Ali's fights. Then Ali was stripped of his title, and having gained an entré to the world of boxing, Arum set up a second corporation called Sports Action, which promoted a lucrative World Elimination Tournament to crown a new heavyweight champion. There was grumbling in Ali's camp about

Arum's infidelity, but when Ali returned to the ring in 1970 it was with Arum as his attorney and closed-circuit promoter.

In the years that followed, Arum left Phillips Nizer, founded and then dissolved his own law firm, and ultimately began to devote his full energy to a third promotional company, Top Rank Inc. Meanwhile, as his power mushroomed, so did his critics, and the word many used in describing him was "liar":

• Jose Sulaiman, president of the World Boxing Council: "Mr. Arum is happy to completely base his life on misrepresentations. He is the biggest liar I have ever known."

• Ferdie Pacheco, former physician for Muhammad Ali, now a network official and color commentator for NBC: "One of the Ph.D. liars in the world is Bob Arum. There's a philosophy I have—if you're a friend of mine, you're doubly a friend of mine in business. I'll be honest with you, and I want you to be honest with me. That rule doesn't hold with Arum."

• Cus D'Amato, former trainer and manager of Jose Torres and Floyd Patterson: "Bob Arum is one of the worst people in the western hemisphere. I don't know the eastern hemisphere very well, but I suspect he'd be one of the worst people there too if he went there. I like to do business with a handshake, but if you make the mistake of doing business with Arum, you get it in writing."

• Bob Biron, former manager of Ken Norton: "The problem with Arum is that he's not trustworthy. I don't know anyone to walk away from an agreement as flagrantly and cynically as he does."

• Bob Waters, *Newsday* columnist: "I was talking with Arum. He told me something, and I said, 'But Bob, yesterday you told me the exact opposite.' 'I know,' Arum answered. 'Today I'm telling the truth; yesterday I was lying.' "

Consternation, surprise, dismay, and perhaps a touch of shock cross Arum's face when the issue of his candor arises. "Maybe it's the caliber of people you deal with in this business," he explains. "I'm a lawyer, and I use very precise language, but no matter what you say, they hear what they want to hear. I'll say, 'Look, I'm going to get you a fight on television if I can sell it to a network,' and they'll leave my office without taking into account the qualifying statement."

Teddy Brenner, who was president of Madison Square Garden Boxing for five years and now works for Arum, concurs with his boss, adding, "If you're a boxing promoter, you go into town and there are fifty managers begging you to use their fighters. You say 'maybe,' but you can only use ten. And later when you don't use the others, someone calls you a liar."

John Branca, former chairman of the New York State Athletic Commission, is also in Arum's corner. "Overall, I found him to be the most qualified and most responsible of the major promoters," says Branca. "I have no qualms about Bob Arum."

But doubts persist. Butch Lewis, who promotes Michael Spinks and James Schuler, dealt with Arum in the late 1970s. "Bob Arum comes across as meek and mild," says Lewis. "Well, let me tell you, Bob Arum is treacherous; he's vicious; he has no morals at all. I worked with the man, putting together the first Ali-Spinks fight for CBS. We signed the contract; we're walking out of the building, and Arum is snickering, 'We can really fuck them.' I looked at him. I said, 'Why do we want to do that? We just made a deal. The ink ain't even dry.' And he says to me, 'I know, but there's a loophole. We can fuck them if there's a rematch.' And he did," says Lewis. "He fucked CBS, and brought the rematch to ABC. Then later he fucked ABC. And he's fucked NBC. He's fucked them all, and they still do business with him because that's the business."

"I'll shake hands with Arum," says British promoter Mickey Duff, "but I'll take my ring off first."

"When Bob Arum pats you on the back," concludes Cus D'Amato," he's just looking for a spot to stick the knife."

"Maybe Arum is his own worst enemy," someone suggests.

"Not while I'm alive," D'Amato answers.

Faced with these attacks, Arum maintains a calm exterior. "People in boxing tend to spout off," he says. "I've been very vitriolic at times myself, so maybe I get what I deserve when people turn around and attack me. Also, I'd have to say there's a strain of antisemitism in the dialogue [unlikely—Duff is Jewish]. . . . I like to outwit an opponent," Arum continues. "I like to get something done cleverly but not by stealing. Stealing makes me very uncomfortable."

Say what you will, Bob Arum revolutionized the business of professional boxing. He was the first promoter to completely package big fights, grossing as much as $30 million for a single event (the first Leonard-Duran bout in 1980). Along the way he also developed a relationship with ESPN, which gave the fledgling sports programming network new life—and accorded Arum a hold over dozens of young fighters. Through a series of alliances and contractual obligations he amassed extraordinary power. For example, when Leon Spinks won the heavyweight crown in 1978, Arum held options on his first six title defenses.

I'm a businessman," Arum once said, explaining the philosophy that brought him to power. "Two guys fighting in a ring, that has nothing to do with me. Fighters bore me."

Yet even as Arum's power was reaching its peak, his standing as boxing's premier promoter was being challenged. Muhammad Ali had found a new ally, a former numbers czar from the streets of Cleveland with schemes and dreams that taxed even the most vivid imagination. The man was Don King, and miraculously his schemes and dreams were coming true.

Don King was born in 1932. When he was nine his father was killed in an industrial accident. King, his sister, and four brothers were raised by their mother. "When you're poor, black, and without formal education," he says, looking back on those early years, "there aren't many things white society allows you to do." What King decided to do was run numbers. "It was statutorily illegal," he acknowledges, "but who knew about statutes? White people were going to church, playing bingo, and nobody was bothering them. They set aside the whole state of Nevada to gamble in. So why did they bother us when we had policy?"

Over time, King graduated from a numbers runner to a numbers czar. "It was good training," he says. "In the numbers business you don't have the luxury of an office with file clerks and telephone answerers. You have to do most of it out of your head, always be on the run, and still come out with a profit. I had to establish liaisons, same as I do now in boxing. I started in numbers when I was nineteen years old, and I went to the top. They called me Kingpin and the Numbers Czar and Donald The Kid King. I was good."

King was an independent operator who took as many bets as possible, kept the ones he was able to cover, and laid the rest off with other bookies. As his operation grew he hired an ex-convict named Sam Garrett to help lay off bets. One day number 347 hit, and Garrett told King he hadn't been able to lay it off. King concluded that Garrett had placed the bet and kept the money for himself. King stood six foot two and weighed well over two hundred pounds. Garrett was nine inches shorter and weighed one-fifty. King's version of what happened next was: "I said, 'Okay, I'm just gonna quit playing with you, because I don't believe the man ain't paid off.' He said, 'You calling me a liar?' I said, 'No, I ain't calling you a liar, but you ain't paid me so I just ain't gonna play with you no more.' He began to hurl expletives. I had about eighteen hundred dollars in my pocket, had a brand new convertible Cadillac. When I was getting in the Cadillac, he challenged me from behind. And in the kicking and fighting of what I call the frustrations of the ghetto expressing themselves, this man's head hit the concrete. Seven, eight days later, he expired."

King was tried, found guilty of second-degree murder (a verdict later reduced to manslaughter), and committed to the Marion Correctional Institute in Ohio. Four years later, on September 30, 1971, he was released from prison. "Jail was my school," he said later. "I had one of the most delightful times under desperate conditions. I read Aristotle and Homer. I got into Sigmund Freud. That almost blew my mind. When I dealt with William Shakespeare, I got to know him very well as a man. I felt he may have been the ghostwriter for King James in writing his version of the Bible. Man, I love Bill Shakespeare. He was some bad dude. Intellectually, I went into jail with a peashooter and came out armed with a nuclear bomb. I made time serve me, rather than me serve time."

The events that followed Don King's release from prison read like the script of a television miniseries. Returning to Cleveland he decided to try his hand at managing a fighter, and settled on heavyweight Earnie Shavers, who at the time was co-managed by baseball player Dean Chance and a Youngstown businessman named Blackie Gennaro. King bought out Chance's share for

$8,000, and soon after added two more fighters—Jeff Merritt and Ray Anderson—to his stable. He helped Merritt conquer a serious drug problem, often sitting up with the boxer until dawn. But King could be rough too. Once during a contract dispute, Anderson hinted at violence, and King told him, "Ray, we come from the same gutter. Let's not jive each other. You could pick up that phone and make me dead in half an hour. I can pick it up and have you dead in five minutes."

Within the next year King branched into promoting fights as well, running several small fight cards in Ohio. In March 1974 he was brought into the Foreman-Norton championship bout as a consultant by Video Techniques, the closed-circuit firm that promoted the match. "I was their token nigger," he remembers. "A black face to deal with the blacks." It was during this period that King also had his first dealings with Bob Arum. Earnie Shavers was knocked out by Jerry Quarry in Madison Square Garden, and adding insult to injury, Arum garnisheed Shaver's purse to make certain he got his money from closed-circuit television rights in Ohio—about $4,000. "I felt emasculated," King says. "The man didn't even give me a chance to pay him." The two clashed again one month later when Arum reneged on what King felt was Arum's promise that King could have Ohio closed-circuit rights on the second Ali-Frazier fight.

Arum for his part today treats his rival with professed equanimity. "I really have no animosity toward Don King," he says. "How King feels about me is his own concern." However, over the years King's bitterness has remained strong. Among other public utterances, he has branded Arum "the master of all evil," "a despicable and unconscionable cad," "a low culprit," and "my greatest foe and nemesis, completely devoid of principle."

Still, boxing is a strange business. And often, under radically different circumstances, old adversaries meet again. Even as King was being "emasculated" by Arum, the seeds of revenge were being sown. In 1972 King had helped promote a charity exhibition for the Forest City Hospital in Cleveland. One of the fighters in attendance was Muhammad Ali, who had lost his title to Joe Frazier the previous year. After the benefit, King spoke with Ali and announced that he wanted to promote the ex-champion's fights.

Ali's response was short and to the point: "Man, you're crazy."

At the time, Ali was managed by Herbert Muhammad—son of Elijah Muhammad, the acknowledged leader of the Black Muslims. "I went to Herbert Muhammad," King remembers, "and I said, 'God has put me here to do this. You must give me the chance because your father said in his holy words that, if you find a black man comparable to a white man in doing his duties, you must remove the white man and give the black man a chance.'"

Herbert Muhammad's response was practical. Black, white, red, yellow, and brown were all secondary. The color of primary concern was green. Ali would fight for King if King could deliver money.

Undaunted, King went next to George Foreman, who had captured the heavyweight crown from Joe Frazier, and offered Foreman $5 million to defend his title against Ali. The sum was unheard of, far more than any fighter including Ali had ever earned. Foreman accepted. Then King returned to Herbert Muhammad with a similar offer, which was satisfactory. Now the would-be promoter had both Ali and Foreman in tow. All he needed was the staggering sum of $10 million. But now Don King had something to trade for it—the heavyweight championship of the world.

Don King is many things—flamboyant, ostentatious, cunning, ruthless, part businessman and part con-man, part riverboat gambler and revivalist preacher. He's also brilliant. Armed with "front money" from The Hemdale Corporation (a British firm that he enlisted as co-promoter), King journeyed to Zaire to secure an audience with President Mobutu Sese Seko, the fledgling African nation's leader. What King wanted from Mobutu was quite simple—$10 million of Zaire's scarce currency. And he asked for it with the promise that the promotion would, in King's words, "bring focus to the plight of their country, tell a story about their country the way they want to tell it. It's a once-in-a-lifetime thing where you can have one billion people focusing in by closed-circuit television. A historic event, two prodigal sons returning home to the land of their heritage, the womb from which they sprang; a black promoter, two black gladiators fighting on black soil. And not incidentally, the promotion promised to spread Mobutu's name across the face of the earth. King got his money.

Certain cosmetic problems followed. A fight poster trumpeting "From the slave ship to the championship" offended Zairans, and had to be replaced. When fight tickets arrived in the African nation they were returned to Philadelphia for reprinting because Mobutu's name had been spelled incorrectly. But the fight was legend. On October 30, 1974, Muhammad Ali knocked out George Foreman to reclaim his crown, and suddenly Don King—not Bob Arum—was Ali's promoter.

"Don King is a man who wants to swallow mountains, walk on oceans, and sleep on clouds," wrote Mark Kram. The business of boxing was never the same again.

In the first six months of 1975, King promoted Ali championship fights against Chuck Wepner, Ron Lyle, and Joe Bugner. Then Ali's demands went beyond the means of individuals and corporations, and King again turned to a foreign power. On March 8, 1971, Don King had listened to reports of the first Muhammad Ali–Joe Frazier fight from his prison cell in Marion, Ohio. On October 1, 1975, four years after his release from prison, it was Don King who promoted the historic third bout between Ali and Frazier in the Philippine capital of Manila. He had become, *Time* magazine wrote, "one of the most successful black businessmen in America."

Whoever controls the heavyweight title controls a sizable chunk of boxing. In the aftermath of Ali-Frazier III, Don King had at least temporary control of that crown, and he moved swiftly to consolidate his power, becoming one of the most recognizable figures in sports. Unseen was an ugly scar across his chest from what should have been simple cyst surgery in prison that went wrong. Externally his image was glitter and sparkling excess—tall, closing in on 250 pounds, fingers studded with diamonds, long cigars, frilled shirts, sequined tuxedos; a gold necklace with more diamonds spelling out the name "Don." Then, too, there was the matter of his hair—the most famous Afro in the world.

"The hair happened by accident," his stepson Carl later recalled. "It was always short and combed straight up. Then with the Ali-Foreman fight he was gone for a couple of months and didn't cut it. It got longer and longer, and he kept combing it up. Finally people started to notice and comment, and he decided it looked like a king's crown, and he liked it."

The result was an Afro that seems to defy the law of gravity, as if its possessor stuck his finger in an electric light socket while the current was flowing. The hair is distinctive, and King likes it that way. His image is stamped on everything he does. "Nobody wanted to be up front before me," he boasts. "They all wanted to sit back, collect their money, and play dirty tricks on each other. But I'm out there, Jack. You can see me. My name's on everything. This ain't no No-Name Productions. It's Don King Productions. I perform."

"Don King dresses like a pimp and speechifies like a storefront preacher," John Schulian has observed. But those who do business with him know that despite his public persona, when it comes to business King can be very quiet and reserved. And in addition to his creativity, King has one superceding advantage. No set formula exists for making it to the top in the business of boxing. A man can be crooked, he can be honest; he can be black, he can be white. But he has to be hard working. Don King is a workaholic, more so than any other promoter in the world. While other people are sleeping, he's awake, making the rounds.

"The man's energy is incredible," says Mort Sharnik, a veteran of *Sports Illustrated* and CBS Sports. "Call Don King at midnight, tell him a fighter is ready to sign, and he'll be on a plane by one A.M. He'll get there by six A.M., sign the papers, be half-dead, and someone will say, 'Don, Joe X just called; he's ready to do business.' Before you can turn around, Don will be off and running again."

"Don King never stops pushing to get a deal done," says Bob Iger, director of program planning for ABC Sports. "I can remember nights, lying in bed with my wife after midnight, screaming into the telephone at Don King who'd just called. When he wants something, he's very persistent. He finds you and he keeps on you until he gets the job done."

"I'm the best promoter in the world," King says, "because I haven't taken a day off from work since I left the penitentiary, and because I have read the great philosophers like St. Thomas Aquinine [sic]. Against all odds I have persevered. I am a true attestation to the American dream. I wasn't invited to any board meetings. I had to kick the door down. I'm with the masses, not the classes. I'm living proof that you don't have to go to Harvard and Yale and Princeton in order to do something in America. I recognize what my limitations are in the system, but there's no shackle put upon you if you can learn and progress. By getting smart you can circumvent the situation and create a new aura. I'm a flag waver. A lot of people think I'm a flag waver for ulterior motives but it isn't about that at all. It's about the country itself with its founding principles. One nation indivisible with liberty and justice for all. We hold these truths to be sacred, and all men are created equal. These principles are very profound, man."

Don King's biggest asset early in his career was his association with Ali. "Because of Muhammad Ali," he acknowledges, "I never had to start at the bottom and work my way up. I started at the top, doing world-title fights." However, there was a second plus in the early days—King wasn't Bob Arum. People in boxing were growing fearful of Arum's power, and wanted a counterweight. "There was only one tune," King remembers, "and if you didn't dance to his music, you didn't dance. I just brought a new tune to town. Where he had Bach and Brahms, I brought rhythm and blues to give them an opportunity to go in another direction."

Still, King was not above adopting some of Arum's tactics when they suited his ends. Through exclusive services contracts, growing numbers of quality fighters were bound to his fold. Anyone challenging a fighter promoted by King for a world title was pressured to sign an agreement giving the promoter options on his first three title defenses should the challenger prevail.

Don King didn't invent the concept of monopoly in boxing. He didn't write the rules, but he played by them better than anyone else ever had. Also, he wasn't above a little deceit to get what he wanted.

Mickey Duff, who manages Uganda's John Mugabi, recalls, "Early in John's career I wanted to get him a fight in the United States, so I called King, and King matched him against Curtis Ramsey in Atlantic City. I brought Mugabi over; then an emergency came up and I had to go home. I hated to do it, but there was no choice. All I could do was tell John's trainer, George Francis, to call with the result the minute the fight was over. So there I was," Duff continues, "sitting in England, biting my nails, when the phone rang, and it was George telling me that Mugabi had knocked Ramsey out in the first round. Then Don King gets on the line and says, 'Mickey, the kid's good but we got a problem. He's begging me to take over his career. He says he wants Don King to run him, but I told him no. I said you and I are friends, Mickey, and I won't take him on unless he lets me keep you as a fifty-fifty partner.' "

"Don," Duff responded, "I didn't know you spoke Swahili."

"I don't," King answered.

"That's very interesting," said Duff, "because Mugabi doesn't speak a word of English."

"King and Arum are alike," Duff summarizes. "One's black and one's white. That's the only difference."

"Don King is the best snake-oil salesman I ever met," says Butch Lewis. "The absolute best."

"If you stay in a room with Don King for an hour," says Larry Holmes, "he'll con you into anything. That's why I talk to him over the phone. So I can hang up." When Holmes defended his world championship against Lucien Rodriguez in Scranton, Pennsylvania, in a bout promoted by King, Scranton Mayor James McNulty was reminded that he had once presented the promoter with a key to the city. "We've changed the locks since then," McNulty answered.

But in the boxing business it's the bottom line that counts. And King delivers. "There's only been three great promoters in this century," he is fond of saying. "P. T. Barnum, Michael Todd, and me. I've made it, Jack. I have coffee and cocktails with presidents and dictators. I'm an international figure, a citizen of the world. I've made it."

If the applicable standards are power, recognition, and the accumulation of wealth, Don King has indeed made it in boxing. He's not a comic, he's not a buffoon. He's a very serious, calculating businessman who controls much of the sport. If catastrophe hit the world, and men could prevail only by living in the jungle, Don King would be a survivor.

"There are two things to remember when doing business with King," says one observer. "The first is that he's been places most people have never been, and it's shaped him. When everything else is gone, when he's been up, working, pushing, grinding for days and all his other resources are exhausted, that's when Don King reaches down and starts to run on hostile energy. It's ugly to watch, but he gets what he wants."

And second?

"Second, whenever you do business with Don King, you can never lose sight of the fact that he's smarter than you are."

7

"White America didn't exactly open up its arms to me," Don King once said. "I had to work harder than most people for what I got."

That statement is true. Yet ironically it was white-controlled "establishment" America—specifically the television networks— that gave King much of his power and continues to give it to him today.

Boxing and the media date back to Homer (the first sportswriter), who recounted the match between Epeios and Euryalos in Book 23 of *The Iliad*. Since then the sport has proven irresistible to chroniclers, and been much publicized by the electronic media. The first world-title fight broadcast on radio was between Jack Dempsey and Georges Carpentier on July 2, 1921. The first major bout televised in the United States was Lou Nova's eleventh-round knockout of Max Baer at Yankee Stadium in 1939. Thereafter, boxing and Milton Berle were responsible for selling many of the nation's first television sets. But in recent years the tables have turned. With small fight clubs on the verge of extinction, boxing is now dependent on television for survival. Yet television views boxing as a programming instrument, nothing more.

Unlike most sports, boxing is not tied to a specific season or calendar date. Fights can be scheduled on short notice, and cost less to produce than most athletic contests. Thus a network will often "counterprogram" a fight opposite another network's major event. "Put even a weak fight against the Kentucky Derby or Masters Golf Tournament," says Bob Iger of ABC Sports, "and the fight draws." Terry O'Neil, executive producer of CBS Sports Saturday and Sports Sunday, further defines the role of boxing in television's eyes. "As far as CBS is concerned," says O'Neil, "boxing is one of many programming tools that make up our sports anthologies; that's all. Each week a hundred proposals come across my desk—bike races, skiing, lumberjack contests. My job is to find the proper mix that brings a show in under budget and attracts an audience for our sponsors."

To fighters, television is crucial. "No matter how good a fighter is," says Emanuel Steward, "he won't make a name for himself until he's on television. He won't be famous without TV, and he won't make any money either." Yet the corollary to Steward's observation is that television is in the ratings business, not the business of boxing. Network executives view selling a fight as a marketing proposition, and how well a man can box is often secondary to his charisma.

"TV means you're developing matinee idols first and fighters second," says Butch Lewis. "You groom your product to the point where the networks want it. In the old days the only fighters who made money were the ones who put asses in seats. Now it's how many people sitting at home turn on their sets, and a fighter's Neilson ratings are as important as his record."

Virtually every big fight has to be sold to television—the networks, Home Box Office, or closed circuit—before it's scheduled. But how does television decide which bouts to take? Alex Wallau, a producer/director for ABC's boxing broadcasts, sheds some light on the criteria used by his network. "Our philosophy," says Wallau, "is to identify the most talented and charismatic champions, and put them in the best match possible. Usually the way we'll get a fight is a promoter or manager calls up and says, 'Fighter X is going to make a defense; let's find an opponent you like.' Other times they'll already have the opponent. Either way, if a match is competitive, if at least one of the fighters is attractive, and if the price is right, we buy it. The problem is, most matches offered aren't competitive."

Why not?

"No good manager wants to put his fighter in an even fight," Wallau answers. "Every one of them is looking for an edge. And beyond that, there are very few competitive matches you can make for a great fighter like Thomas Hearns or Marvin Hagler. The result is that, like the other networks, ABC puts on a few great fights, a lot of decent ones, and our share of mismatches. We'd love it if every fight was an all-out war between evenly matched fighters. That would be great for our audience and great for us, but you'd be looking at the worst-managed fighters in the world."

Mort Sharnik of CBS is in accord with Wallau. "A should fight B, and X should fight Y," says Sharnik. "But the dynamics of the game are that too often A winds up fighting Y, and B fights X. The matches would be better if we could make them ourselves, but then we'd run into antitrust problems. What CBS looks for," Sharnik continues, "are fights that take a fighter someplace, that are important career building blocks, part of an ongoing story."

The bottom line is that it's television executives acting in concert with a few key promoters who make virtually all of today's major fights. And it's television executives who supply most of the money that allows people like Bob Arum and Don King to operate. Yet almost without exception, these same executives disclaim responsibility for boxing's troubles.

"ABC is not a sports organization," says Iger. "We broadcast fights. We don't govern them."

"We feel we should do everything possible to put on a good show and be honest with the public," says Wallau. "But it's not our proper role to turn activist and clean up the sport of boxing. We're supposed to report the news, not manage it."

Terry O'Neil of CBS acknowledges, "I'm troubled by the essential nature of boxing, the dangers and physical risks. I know that, often, television is the catalyst for young men's dreams, and leads them to do things I might not want them to do. But let's face it, no matter what anyone at CBS, NBC, or ABC does, boxing will continue. I don't see myself as someone on a white horse trying to clean up boxing. I'm a businessman with a very straightforward responsibility."

Mort Sharnik concurs with O'Neil, and then goes him one further. "I feel very strongly that television has a positive influence on boxing," says Sharnik. "We investigate records. The glaring eye of the TV camera encourages honesty in judges' decisions. We get rid of more mismatches in a week by turning down prospective opponents for champions than the public could possibly imagine."

Still, newspapers and magazines that cover boxing expect their reporters to be critically honest. By contrast, television demands considerable "puffing" and promotion from its commentators. The line between honest reporting and concern for ratings is often too fine to be clearly drawn. And on occasion the marriage of boxing and television leads to scandal.

Perhaps the best-documented example of television's involvement with professional boxing having gone astray is the "United States Boxing Championships" tournament promoted by Don King for ABC Sports. For many years ABC had lagged behind CBS and NBC in most respects. Then Roone Arledge developed ABC Sports as the network's first prestige arm, and began to utilize boxing as one of several keys to sports programming. It was ABC that brought Ray Leonard, Howard Davis, Leon and Michael Spinks, and other Olympic heroes into millions of livingrooms during the Montreal Olympics. It was also ABC that exploded the myth that fighters had to be American to draw well on American television.

In April 1976 Don King approached ABC Sports with a plan to promote a tournament that would produce United States Boxing Champions in eight weight divisions. As ultimately agreed between the parties, the tournament was to be held between January and June of 1977. ABC committed 23 hours of air time to the project, and contracted to pay Don King Productions $2,035,000. King, in turn, agreed to build the tournament around ratings provided by *Ring Magazine.* *

The *Ring* connection was crucial. Founded by Nat Fleischer in 1922, the magazine had long been regarded as boxing's version of *The New York Times.* Its monthly circulation was small, only 150,000, but under Fleischer's guidance the publication had developed a reputation for accuracy and integrity. It was *Ring* that pioneered the boxer ranking system used throughout the world when, in its February 1925 issue, Tex Rickard rated the top ten

---

* King's proposed budget was broken down as follows: $1,135,000 for fighters' purses; $50,000 for standby fighters; $70,000 for *Ring Magazine;* a $250,000 promoter's fee; a $200,000 matchmaker's fee; $70,000 for committee expenses; $260,000 miscellaneous.

fighters in each weight division. Those ratings were repeated annually in 1926 and 1927 with Jack Dempsey doing the selecting, and soon after were converted to a monthly basis. Starting in 1941, *Ring* had also published the annual *Ring Record Book.* Known as the "Bible of Boxing," it contained the won-lost records of every active fighter and a career summary of every world champion ever. When Fleischer died in 1972, his son-in-law Nat Loubet took control of both publications. Thereafter Johnny Ort was named Associate Editor of *Ring Magazine.*

As part of his contract with ABC, Don King agreed to pay *Ring* $70,000. In return, *Ring* was to provide Don King Productions with ratings and records for the top American fighters in each weight division, and lend its name to the tournament for use in advertising and as a sponsor. *Ring*'s records and ratings were critical to the integrity of the tournament. Indeed, the contract between ABC and Don King Productions specified that the "essence of the agreement" was that "the quality of fighters participating in each weight category be the best possible, determined by rankings established by *Ring Magazine.*" King himself later acknowledged, "This was the heart of the tournament. I needed their reputation, their ratings, and their sanction to give validity and authority to the tournament." King also agreed to pay $20,000 each to managers Al Braverman and Paddy Flood to serve as consultants in the organization and administration of the tournament.

Thereafter *Ring* designated the top twelve United States fighters in the heavyweight, lightheavyweight, middleweight, welterweight, lightweight, and featherweight divisions, and the top six fly- and bantamweights. The tournament was announced in September 1976, and invitations distributed soon after. Fighters who accepted were signed in order of rank. There were eight openings in each of the top six weight divisions, and four openings for the two lightest weight categories. As a condition of entry, each fighter had to sign a contract giving Don King Productions three options should he win a tournament title. Because the bouts were to be staged in such unique and diverse locations as the Marion Correctional Institute and a United States Navy aircraft carrier, no state boxing commission had jurisdiction over the tournament, and only three of six tournament sites were subject to state inspection.

Problems abounded from the start. Among the fighters excluded from the tournament, despite a request by his manager that he be allowed to fight, was a Massachusetts middleweight with a 38–2–1 record—Marvin Hagler. Yet three men Hagler had beaten were invited to the tournament. Other omissions were similarly glaring, and Teddy Brenner, president of Madison Square Garden Boxing, publicly criticized the ratings with the declaration, "If *Ring* is the Bible of Boxing, then boxing needs a New Testament." Then on December 11, 1976, Alex Wallau sent an internal memorandum to Jim Spence, vice-president of programming for ABC Sports. In it, Wallau expressed concern over the quality of fighters in the tournament, and questioned the integrity of the selection process. Among his observations concerning the fighters who would be on the first televised card, Wallau declared:

• Tom Prater: "Prater has no right to be in the tournament on the basis of his record."

• Mike Colbert: "A Portland prospect who has been unconscionably promoted by [*Ring Magazine* associate editor] Ort on behalf of his rumored partner Mike Morton of Seattle who manages Colbert. His number one ranking in *Ring Magazine* is laughable."

• Paddy Dolan and John Sullivan: "White club fighters who have never fought a main event or an opponent of any reputation. No other group or publication ranks them at all. They are two disgraceful examples of King handing $15,000 to Paddy Flood [Dolan's manager] and his friends."

• Hilbert Stevenson: "An unknown unproven nonentity, who has been inserted in the tournament only because he is managed by Chris Cline [a Baltimore-based manager who was a friend and alleged business associate of Ort]. Stevenson has nothing to justify his inclusion in the U.S. Championships."

• Juan Cantres: "The biggest embarrassment in the first quarterfinal; an unskilled club fighter. He has not fought since May 1976, has never gone more than six rounds, and has never scored a professional KO."

On December 21, Wallau sent Spence a second memorandum, covering all 56 tournament fighters. Only 25 were deemed by

Wallau to be "qualified by virtue of ranking in the U.S. top twelve according to my estimation." Fourteen were listed as "disgraces." Among Wallau's observations:

- Biff Cline: "Perhaps the greatest example of King's payoffs to Ort and Ort's lack of integrity lies in the inclusion of Donald 'Biff' Cline in the lightheavyweight division. He has never even fought as a lightheavyweight. The only reason he will collect a paycheck of $10,000 is his father, Chris Cline." Dripping with sarcasm, Wallau proceeded to describe some of Cline's fights. "The Terror made his pro debut in 1971 against Jimmy Brown alias Sonny Brown, Joe Brown and Melody Brown—a pathetic club fighter who was knocked out in his first twelve bouts and was 0–15–2 when he fought Cline." Then Wallau moved to another of Cline's opponents. "Cline's fight on April 5, 1976, was against the infamous Al Byrd of Winston-Salem. Byrd was billed as the North Carolina heavyweight champion. Since Byrd's pro record contains only one win and twelve losses, ten by knockout, it can be assumed that he won this title in that lone win. Then The Terror marched on. His next win was over Jimmy Davis. The attached clip from the *Washington Post* conveys some sense of that battle."

The clip Wallau included was from page one of the *Washington Post* sports section. Featured was a photo of five-foot-nine-inch, 231-pound Jimmy Davis, referred to by the *Post* as, "A Moby Dick lookalike, who threw in the towel after one round. . . . His weight was lumped over a frame that must have inspired the model for the Pillsbury dough boy. Davis' game was obviously overeating, not boxing."

Next, Wallau offered an evaluation of several more fighters "ranked" by *Ring* and included in the Don King tournament:

- Jerry Kornele: "Kornele's record contains the classic earmarks of phony listings. On April 4, 1974, he knocked out a Refugio Rios. One week later, he knocked out a Refugio Ramos. Oftentimes, Ort and/or managers have difficulty thinking up original names for their fictional opponents. Later in 1974, Kornele kayoed Baby Rodriguez on December 15th and Roberto Rodriguez on

December 16th. Having repeated first names once and surnames once, Kornele's people decided to repeat both. Jerry beat Jorge Martinez on March 21st and April 4th of 1974."

• Vinnie Deborros: Here Wallau listed some of Deborros's opponents: Terry Rondeau, who had lost seventeen of his last nineteen fights when he met Deborros; Jose Pagan, a fighter with seventy professional losses. Wallau closed this paragraph with the warning, "Deborros has never fought outside of Connecticut, never beaten a decent opponent, and has no legitimate claim to a place in the United States Boxing Championships."

Alex Wallau was, and remains, one of the most respected people in network sports. His job is to cover boxing 365 days a year. It's a persistent, never-ending chore that involves calling around the world, viewing tapes, watching fighters in arenas and gyms, interviewing, and making judgments that more often than not turn out to be right. Yet incredibly, despite his warnings, ABC Sports let the tournament begin. On January 16, 1977, the first bouts were held onboard the United States Naval Aircraft Carrier *Lexington* anchored off the coast of Florida. On February 13 the second telecast took place, with Biff Cline knocked out in the fourth round. There were two other knockouts and three decisions that day, the most controversial of which saw Johnny Boudreaux awarded an eight-round decision over Scott LeDoux, who had knocked Boudreaux down early in the fight. The decision appeared to be a bad one, as ABC commentator Howard Cosell stated when the result was announced: "They gave it to Johnny Boudreaux! The crowd doesn't believe it! Scott LeDoux doesn't believe it! Look at LeDoux lean over the ropes. The crowd does not believe this decision!"

In the chaos that followed, an enraged LeDoux started shouting "fix" and tried to kick Boudreaux in the head. The blow missed, and instead hit Cosell, knocking the commentator's toupee askew. It was an ugly scene, and LeDoux's charges focused public attention on criticisms of the tournament and intensified press coverage of alleged irregularities.

The third telecast took place on March 6 from the Marion Correctional Institute in Ohio. By now the air was rife with allegations of "booking fees" and kickbacks that fighters had been forced to pay to associates of Don King Productions as a cost of entering the tournament. Additional bouts were held on March 27 at the Randolph Air Force base near San Antonio; April 2 in San Antonio; and April 10 in Miami Beach.

Meanwhile, as April progressed, evidence of massive improprieties began to flow into ABC. On April 13, 1977, Al Rose, the manager of a tournament fighter, told the network that he'd been forced to kickback 40 percent of his purse in order to participate. The next day, Nat Loubet, editor of *Ring Magazine,* admitted that *Ring* had published inaccurate records, but claimed that *Ring* was the unknowing victim of false reports by various fight managers. Finally, on April 16, ABC announced that it was suspending telecasts of the tournament. A press release marking the occasion declared, "ABC has determined that the records of numerous fighters in the tournament, as listed in the 1977 *Ring Record Book,* are inaccurate and contain many fights which apparently never took place. ABC believes that the very basis of the tournament has been severely compromised. As a result of these facts, ABC has suspended telecasts of the tournament until such time as it is satisfied that a more adequate mechanism has been put into effect that will guarantee the honesty and integrity of the tournament." Twenty-seven bouts on six dates had occurred. Thereafter, Don King Productions canceled the remaining fights. Still, the file on the United States Boxing Championships was not closed.

On April 19, 1977, ABC retained the law firm of Barrett Smith Shapiro Simon and Armstrong to investigate the tournament. The Armstrong Investigation, as the inquiry became known, was conducted under the guidance of the firm's chief litigator, Michael Armstrong. Three partners, seven associates, five law students, one paralegal, and a detective were engaged in the inquiry. Eighty-three alleged irregularities were probed. More than two hundred people were interviewed by the investigators, not including telephone interviews with various state boxing commission officials and local reporters in an attempt to verify fighters' records. The investigators acknowledged that they were hampered by a lack of subpoena power and the inability to compel testimony under oath. Still, they persevered, and eventually submitted their findings to the network in the form of a voluminous internal document consisting of a 133-page statement of facts, a 327-page report, and 119 exhibits.

The report began by acknowledging its weaknesses: "In certain instances," the investigators acknowledged, "key people refused to talk to us or produce relevant records. Others would discuss the tournament in general terms, but balked at supplying us with specific information because they felt that making allegations against King, Flood, Braverman and *Ring* would adversely affect their ability to make a living from boxing." Still, the investigators were able to confirm that Don King had a financial interest in the management of at least five boxers participating in the tournament. His "consultants"—Paddy Flood and Al Braverman—had a financial interest in six and three participating fighters respectively. "It is clear," the report read, "that Flood and Braverman, both of whom had financial interests in fighters, had serious conflicts of interest in carrying out their assigned roles in the tournament. King was aware of the facts giving rise to the conflicts of interest, but failed to take appropriate steps to deal with the problems."

Then the report turned to more serious allegations: "Based upon all available evidence, we have concluded that the process of invitation and selection of participants for the tournament was seriously deficient. Furthermore, we believe that in some cases the evidence established deliberate manipulation of the process in order to assure the inclusion of fighters whose managers or representatives were associated with or friendly to King, Ort, Flood or Braverman at the expense of other more highly qualified fighters. In six instances, the evidence indicates that improper payments were paid or requested, purportedly in return for getting fighters into the tournament. Each of these cases involved a fighter who was selected to participate in the tournament, and in five instances the recipient or potential recipient was an associate of Don King Productions. In instances involving nineteen other fighters," the report noted, there was "evidence to support the allegation that a payment was made or requested," but the evidence was "insufficient upon which one could fairly draw any definitive conclusions."

As for phony records, the report concluded that twenty tournament participants had "inaccurate" listings in the *Ring Record Book,* and eight more had records that were "unverifiable." Biff

Cline, the report concluded, had been credited with five "undisputedly phony" first-round knockouts in fights that never took place. Other false entries included:

- Pat Dolan: four fake 1975 wins.
- Hilbert Stevenson: five fake 1976 wins.
- Anthony House: seven fake 1975 and 1976 wins.

One boxer, Ike Fluellen of Houston, was credited with two 1976 wins in Mexico, rated third in the United States junior-middleweight class, and given an honorable mention for *Ring*'s 1976 Progress Award when in fact he hadn't fought at all during that year.

The investigators further determined that in 1976 Don King had given John Ort at least $5,000 in cash for "consulting services." In this regard, the Armstrong Report declared, "The most disturbing action by King for which we were able to acquire direct evidence of personal involvement was his clearly improper payment of $5,000 to John Ort which seriously compromised the integrity of the selection process. In this tournament, the allegedly independent and automatic selection process was supposed to minimize the dangers inherent in such potential conflicts of interest. As we have seen, the selection process did not work in the intended fashion, and the credibility of the tournament was seriously impaired by allegations regarding King's interests in fighters."

For ABC the 1977 tournament was a disaster, the network's "darkest day" in boxing. In the months that followed, network officials gave serious consideration to dropping the sport or, as a less severe measure, severing all ties with Don King. However, in the end, neither step was taken.

"You can't believe anything anybody tells you in boxing," Don King said later. "The business is predicated on lies. You are dealing with people who very rarely tell the truth."

Much to their chagrin, ABC officials found this to be so. But what was most remarkable about the 1977 tournament's unseemly end was that it gave rise to a new set of powers in boxing. And soon Don King would cement an alliance with one of those powers that would make him the most powerful promoter in boxing history.

In the aftermath of the 1977 Don King tournament, America's television networks had a problem. Muhammad Ali was as charismatic a champion as boxing had known.
The success of *Rocky* had brought a vast new audience to the
sport. The Montreal Olympic fighters were coming into their own.
In sum, the popularity of professional boxing was at its peak,
and television desperately needed respectable ratings and true
champions to cash in on the phenomenon.

Two organizations—the World Boxing Association (WBA)
and World Boxing Council (WBC)—stepped into the void. Both
organizations were formed to control championships, not regulate boxing at lower levels. They sanction only championship
matches and official title-elimination bouts. Each is comprised
of foreign national boxing commissions and some state bodies.
They set their own rules, establish their own medical and safety
standards, make their own rankings, and designate their own
"world champions." Neither organization has formal authority
to impose its will on any state boxing commission. However,
as a practical matter, virtually all jurisdictions bow to their
power, and those that don't go without world title fights within
their borders.

To hold a title in either the WBA or WBC, a fighter must
compete in places, against opponents, and under conditions specified by the sanctioning body. If he refuses he may be stripped
of his title. If a state commission fails to submit to the rules of

the WBA or WBC, a fighter, rather than lose his title, will move his match to a state with more compatible rules or with no regulation at all. Assaying the situation, Pat Putnam, *Sports Illustrated*'s premier boxing analyst for much of the past quarter-century, declared, "Two nickel and dime outfits, the WBC and WBA, run the fights to their own aggrandizement and the detriment of the sport." Teddy Brenner, in an attack on the WBC that held equally true for the WBA, proclaimed, "For reasons of expediency and commercial necessity, the television networks have propitiated the World Boxing Council by giving it an imprimatur which it has not earned." To these thoughts, Butch Lewis adds, "The WBC and WBA are like private clubs with their own arbitrary rules and regulations. And what you have to do, because the networks force you to do it, is join one or both of those clubs and play by their rules."

Advancement in boxing is arbitrary and capricious. Team sports such as baseball and football are structured by leagues with each team having a vested interest in signing the best players. Individual sports like golf and tennis have qualifying procedures that enable the best competitors to rise. But in boxing a handful of men—too many of them corrupt—determine who fights, and fighters do their best to avoid opponents who can beat them. The result parallels a situation whereby John McEnroe would not be allowed to compete at Wimbledon and Jack Nicklaus would be able to "duck" Tom Watson at The Masters. The professional worlds of tennis and golf would never tolerate such a situation. But looking first at the World Boxing Association, it's clear that boxing's major sanctioning bodies often operate in precisely that manner.

The World Boxing Association, headquartered in Panama, is an outgrowth of the old National Boxing Association. The NBA was incorporated in 1920, and consisted of representatives from various state and local boxing commissions in the United States and Canada. Few people took the NBA seriously. Its self-imposed functions were largely ceremonial, and little notice was paid in 1962 when the group reincorporated as the World Boxing Association. The WBA issued monthly ratings, which were largely ignored, and continued under American domination. Indeed, from 1921 through 1973, the group's presidency remained exclusively in American hands, except for two year-long hiatuses when it was held by a Canadian.

In 1974 two Panamanians, Elias Cordova and Rodrigo Sanchez, orchestrated a coup that brought the WBA into a Latin orbit. Under the organization's constitution, any athletic commission or other body that regulated boxing in any country, province, city, or other political subdivision was eligible for membership and entitled to vote in WBA elections. The constitution further provided that only delegates present at the WBA's annual convention could cast ballots. Beginning in 1974, Cordova and Sanchez imported "delegates" from such countries as Panama (four registered commissions), Venezuela (six), and El Salvador (four). The Virgin Islands was represented by three "commissions," despite the fact that no official boxing commission existed on any of its islands. Indeed, one of the Virgin Islands "commissions" was listed as representing Saint Maarten, which is actually in the Netherlands Antilles. Still, the power play succeeded. Cordova was elected president, and served in that capacity from 1974 through 1977. Then after a two-year reign by Fernando Mandry Galindez, Sanchez took office and held power until dying of cancer in 1982. He was succeeded by Gilberto Mendoza, also of Panama.

Most knowledgeable observers regard the WBA as little more than a corrupt joke. A two-part investigative report in *Sports Illustrated* branded the organization "a fraternal club for Latin Americans," and proceeded to detail some of the WBA's more flagrant abuses and shadowy characters. High on the list was Pepito Cordero of Puerto Rico, a longtime confidant of Sanchez and Cordova. In 1964 Cordero was convicted on two counts of burglary, and sentenced to two to five years on one count, five to ten years on the other. After his release from prison he moved into boxing and acquired a managerial interest in three WBA champions—Ernesto Espana, Angel Espada, and Sammy Serrano. Pat Putnam, who wrote the report for *Sports Illustrated,* no longer attends fights in Puerto Rico. After the report was published, he received anonymous telephone calls threatening to kill him if he ever again set foot on the island. "Some of these guys aren't Jewish," said a colleague of Putnam's. "If they get mad, they don't sue you. They'll blow you away."

Still, public criticism of the WBA and Cordero has continued. "There's one bagman in the WBA," says Bob Arum, "and that's Pepe Cordero. Anytime you want a fix in the WBA, you bribe Cordero and he takes care of it. When I want something done, I have to pay off Cordero."

Arum knows of what he speaks. In 1981 he promoted thirteen WBA title fights; in 1982 eleven; ten in 1983. To get Ray Mancini a shot at the WBA lightweight crown, Arum paid Pepe Cordero a $10,000 bonus plus $25,000 each of the first three times Mancini defended his title. In addition, Arum agreed to give Cordero's fighter, Ernesto Espana, a title fight with Mancini for an inflated purse of $250,000, one-third of which went to Cordero. "We shouldn't really call it a bribe," says Arum, "because you can't bribe a person who's not in a position of authority. Cordero has no office at all in the WBA. He's just a promoter, supposedly. But anyone who wants anything done in the WBA has to pay Cordero."

"I gave up on the WBA a long time ago," says Pat Putnam. "They just do what they want to do, name their champions, and nobody gives a damn." Putnam's assessment is widely shared within the boxing community. WBA titles seem to exist largely so that television networks can ballyhoo fights as "championship matches." But there is another, larger, world sanctioning body—the World Boxing Council. And that organization merits close attention.

The WBC was the brainchild of a Californian named George Parnassus, who had made a career of promoting Mexican and Mexican-American fighters. Parnassus wanted a sanctioning body that would rate his fighters, and at the time the WBA was dominated by parochial American interests. Thus he bankrolled his own world sanctioning organization. Sixteen countries were represented at the WBC's inaugural meeting in Mexico City on February 14, 1963. They adopted a constitution styling themselves "a nonprofit organization dedicated to promote and serve the sport of boxing," and divided their group into seven federations, representing North America, Europe, Africa, Great Britain, South America, Central America/Caribbean, and the Orient. Each federation was given two votes in council matters. Because the United States shared North America's votes with Mexico and

Canada, its total representation came to two-thirds of one vote. Control of the WBC began, and remains, with third-world powers.

The growth of the World Boxing Council to the point where it is now the most powerful regulatory authority in boxing has been due largely to the efforts of one man. Jose Sulaiman was born in Tamaulipas, Mexico, on May 30, 1931. The son of a Lebanese immigrant, he grew up in San Luis Potosi, and was introduced to boxing in 1939. "I was eight years old," Sulaiman remembers. "A group of friends went to a boxing match, and I asked my father for money to buy a ticket. He refused. The thought of spending to watch two men punch each other in the head outraged him, so I went to the stadium and begged to get in. The gatekeeper told me I could go for free if I participated in the hors d'oeuvres."

The hors d'oeuvres was a long-established custom in Mexico. Before each fight card, two children would square off and fight to excite the crowd. "My opponent was a Mexican Indian," Sulaiman continues, "much taller than I was, about ten years old. At first, he was very scared of me, but I didn't know how to fight and he won, although he never knocked me down." During the hors d'oeuvres, tradition dictated that the crowd throw coins into the ring. "After the fight," says Sulaiman, "while my opponent was waiting for the decision to be announced, I took off my gloves and picked up the coins. He won the fight, but I won most of the money. After that, I kept going back to the hors d'oeuvres. I kept losing fights, and I kept getting most of the coins."

Sulaiman today is a wealthy man. Short, heavyset, with a receding hairline and large hooked nose, he carries himself with an aura of graciousness and Latin aristocracy. His wealth comes largely from his position as president and chief executive officer of Controles Graphicos, a company that produces paper for electrocardiograms and electroencephalograms. He is also on the board of directors of several corporations, and has extensive real-estate holdings, including a movie theater and ranch. But his primary love is boxing. He assumed his first administrative post within the sport's hierarchy in 1946 when, at age fifteen, he became secretary of the local boxing commission in the town of Valles. In 1953 he was named president of the San Luis Potosi

State Athletic Commission, and fourteen years later vice-president of the Mexican Boxing Federation. Thereafter he rose swiftly—in 1968 president of the Mexican Boxing Federation; 1969 vice-president of the North American Boxing Federation; 1970 president of the North American Boxing Federation; 1971 secretary-general of the World Boxing Council. In 1975 he was elected president of the WBC at the Council's convention in Tunis, North Africa. Under his guidance the organization's membership has grown to 104 nations. He is a hero-worshipper who looks up to fighters, loves to be around them, and desperately wants his heroes to adore him. He's also a brilliant diplomat, fluent in six languages, and has made the World Boxing Council his personal fiefdom. "With Jose," says Bob Busse, one of the few members of the WBC hierarchy willing to be openly critical of his boss, "there are no in-betweens. He's on an ego trip. If you agree with him, you're his friend. If you disagree, you're his enemy."

On paper, power within the World Boxing Council resides with an "Executive Council" that consists of two representatives from each of seven continental federations, five vice-presidents, the secretary-general, and president. The president and vice-presidents are elected to four-year terms by the fourteen federation delegates. All other officers, including the secretary-general, treasurer, and comptroller are appointed by the president. The president also makes committee appointments, including the designation of chairmen for each of the WBC's twenty-three committees. In practice, the Executive Council rarely meets. Most votes are held by telephone, with the president calling each member. In this regard Sulaiman defines his role as "coordinating the committees, to inform everybody of what is happening, to try to see that the votes are taken." This gives him enormous power, which is augmented by the WBC constitution. Pursuant to that document, if the president determines that an "emergency situation" exists, he may act by polling seven Executive Council members, one from each federation. Also, when the president polls the Executive Council he may make a recommendation as to how the Council should vote, and if a Council member does not respond within seven days, his vote is deemed to be in accord with the president's recommendation.

Sulaiman's critics are extremely vocal. Bob Busse, who doubles as president of the North American Boxing Federation and chairman of the WBC Ratings Committee, states, "One of the WBC's problems is that it refuses to recognize that the United States represents the heart of professional boxing. Jose will say time and time again that the United States is only one of 104 countries, but that's ridiculous. You can't compare boxing in the United States with boxing in Barbados, and, too often, American fighters are treated unfairly by the WBC as the price of appeasing other countries."

Teddy Brenner goes further. In an affidavit filed with the United States District Court for the Southern District of New York, Brenner declared, "At no time in my experience has more violence been done to the basic rules of fair play than the practices and procedures of the World Boxing Council under the regime of Jose Sulaiman. These abuses have affected every aspect of the sport."

Part of the basis for these criticisms lies with the fact that WBC rules are extremely flexible. "Yes, my rules are flexible," Sulaiman responds, "but that is necessary for fairness and compromise."

Maybe so. But the counter view, expressed by Michael Katz of *The New York Times,* is that "WBC rules are like the Soviet Constitution. They only work on paper." And Bob Arum declares, "The rules are an ever-changing series of directives that apply to certain people and certain entities at different times and not to others."

The biggest question regarding WBC rules is the extent to which they apply to Don King. Sulaiman says that King is treated like any other promoter. Others dispute that contention. What is clear, however, is that Don King and Jose Sulaiman have cemented a mutually profitable alliance. In 1982 King promoted sixteen WBC championship fights; in 1983 the same number; seventeen in 1984. Each of those fights generated substantial revenue for Don King Productions. And those fights were also life's blood for the WBC. The WBC has substantial expenses. Executive Council members serve without salary, but are reimbursed for travel expenses, which are often considerable. The WBC's headquarters in Mexico City handles 82,000 telephone calls annually, and approximately six feet of documents relating to income and expenditures are processed each year. To run this organization it's necessary to rely on income from three sources: a $2,100 annual authorization fee paid by persons who promote or register option contracts for world title bouts; a promotional fee ranging from $1,500 to $2,000 for each championship bout; and most important, a sanctioning fee that has risen to 2½ percent of each fighter's gross purse from every WBC championship fight. Over the years Don King has controlled or been involved with the promotion of most of the big names in boxing. Without Don King–promoted fights, the WBC would lose substantial sanctioning fees and be sorely lacking for money.

Ironically, the King-Sulaiman friendship—and the two men acknowledge that they are close friends—had an inauspicious start. On the eve of the Ali-Foreman championship bout in 1974, Sulaiman, who was then secretary-general of the WBC, went to Zaire to discuss the organization's rules and regulations with King, the fight's promoter. "I was feeling very important," Sulaiman recalls. "Then, to my great consternation, King said he would only meet with the president of the World Boxing Council. This left me very hurt, and out of my well-known pride I left Zaire, only to arrive in Paris to learn that Foreman had suffered a cut during training and the bout was postponed. For the anguish I knew this would cause Mr. King, I was the happiest man on earth."

Sulaiman later watched the Ali-Foreman bout on closed-circuit television. Subsequently he and King reached a meeting of the minds, and when a 1978 attempted coup by Bob Arum failed to emasculate then-president Sulaiman's power, King declared, "A display of devotion and love for right and democracy was shown by the delegates. Jose is the best thing that has ever happened to boxing. I was happy and proud to see him given the vote of confidence he deserves." Later King added, "Jose Sulaiman is the greatest boxing man I've ever met. I think he's a knight in shining armor for the boxer."

Others, however, are not so sure. In June 1983, Bert Sugar (who had replaced Nat Loubet as editor of *Ring Magazine*), wrote an editorial calling Sulaiman the "personal lap dog" of Don King. British promoter Mickey Duff concurred. "My complaint," said Duff, "is that Jose Sulaiman is not happy his friend Don King is the biggest promoter in boxing. Sulaiman will only be happy when Don King is the *only* promoter in boxing." *Sports Illustrated* added fuel to the fire, charging, "Under Jose Sulaiman, the WBC has produced some of the most dubious boxer ratings in the history of the sport." Were those ratings designed to give Don King–controlled fighters an unfair advantage? "The quirks of Sulaiman's complex character are most likely responsible for many of the mysteries of the WBC's ratings and its title fight sanctions," *Sports Illustrated* concluded, "although to the objective observer these appear at times to be geopolitical payoffs in exchange for pledges of fidelity to good king Jose."

Ratings are a fighter's future. They spell the difference between fame and oblivion, poverty and fortune. A boxer must be rated among the top ten fighters in his division to qualify for a WBC title fight. Should he advance to the position of number-one challenger, the champion *must* face him within one year of the division's last "mandatory" defense.

The truth is that it's very difficult to rate boxers. All one has to do is look at the diverse balloting for the number-one college football team in America to see the problem. Now magnify that by fifteen weight divisions with a pool of ten thousand boxers who fight in one hundred countries anywhere from one to a dozen or more times a year, and the task becomes quite complicated.

Under the WBC Constitution, ratings fall within the domain of a "Ratings Committee." According to Committee chairman Bob Busse, "Two times a year we all attend a meeting and do the ratings together. Once it's at the annual convention, and once at a meeting in Mexico City. The members from each continental federation attend, as do four or five ratings advisers. In the months in between, each federation mails in information and recommendations. The secretary, Eduardo Lamazon, coordinates it and puts together the first set of ratings. On the nineteenth of the month, he calls me and we spend whatever time is necessary to make changes and a final set of ratings. The week of the twentieth, I finalize the ratings and they're sent out."

It sounds good. And certainly it's an improvement over times past when Busse admitted that 90 percent of the ratings were made by Sulaiman. "How some of the people get in our ratings," he told *Sports Illustrated* in 1981, "I couldn't tell you. Promoters call me and ask about fighters they say we have ranked, and I didn't even know they were ranked. What can I do about it?"

Still, even today, Busse concedes, there are "special cases where Jose gets involved," and the recent plight of Howard Davis exemplifies the hazards of the system.

In June 1983, Davis was the second-ranked lightweight in the world but was unable to get a bout with WBC title holder Edwin Rosario, who owed options on his first three title defenses to Don King. "Davis is not one of our fighters," said Bobby Goodman of Don King Productions. "Why should he get a title shot?" Then on June 18 Davis fought highly touted Greg Coverson (the number-four WBC contender), and in one of his finest efforts as a professional knocked Coverson out in the eighth round. Yet in the next set of WBC ratings Davis was dropped to number three, one spot below Roberto Elizondo, a boxer with promotional ties to Don King. How could Davis drop from two to three by beating the number-four contender? "Maybe," explained Sulaiman, "the result was not known." But it was known. The fight was on national television, and as a result of being knocked out Coverson had been removed from the WBC's top ten. One year later Howard Davis got a title shot—after signing a multibout option contract with Don King.

Is Jose Sulaiman on the take from Don King? The general view among boxing insiders is "no."

"If Jose was going to solicit money from anyone," says Mike Jones, "he had plenty of opportunities to come to me. I've had five fighters challenge for WBC titles, and Jose Sulaiman never asked me for a dime."

"It's not the corruption of money," says Michael Katz. "It's the corruption of loyalty and friendship. But whether a man gets paid off in dollars or in strokes to the ego, it's still wrong."

The prevailing view is that Jose Sulaiman is basically a decent man. He cares deeply for boxing as a sport, and for boxers as people. He holds the World Boxing Council together in masterful fashion by engendering a mixture of personal loyalty, respect, and fear. His decisions are sometimes unwise, but once his word is given he keeps it. The problem is that Sulaiman wants to be more—he wants to be boxing's savior, a benevolent monarch, and he wants everybody to like him. "To those who bend at the knee," writes Pat Putnam, "he dispenses favors." Others feel his wrath.

"I have given my life to boxing," says Jose Sulaiman. "And in return, all I have asked for is the friendship of boxers. I am not perfect; even God makes mistakes. But I have done my best to build a sense of trust and confidence in the World Boxing Council, and sometimes I do not understand the criticisms people make of me. I go to countries in the Orient and Africa, and the King and Prime Minister are at the airport to greet me. I come to the United States, and at the airport I am attacked by Michael Katz of *The New York Times*. Still," concludes Sulaiman, "I thank my enemies for inspiring me to get up earlier each morning and forcing me to work even harder for the good of boxing."

Testifying before Congress in support of a bill that would have established a Federal Advisory Committee on professional boxing, Howard Cosell declared, "If we had our own national rating system and created our own system for the development of world champions, the WBC and WBA would shortly perish. The WBA is a joke to begin with, and the WBC is not much above it." More bluntly, Bob Arum declared, "Boxing is the most poorly regulated, most corrupt big time sport in America. To take the WBA seriously, to take the WBC seriously, you've got to be a moron. Unless there's a federal boxing commission, these two asshole jokes—the WBA and the WBC—will continue to do whatever they want." Bert Sugar, with a touch of chauvinism, echoed Cosell and Arum. "Most of your boxers," said Sugar, "are American. The great majority of world class fighters are American. The TV money is overwhelmingly American. And boxing is run by a fat little Mexican dictator and a group of corrupt Panamanians. A national government commission of some sort is the only answer."

"What can I tell you?" says Mike Jones, his hands held out, palms upward. "We don't have a federal commission. And the people I had to deal with weren't Pete Rozelle or Bowie Kuhn; they were Jose Sulaiman and Don King. My job was to get Billy Costello a shot at the title. It wasn't easy, but we got the job done. We did it."

9

"Boxing goes through stages," says Ray Arcel, the venerable trainer and manager. "I've seen it grow and deteriorate, grow and deteriorate; but it will always be there."

In 1983 when Mike Jones began serious pursuit of a title shot for Billy Costello, boxing was there, but it was in a period of retrenchment. Muhammad Ali was gone. His heir apparent, Sugar Ray Leonard, had been forced into retirement by a detached retina. And the sport was reeling from four incidents that occurred within the space of a month—four championship fights that went sour.

Boxing's most traumatic month began with a great fight. On November 12, 1982, Alexis Arguello challenged Aaron Pryor for the World Boxing Association's 140-pound title. Pryor was undefeated, a nonstop fighter with 31 consecutive wins and 29 knockouts. Arquello was widely regarded as one of the great fighters of his time, with 76 wins in 80 fights, and world championships in three weight divisions.

Television glamorizes boxing. Viewers rarely see seedy dressing rooms and the hundred-dollar paychecks paid to preliminary fighters. The one-dimensional nature of the medium cosmetizes violence in that the full impact of punches is seldom seen. For thirteen rounds, Alexis Arguello and Aaron Pryor engaged in a brutal, brilliant, stunningly violent bout. Then midway through round fourteen, Pryor landed a blow that shattered Arguello's nose and brought a look of terror to the challenger's eyes. A dozen more unanswered blows followed, sending Arguello to the canvas. Exceptional camera work caught it all. The challenger was still unconscious four minutes later when the telecast went off the air.

The Pryor-Arguello bout was brutal, but if one accepts the underlying premise of boxing, one also accepts the fact that injuries occur. Still, the sight of a man battered so thoroughly into submission was disturbing, and less than twenty-four hours later a more serious incident occurred. Boxing in recent years has been swamped with "champions." Once, there were eight weight divisions and eight world-title holders. However, by 1982 both the WBA and WBC had expanded to fifteen weight classes. In many respects the proliferation of titles was good for boxers. Fifteen divisions times two world sanctioning bodies meant that thirty fighters could share championship glory. Also, fighters who outgrew a weight division no longer had to choose between being overmatched against heavier opponents and making health-threatening sacrifices to lose extra pounds. However, the down-side of having thirty champions is that some title holders are no longer the genuine article. And from television's point of view, the average viewer can't keep track of titles. Thus to sell their product, the networks have been forced to focus on three categories—great fighters, heavyweights, and champions with charisma.

Ray Mancini was a network darling. Born and raised in Youngstown, Ohio, the son of a former contender who had lost his chance to fight for the title when drafted into the Army and wounded during World War II, he had charisma galore. White, outgoing, fighting to win the championship that eluded his father, Ray Mancini would have been a good story in any sport. For boxing he was phenomenal. "Both in image and ring style," said Mort Sharnik of CBS, "Ray Mancini is Teddy Roosevelt charging up San Juan Hill. He's a throwback to an earlier era when God, family, and country reigned. There's a blue-collar hometown. His father lost a chance to fight for the title by serving America. What more could you want?"

In 1981 Mancini had challenged Alexis Arguello for the WBC lightweight title, and had been knocked out in the fourteenth round. Seven months later he switched sanctioning bodies, and defeated Arturo Frias for the WBA crown. "You can't help but think that everything was set up for Mancini," says Michael Katz. "He fought a stiff for the title. Most of his defenses sanctioned by the WBA were against bums." On November 13, 1982, one day after Aaron Pryor destroyed Alexis Arguello, Ray Mancini defended his title against South Korea's Duk Koo Kim. Kim was unranked by *Ring Magazine*. One year earlier the Korean Boxing Association had compiled a list of its top forty fighters, and Kim was not among them. Yet the World Boxing Association had him rated as the number-one challenger for Mancini's crown.

The fight was televised nationally by CBS. Mancini knocked Kim out at the nineteen-second mark of the fourteenth round. Moments after the bout's end, Kim lost consciousness. He died four days later from a cerebral edema, swelling of the brain. Two brutal events had now been showcased on national television within a span of eighteen hours, and more was to come.

On November 26, 1982, WBC heavyweight champ Larry Holmes stepped into the ring to defend his title against Randall "Tex" Cobb. Holmes's credentials were well known. He was the premier heavyweight of the post-Ali era, undefeated and untied in forty bouts. Eleven of his twelve title defenses had resulted in knockouts. Cobb was an unpolished brawler with lots of courage but little more. "I'm a whore who sells his blood instead of his ass," Cobb told reporters, "but that comes with the sport. I never made much money being good looking, but there's always somebody who'll pay me to take a punch. And I can take a punch, darlin'. It's a natural gift. This piece of granite on my shoulders can absorb a lot of punishment. They don't pay me to be bright."

The Holmes-Cobb championship fight was broadcast by ABC in prime time on a Friday night. Howard Cosell was the blow-by-blow commentator. Cosell's presence was regarded by ABC as crucial to the ratings success of the program. He had the most recognizable voice in America, and was boxing's only nationally known commentator. He had the ability to go before a major sports audience, and simply by virtue of his presence make an event important. Yet in recent years Cosell had grown increasingly disenchanted with professional boxing. Indeed, near the end of a bout between WBC junior-featherweight champion Wilfredo Gomez and Eddie Ndukwu—a patent mismatch that resulted in a fourth-round knockout—Cosell had told a national audience, "Look at this! It's a public and a national embarrassment. This fight should be stopped. It should not have been held in the first place, and we apologize to you for it."

Then came Larry Holmes versus Randall "Tex" Cobb. After the fact, Jim Spence, who had been elevated to senior vice-president at ABC Sports, was to testify before a Congressional subcommittee as follows: "Did we think that Tex Cobb was going to defeat Larry Holmes? No, we didn't. Did we think that the fight was going to turn out as it did? Absolutely not. If we had known the fight was going to be as one-sided as it obviously was, and it was an awful fight, we would not have televised it. We thought it would be more competitive than it was."

Did they? Testifying before the same subcommittee, Bert Sugar gave his version of what the ABC hierarchy thought: "They knew that it was going to be the ninth-highest rated show that week on television," said Sugar. "I also think that they knew Larry Holmes was going to do exactly what he did to Randy Cobb. The problem was, they didn't tell Howard."

As for the fight itself, Cobb took a merciless beating but refused to go down. All three judges scored one round even. The rest of the bout belonged to Holmes. Rounds one through five saw Cosell voice a mixture of skepticism over the fight's merits and admiration for Cobb's courage. From round six on, before a national audience, he savaged it all:

• Round Six: "Tex Cobb's left eye is half-closed. His head must have been carved out of Mount Rushmore and he certainly has a granite chin, but is this a palatable match?"

• Round Seven: "Imagine the number of combinations against this man's head; the punishment he's been taking."

• Round Eight: "Cobb is heavy-legged, ponderous, with a bravery about him. However, we are not in the age of the Roman Coliseum and the lions. You can see Cobb's face all bruised and swollen."

• Round Nine: "This is a strong decent man, Randy Tex Cobb, and I hate to see anybody take this kind of punishment. This is brutalization. The referee should think about stopping this fight fast. This is not right. You can't measure the aftermath of a fight like this, with this kind of punishment. He won't go down; the courage of a lion; but why?"

- Round Ten: "Why don't they stop it? The punishment inflicted is simply enormous. This is just terrible."

- Round Eleven: "Look at that head snap back from the Holmes left, again and again. Lord knows, maybe this man can stand up and take this for fifteen rounds. What does that prove? Who knows what the aftereffects will be?"

- Round Twelve: "This kind of savagery doesn't deserve commentation. I'll tell you something; this is as brutal a mismatch as I think I've ever seen."

- Round Thirteen: "This fellow, the referee Steve Crosson. I don't understand his judgment or thinking. What is achieved by letting this man take this kind of beating? From the point of view of boxing, which is under fire and deservedly so, this fight could not have come at a worse time."

- Round Fourteen: "Obviously this referee has no intention of stopping this fight. The blood is all over Cobb's face now. I wonder if that referee understands that he's constructing an advertisement for the abolition of the very sport that he's a part of."

- Round Fifteen: "Look at how swollen the poor man's face is. I can't believe this referee. It's outrageous."

Then came the final bell and, after the decision was announced, the ironic sign-off with Cosell biting off the words, "This has been a presentation of ABC Sports—the leader in sports television."

Six days later, on December 2, 1982, Howard Cosell announced that he would never again announce a professional boxing match on television. "The Cobb fight did it for me," he told a reporter for the *Washington Post*. "I was leaving the ring and people were shouting, 'That Texan sure can take a punch, can't he.' Don't they realize what's happening? Four days or four weeks or four years later, that man is going to pay for the pounding he took. I'm past the point where I want to be a part of it. I don't want to be a party to the sleaziness. I'm worn out by it all."

Later, Cosell elaborated on his views regarding the sport and business of professional boxing, which he had helped popularize and which had made him famous in return: "Boxing once had appeal to me. It was the romantic appeal of a way out of the ghetto, and I've always had great unwavering respect for men who fight for a living. I've been in more rings than most fighters ever have, and I know how small it is in there. I know that, no matter how skilled and courageous a fighter is, every time he walks down that aisle and goes up those three steps in between the ropes and into the ring, he wonders what it's going to be when the bout is over. I admire that. I really do. But," Cosell continued, "professional boxing is no longer worthy of civilized society. It's run by self-serving crooks, who are called promoters. They are buttressed with the look of nicety about them by the television networks, which are in fact corrupt and unprincipled in putting up the front money that continues boxing in its present form. Quite frankly, I now find the whole subject of professional boxing disgusting. Except for the fighters, you're talking about human scum, nothing more. Professional boxing is utterly immoral. It's not capable of reformation. I now favor the abolition of professional boxing. You'll never clean it up. Mud can never be clean."

No sports commentator in America has more critics than Howard Cosell—and none is more respected. Cosell's remarks during and after the Holmes-Cobb bout shook boxing. Then, two weeks later, the sport sustained yet another blow.

In many states, it is illegal for the same man to both manage and promote a fighter. The rule exists to prevent the concentration of power in too few hands; and also protect the public and the fighter. "You're either a promoter or a manager," says Ferdie Pacheco of NBC. "The promoter's interest should be, what's the best fight for the public and the least money I can pay for it. The manager's viewpoint should be, what's the best fight I can take for my fighter and the most money I can get for him. When you come from those two divergent viewpoints, there's no way to meet them."

Yet the advantages inherent in one man promoting and managing the same fighter are obvious—twice the profits and twice the control. Both of those products were appealing to Don King, and thus to circumvent the proscription against managing and promoting, he arrived at a simple solution—turn his stepson into a manager.

Carl King was born in Cleveland on February 18, 1957. His father died the day before his fourth birthday, six months before Carl's sister was born. Looking back on those early days, Carl King recalls, "Don moved in with my mother when I was four. It's hard for me to remember life before he was around. People criticize his involvement with numbers and all that, but the numbers fed me and gave me clothes. Don King," Carl continues, "is my idol and one of my best friends. I respect his strength; I admire what he's done. What I remember most about growing up was his telling me that the words 'can't' and 'failure' shouldn't be in my vocabulary. I love him."

Today Carl King is a tall, slender, garrulous man, a graduate of Baldwin-Wallace College with a degree in promotional management and international marketing. He is also president, chief executive officer, and sole shareholder of Monarch Boxing—a sports management company in Orwell, Ohio. His sister Debbie is first vice-president. Through Monarch Boxing, Carl King manages some two dozen fighters, including present or past world champions Tim Witherspoon, Leroy Haley, Carlos DeLeon, Leon Spinks, Azumah Nelson, Michael Dokes, and Saoul Mamby. Among the contenders in his stable are James Kinchen, Julian Jackson, Dwight Davison, Johnny DeLarosa, and David Bey.

Having Carl King manage fighters is a necessary technicality, like having George Wallace's wife, Lurleen, serve as governor of Alabama when Wallace was constitutionally ineligible to succeed himself. Yet the arrangement gave Don King even greater power than he had previously enjoyed. Indeed, on at least three occasions the boxing world was treated to the bizarre spectacle of televised fights promoted by King in which Carl King was the manager of both fighters. Summing up the situation, Michael Katz observed, "First, the fighter signs a promotional contract with Don King. Then the manager signs over a piece of the boxer to Carl King. Finally, the fighter gets a title bout. In this corner, a Don King fighter. In that corner, a Don King fighter. Guess who wins."

On December 10, 1982, two weeks after Larry Holmes brutalized Randall Cobb to retain the WBC heavyweight championship, Michael Dokes stepped into the ring to challenge Mike Weaver for the WBA heavyweight crown. The bout was promoted at Caesar's Palace in Las Vegas by Don King Productions. Weaver was managed by a Californian named Don Manuel. Dokes was managed by Carl King. Thirty seconds into the first round, Dokes floored Weaver with a left hook. The champion rose, stepped back against the ropes in a defensive posture with his arms high, and successfully blocked most of the punches that followed. Then, with the bout 63 seconds old, referee Joey Curtis stepped between the fighters and ended the fight. Michael Dokes was the new WBA heavyweight champion. Pandemonium followed. Inside the arena, the crowd began to chant, "Bullshit . . . Bullshit . . ." The cry lasted for over a minute, until it turned to "Fix . . . Fix . . ." Then, over national television, came the intonation, "Don King sucks . . . Don King sucks . . ." "They shouldn't have stopped it," said ringside physician Donald Romeo. "The referee was wrong. Weaver was fine."

A referee's decision as to whether or not to stop a fight is an enormous responsibility. The wrong decision can kill a career if a fight is stopped too soon. The wrong decision can kill a fighter if it's stopped too late. Defending his actions, Curtis told reporters, "I wasn't going to have another Duk Koo Kim. You're not going to see anyone killed, not in my fights." Curtis then went on to say that after the knockdown he'd asked Weaver if he was all right, and Weaver "did not give the correct answer."

"Joey Curtis is a liar," Weaver countered at a postfight news conference. "I told him I was all right. I could see stopping it if the referee came and looked in my eyes, but he didn't. He just stepped in and stopped the fight." Also, Weaver's manager Don Manuel pointed out, Curtis had let the fight continue for thirty seconds after Weaver had risen from the canvas and given the referee his allegedly incorrect answer.

"Was it a fix?" Weaver was asked.

"Definitely," the fighter answered.

It's very difficult to make boxing a safe sport, but at the very least it should be a fair one. In the aftermath of the Michael Dokes–Mike Weaver fight, public indignation reached new heights. First, three brutal bouts had been witnessed on national television within two weeks. And then an alleged Don King conspiracy had stripped a champion of his title. Whether the bout had actually been "scripted," as charged by Weaver and his manager, was almost irrelevant. What mattered was that the public was taking a long look at boxing and its premier promoter. And some people didn't like what they saw.

Don King had a five-story office building and an eastside townhouse in Manhattan worth several million dollars. He also owned a home on Star Island and a five-hundred-acre farm in Ohio where, at any given time, twenty professional fighters were in training. His New York office had fourteen employees. A total of *thirteen* active world champions were under promotional contract to Don King Productions. Altogether, Don King had promotional ties with over one hundred fighters, and assets estimated by *The New York Times* at $45 million.

The heavyweight division—boxing's flagship division—was King's personal empire. Indeed, the full scope of King's domination of heavyweight ranks was revealed when promoter Butch Lewis filed a lawsuit against King, charging that Don King Productions had interfered with Lewis's exclusive promotional contract with heavyweight contender Greg Page. King countered by claiming, first, that Lewis's contract wasn't valid, and second, that he hadn't interfered with the contract at all. Rather, King claimed, Page had come to him because it was the only way for the fighter to advance through the heavyweight ranks. King's promotional ties with Larry Holmes were a matter of record. In a remarkable affidavit submitted to the court, King listed the top twelve WBC heavyweight challengers and set forth their promotional ties to Don King Productions (DKP):

1. Gerry Cooney—At present, he is under contract to King-Tiffany, Inc., a company half owned by Don King Productions, to fight Larry Holmes. Cooney has fought for me in the past (i.e., against Jimmy Young) and to my knowledge has never fought for Butch Lewis.

2. Mike Dokes—Is under a promotional agreement with Don King Productions, and has been for several years. In fact, Dokes' manager is my son, Carl King.

3. Greg Page—[promotional ties in dispute].

4. Trevor Berbick—Is under contract to Don King Productions.

5. Randy "Tex" Cobb—Is under contract to Don King Productions for his next three fights.

6. Leon Spinks—Is under contract to Don King Productions, and, in fact, fought in Atlantic City under such contract for DKP against Ivy Brown.

7. Renaldo Snipes—Is under contract to DKP for his next three fights, and is right now scheduled to fight Scott Frank for DKP.

8. Jimmy Young—Is under contract to DKP, and has been for several years.

9. Lynn Ball—Is under contract to DKP, fought for DKP against Mike Dokes, and is scheduled to fight George Chaplin for DKP.

10. Bernardo Mercado—Is under contract to DKP, and fought for DKP against "Tex" Cobb.

11. Larry Frazier—Is under contract to DKP and scheduled to fight for DKP.

12. James "Quick" Tillis—Has executed a letter agreement with DKP, and contract is now in process of preparation.

"In sum," the King affidavit concluded, "Greg Page must, if his career is to develop properly, fight only top ranked opponents. I respectfully submit that, unless Greg Page can fight opponents who are under contract to DKP, his career will be at a standstill. And under DKP's promotional contracts with top contenders, they cannot fight for any other promoter without DKP's consent. In light of Butch Lewis' past and present conduct toward both me and Greg Page, such consent will not be forthcoming."

Ultimately, the Butch Lewis lawsuit was settled. King paid Lewis some money, and Greg Page became a Don King Productions fighter. Still, Lewis is not entirely satisfied with the outcome. "Don King is something else," Lewis says, a touch of bitterness in his voice. "The man comes in and says, 'Make a deal, or you're gonna lose everything.' And you make the deal because, nine times out of ten, he's gonna be right. To be a successful promoter," Lewis continues, "you have to tie up quality fighters. And I mean, really tie them up, because if you don't someone else will come along and steal them. I was kissing Greg Page's ass from the time he was fourteen. I was with Michael Spinks from his first pro fight. King and Arum do the same thing, only they have a built-in advantage because they do regular cable telecasts which lets them promise young fighters TV exposure. And King, in particular, controls so many titles that he's got an unbeatable edge. Don King is like a spoiled kid," concludes Lewis. "He's got so many toys he can't possibly play with all of them, but he still won't let you have one."

Butch Lewis's thoughts are not uncommon. Big fish eat little fish every day in the world of boxing. "It's sad," says Jimmy Glenn, who's spent much of his life teaching amateurs and occasionally ventures into professional waters. "Managers and trainers dream too. You teach a kid. You give him thousands of hours. The kid quits; you bring him back. He gets in trouble with the law or with a girl, and you help him out. You put a foundation under him. You give him your heart. Then," Glenn continues, "the kid starts to look good. He turns out to be that one in a thousand who's really good. And all of a sudden, some guy walks in, offers the kid a salary, a bonus, and he's gone. That's always the way it is with amateurs on account of you can't sign an amateur to a contract. And with a pro, even if you have a contract, where are you gonna get the forty thousand dollars in legal fees to enforce it? So you sell the contract or it isn't renewed when it expires. Guys like me dream of a champion, but when a fighter hits ten rounds, big money pushes the little guys out."

Those who cover boxing for the electronic and print media are well aware of how the game works. "You can't be a thinking person and not have moments when you're repelled by it all," says Alex Wallau of ABC Sports. "Sometimes you get worn down," adds Pat Putnam of *Sports Illustrated*. "You get battered from all the things that are going on outside the ring, from who's screwing who, and you get to the point where you're ready to say that's it, I've had it. All the good writers who cover the sport go through it. I'm surprised more of us don't quit."

Still, the business of professional boxing goes on. And one

of the most ardent proponents of the status quo is Don King. "How many professions do you know of," asks King, "where a black businessman—I said businessman, not athlete or rock singer—can come in, and without a college education make one hundred or two hundred thousand dollars? How many black general managers are there in major league baseball, or black head coaches in the NFL? As far as antitrust goes," King continues, "if the fighter asks me, I sign him up. They've been asking me because they know I perform. I see no difference between what I do and what Mark McCormack does when he signs up all the leading golfers. Why is it all right for him to have Arnold Palmer, Gary Player, Jack Nicklaus, and Lee Trevino at the same time? There's nothing wrong with that unless a black man does it. A nigger starts doing it, and the next thing you know they call out the FBI, the CIA, and IRS. Why can't you look at it the way it really is? They walked into this office. I didn't send for them. I didn't put no gun to their head. I didn't coerce, intimidate, or bribe to get them to come. They came because they thought I was the best promoter in the world.

"Life within the law," King continues, "is where the real villains are. I didn't invent the rules, but I played within the rules and I've been successful. There's nothing wrong with options. Options are everywhere. In movies, in sports. Options is not a dirty word. My morals are no different from those of any other chief executive officer. I'm a promoter in business to make money. All I'm doing is working in the tradition of America. This nonsense, complaining about me and my son. Lou Duva trains and manages fighters. His son Dan promotes them. And he's got another son and a daughter and I don't know who else in the business. I dig it. I like it. But with the white populace, which controls the media, they extol Lou. He's got 'the first family of boxing'; the whole family working together. Me, I got one little son. People just don't like me for the same reason they didn't like Muhammad Ali. We're the wrong kind of nigger. We're not quiet. We stand up to be counted. We're the best, and we're heard. I'm getting very tired of everyone making me out to be a nigger; like I can't do anything right on my own; like I can't get anything done without breaking the law. Every day is a struggle for me. I've always had to go out and fight because I'm a black man. It's not fair."

Thomas Hauser

There are certain individuals it helps to please if a man is to have a future in boxing. Don King is first among them.

"I'm not God's policeman," says Mike Jones. "I do what's honest and fair and best for my fighters. To get a shot at any world title you need a godfather. To get Billy his shot, I went to Don King."

10

It was late 1983 when Mike Jones took aim at a championship shot for Billy Costello. Despite the existence of two world sanctioning bodies, there was really only one option. Aaron Pryor held the World Boxing Association's 140-pound crown, and Billy hadn't evolved to the point where he was ready for Pryor. Also, Mike's contacts with the WBA were minimal. That left World Boxing Council superlightweight champion Bruce Curry as a potential foe.

Curry was a seasoned professional, 27 years old. His amateur record included four Texas Golden Gloves titles and a victory over Sugar Ray Leonard. As a professional he'd had 41 bouts and 34 wins. Two of his losses were to Wilfred Benitez, one to Thomas Hearns. He'd won the title in May 1983, and defended it successfully twice since then. As for opponents in common, Billy Costello had won a ten-round decision over Willie Rodriguez. Curry had knocked out Rodriguez in the twelfth round.

"How did I get Billy the fight with Curry?" Mike asks rhetorically. "I'll tell you one thing, there was no pride involved." Curry was managed by Bill Baxter, and under promotional contract to Don King. "I put my pride in my pocket," Mike continues, "and I chased King and Baxter all over the country. Don King was the man I really had to sell. I kept telling him how exciting Billy was as a fighter; how when Billy was in the ring you couldn't

117

turn away because at any moment—boom—anything might happen."

Eventually, Mike Jones followed King to Las Vegas, where the promoter was staying at the Dunes Hotel. "We had three appointments," Mike remembers, "and he stood me up each time. Finally, I went up to his room, knocked on the door, and Don asked who it was."

"Room service," Mike answered.

Dressed in his underwear, King opened the door.

"Jones, what do you want?"

"You know what I want."

Soon after, Mike had his contract. Billy Costello would get $25,000 and a shot at Bruce Curry's World Boxing Council superlightweight crown. In the event Billy won, King would have options on his first three title defenses for an amount to be mutually agreed on, but not less than $125,000, $150,000 and $175,000. The $25,000 wasn't much, but it gave Mike, Billy, and Victor Valle what they wanted. "There's a time to be strong and a time to make a deal," Mike would say later. "Other managers chasing after Curry were talking about money. I was just talking fight. If you want the truth, I'd have taken that fight for nothing."

As for Don King, he was equally pleased. None of the other challengers in the 140-pound division was likely to make more money for him than Billy Costello, and the deal was a way of keeping open lines of communication with Mike Jones. That was important. Lest anyone forget, Mike and Dennis Rappaport (whom King abhored) were Gerry Cooney's co-managers. If Cooney ever returned to the ring, Don King wanted a piece of the action.

The fight, televised nationally by CBS, took place on January 29, 1984, in Beaumont, Texas—Bruce Curry's backyard. "Not too many people were rooting for me," Billy recalls. "There was a group of friends who flew down from Kingston—Joe LaLima, Pete Esposito, Aaron Ball, Rocky Secreto, Jack Becker, Mike Jubie, Jeff Boyle, a few more. 'Costello's crazies,' people called them. There was my wife; and there was Mike and Victor. Mike and Victor have been in my corner for every one of my fights. They're always there."

As Billy entered the ring, the difference between winning

and losing was painfully clear. One bad punch, one mistake, and his title hopes would be gone forever. Winning held out the prospect of bigger things in the years to come. Losing all but guaranteed that there would be no money in a career that by definition would end while he was still a young man.

The fighters were introduced: "Ladies and gentlemen; twelve rounds of boxing for the World Boxing Council superlightweight championship; in this corner . . ."

"I looked across the ring," Billy remembers, "and I said to myself, I'm here. People put me down all my life, but I'm here. Now all I got to do is beat this motherfucker."

Fighting is a young man's game. In boxing history, only two men have held titles over the age of 40; less than two dozen over the age of 35. Billy Costello and Bruce Curry were both 27 years old, but it's not just years that wear a man down; it's the wars he's survived. Curry was a young man, but an old fighter. His legs were shot. They no longer gave him power, held him up strongly, or moved him swiftly around the ring. The assets he brought into the ring against Billy Costello were courage and a will of iron.

There's a story a former world champion tells that says a lot about the desire to win. It's embarrassing in part, and he tells it on the condition of anonymity. This fighter once went into the ring against a younger, faster, stronger foe. For the first eight rounds he was beaten badly. Then against all odds he rallied to salvage his crown.

"How did you do it?" the fighter was asked. "I know about courage, but where did you find the strength and inner resources to do what you had to do?"

And the fighter answered, "Sometimes, it's like you do things that physically you don't think you can. It's like, one time when I was seventeen, I was on a date with this girl in the park. I had to shit, so I went to the men's room, but it was locked. I had to go real bad so we looked for another men's room but we couldn't find one, and it was getting worse so we started to walk out of the park to go to a restaurant or bar. I was wearing white shorts and a T-shirt to show off my body. I liked this girl. I wanted to impress her because I liked her a lot. My stomach got worse. My bowels were pushing or whatever, and suddenly

I realized I was going to shit in my pants. I fought it. It was like every ounce of strength I had was working to keep it in. I had to keep it in because, if I shitted in my pants in front of this girl, I'd die. And we walked. I could hardly talk, and I felt it slipping, but I held it in. I controlled myself physically, and we got to a bar, and I made it into the men's room and practically shitted all over the floor. That's the kind of effort you need in the ring. When you're getting pounded, when you're getting beat bad, you say to yourself, if I lose this fight I'll die."

With 25 seconds left in the first round, Billy Costello rocked Bruce Curry with a straight right to the jaw and a left hook to the point of the chin. Curry wobbled backward against the ropes and survived the round, but the pattern of the bout was set from then on. Curry, reaching in, throwing punches that left him open for short crisp counters. Curry, coming in, absorbing punches until he couldn't take it anymore.

In the fourth round, Billy again staggered the champion with left hooks to the body and jaw. Three smashing rights. Another hook. A chopping right to the head. Enormous punishment. Curry, his legs rubbery, was saved by the bell.

Round five: more of the same. In round six, blood started to stream from a cut above Curry's left eye. Round seven: Billy began landing four, five, six blows in succession; just teeing off, landing to Curry's jaw. In the corner, watching the carnage, Victor Valle stared at the champion who wouldn't fall. "What a courage," Victor murmured. "What a courage that son-of-a-bitch has."

Round eight: more punishment. Round nine: again Billy began to load up, ripping punches to Curry's head and body. Unsteady, taking a ferocious beating, the champion staggered forward, surviving on instinct alone.

Fifteen seconds into the tenth round, a barrage of punches sent Curry down. He rose, arms at his side, and backed into a neutral corner. Fighters live for an opponent's vulnerability— the moment their foe is dazed, groggy, unable to defend himself. That's when a fighter moves in and smashes his opponent with finishing blows. Fifty-five seconds into the tenth round, with Bruce Curry pinned helpless against the ropes, referee Richard Steele stepped between the fighters. Billy Costello was superlightweight champion of the world.

An hour later, Mike, Victor and the newly crowned champion left the arena together. "It was pouring rain," Mike remembers. "I couldn't have cared less. Billy was the first fighter I'd managed on my own, and now I had my first world champion. I was happy for me; I was happy for Victor; but most of all I was happy for Billy. For five years we'd been together. I knew how hard Billy had worked and what a decent person he was. I loved him."

Win, lose, or draw, Mike had resolved that Billy was going to leave the arena in style. By prearrangement a huge black limousine was waiting to take the victors back to their hotel. As Mike strode through the downpour, Billy looked back toward the arena. There, huddled together, were Bruce Curry and his mother, with Curry's brother at their side.

"Mike," Billy said softly, "tell Curry he can have the limousine. We'll take a bus back to the hotel."

* * *

There are very few things that live on after a man is gone. The money he's saved is dispersed to future generations that ultimately don't even know his name. The possessions he's owned are scrapped or discarded as time wears on. What is left are children and succeeding generations of children. And if a man is lucky there is something more, a touch of immortality that lasts through time.

Billy Costello had become a world champion. Within his division, he could trace his lineage to Tony Canzoneri, Jackie "Kid" Berg, and Barney Ross. He now shared a common heritage with Joe Louis, Muhammad Ali, and Sugar Ray Robinson. He was immortal, and an emotional high swept his camp just as emotional despair would descend over Bruce Curry's.

"Winning that title," Billy said later, "was the greatest feeling in the world. I knew I'd do it; I had to. After all the work and preparation I'd put in, losing to Curry would have been like praying to God and then going out and committing sin."

Still, to most observers, it was unlikely that Billy Costello would remain champion for long. The flaws were obvious. Against Curry he'd shown virtually no finesse, and backed away from punches instead of slipping them. His jab had been close to nonexistent. He'd stood too straight, and his balance was poor. Bruce Curry had walked into the ring a spent fighter who just didn't have it anymore. Billy Costello was an awkward fighter with a good left hook, that's all.

"After a few days," Billy remembers, "I didn't even feel like a champion. All I'd gotten for Curry was twenty-five thousand dollars, and I owed more than that. No one recognized me on the street. And all the time I heard the chirping. 'Billy Costello's hands are too slow; he can't do this; he can't do that.' No one ever said anything to my face. It was always behind my back, but I heard them. And then all I started hearing about was Ronnie Shields."

Ronnie Shields, born in Port Arthur, Texas, 26 years old, black, the son of a laborer, one of six children. As an amateur, Shields had won 242 fights, six regional Golden Gloves championships, and three national Golden Gloves crowns. His professional record was 20 and 2; including a win over former super-lightweight champion Saoul Mamby. Both the World Boxing Council and World Boxing Association rated Shields the number-one challenger in the 140-pound division. He had power and the best jab in his class. Worse, Billy had no choice—he had to fight Shields.

Under the World Boxing Council Constitution, a champion may defend his title against anyone in the top ten. However, at least once a year he must make a "mandatory" defense against the designated number-one challenger. Moreover, a new champion inherits the obligation of his predecessor. The rule is a good one. Too often in the past, fighters treated titles as belonging solely to them rather than to the sport. Floyd Patterson ducked legitimate challengers for years while defending his championship against Pete Rademacher and Tom McNeeley. Jack Dempsey didn't defend his title from September 14, 1923, when he knocked out Luis Firpo, until September 23, 1926, when he lost it to Gene Tunney. Great fighters like Archie Moore languished for years, or in some cases were never afforded an opportunity to fight for the title. Still, for Billy Costello, the rule was a burden. His mandatory defense was due immediately. Either he fought Ronnie Shields or he relinquished his crown.

The bout was signed for July 15, 1984, in Kingston, New York. Don King agreed to pay Billy $140,000; Shields $50,000. "It won't be no problem," said Shields's manager Willie Savannah. "Ronnie Shields will pick Billy Costello apart. Besides," Savannah added, "Billy Costello has no heart."

"Willie Savannah could get his fighter hurt saying things like that," Mike Jones countered.

Still, for Billy Costello, Mike Jones, and Victor Valle, the weeks leading up to the fight against Shields were a time of doubt. "What can I tell you," Mike said a few days before the bout. "It's a fight. If Billy loses, he loses. You have to accept the possibility of something like that or else you go batty in boxing."

"Billy can win," said Victor Valle. "He's as good right now as I can help him to get. But once the bell rings, what he does is up to him. It's his ability, his desire. To win this fight, Billy is gonna have to go places inside himself he's never been."

The night before the fight, Billy Costello sat in Room 105 of the Ramada Inn in Kingston. Sugar Ray Leonard, who had flown in to do the broadcast commentary for CBS, was at his side. A few minutes before seven o'clock, Billy's wife Jane came by with their fifteen-month-old daughter Christine. "You're adorable," said Leonard, picking the infant up and carrying her to the mirror, where she could see her reflection in the glass. "My wife and I want one just like you someday to go with our boys."

Jane and Christine left. Ray Leonard excused himself, and Billy turned to a friend who had stayed behind. "I guess to be the best in the world you got to beat the best," he said softly. "When the time comes, you got to fight the man." Then he looked down. "If I lose tomorrow, it's not like I died."

The fight was held in stifling hundred-degree heat at Kingston's Midtown Neighborhood Center, capacity 1,600. Don King Productions had wanted to stage the event in the gym at nearby Ulster County Community College, which had air conditioning and seated three thousand, but CBS vetoed the proposal. The network wanted a sellout crowd and cramped quarters to generate excitement for home viewers. Under the hot glare of ring lights, the fighters were introduced. "When I get in that ring," Billy would say later, "I look across at that other fighter and I say to myself, 'Man, you're on my turf. This square is mine.'"

Shields started fast, circling, scoring with his jab. Then, surprisingly, in the last minute of the first round, he chose to fight inside, pushing Billy back against the ropes, landing with repeated blows to the body. Clearly it was Shields's round, and round two began in much the same fashion. Shields with a jab. Shields with a hook to the body. Shields with another jab. Then Billy launched his counteroffensive.

"Shields *looks* like he's a good defensive fighter," Victor Valle had said before the fight. "He holds his hands in the right place, but he don't always know what to do with them. His jab is good but, also, he can be hit with the jab. What Billy's got to do is go in there and outjab him."

Midway through the second round, Billy began to jab. Left hook. Jab. Straight right. Jab. Then after a missed right, a left hook to the chin stunned Shields, sent him staggering backward and down. He rose quickly to one knee, and was up at seven. Cautiously, Billy came on. Left hook to the body; another hook. One second before the round's end, Billy launched a straight right and Shields countered with a perfect hook to the jaw, knocking the champion down. There was no count. Billy was on his feet at the bell. The brawl had begun.

"Billy is a funny fighter," Mike Jones would say later. "For all his ability, the thing that always held him back was a lack of confidence. He'd get in the ring, and no matter who he was against you could see he was tight. One of the best things about his becoming champion was it gave him confidence and a sense of presence in the ring."

In round three the confidence showed. Billy was landing his own jab, neutralizing the primary weapon in Shields's arsenal. A Costello jab. A Costello hook. Forty-five seconds into the round, Billy landed an overhand right just above Shields's left eye. Instinctively the challenger moved in to avoid the hook that was coming next, and as Billy's momentum carried him forward, their heads clashed. When the fighters drew back, blood was streaming from a gash above the challenger's eye.

Between rounds Shields's corner stemmed the flow of blood. For round four he came out jabbing, moving, pushing Billy to the ropes, hammering to the body with both hands. Billy countered with left hooks, but the challenger kept punching. Billy tried to spin away from the ropes. Shields kept him pinned in. Then in the waning seconds of the round, Billy fired several hard shots to the body, and Shields retreated. It was the challenger's round, but as he went to his corner something bad showed in his eyes. He'd thrown his best. Billy Costello had taken it, and had come back harder with more.

Round five. Shields no longer wanted to mix it up. He jabbed and moved laterally, not forward as before. Billy waited patiently for an opportunity to drop his right hand over the jab. The round was even until the last minute when the champion began to advance behind his own jab. A hard left hook with twenty seconds left shook Shields. Clearly, it was Billy's round, and more important, he had taken control.

Round six. The ring mats were wet from the fighters' soaked trunks and bodies. Battling the sweltering hundred-degree heat, their handlers had doused them with ice water between rounds. Again, it was the champion advancing against Shields's now-ineffective jab. More left hooks to the body started to land. With fifty seconds left in the round, Billy shot a left hook to the head and a short right to the neck. Shields stumbled and went down. He was up at two, and moved into a neutral corner as referee Davey Pearl's count reached eight. Then the fight resumed, and Billy came on. Jab, jab, left hook, right-hand lead, left uppercut. With nine seconds left, a double jab was followed by a straight right that smashed against Shields's cheek, contorted his entire face, and sent him plummeting to the canvas. Miraculously, he rose; but for all practical purposes the fight was over. Shields was fatigued; Billy was strong. Billy had the punch. He was in total control.

Ronnie Shields, it had once been said, discouraged his opponents. Billy Costello didn't just discourage Shields. He cut his heart out. The judges' decision was anticlimactic after twelve rounds. Rudy Jordan, 119–110 for Costello. Rudy Ortega, 117–111 for Costello. Vince Delgado, 117–110 for Costello. "Billy Costello fought one hell of a fight," Shields said when the battle was done. "He just went out and did everything right."

"It's incredible," said Gil Clancy, who along with Tim Ryan and Ray Leonard had covered the fight for CBS. "I can't believe how much Billy has improved since the Curry fight. He's jabbing better, moving better, punching better. He looks like a champion. No one expected him to beat Shields this decisively."

It was a good fight, and a good win for Billy Costello. He'd retained his title. He had earned respect, proving he could box as well as punch. There had been twelve rounds of solid action with four knockdowns, which meant the television networks would want him again.

"What are you going to do with all the money?" someone asked after the fight.

"You want a real answer?"

"Yeah."

A serious look crossed Billy's face. "All right. For this fight I got a hundred and forty thousand dollars. Ten percent goes to Victor and thirty percent to Mike. That leaves eighty-four thousand. I owe twenty-seven thousand to Mike that I borrowed, and next April you know I'll be paying taxes. The apartment needs furniture. I promised my wife I'd buy an air conditioner and new television set. When everything's done, I'll have ten thousand dollars."

"That's all?"

"That's all. And you know something? I'm putting it in the bank. It's the first real money I've ever had."

PART
3

Fighters are like beautiful women; too many times they'll break your heart. But in all my life I never had a fighter like Billy. No one works harder. When you scold him, he don't walk away mad—he thinks about what he's done wrong and how to do better. He puts in the same effort every day at the gym whether he feels good or not. And he listens. Some fighters, you tell them something and they forget it like you're writing on ice. With Billy, you say something once, and it's etched in marble. He's a trainer's dream.

—Victor Valle

11

On Thursday, August 9, 1984, a muscular olive-skinned young man rode the subway into Manhattan from his apartment in Queens. Twenty-four days had passed since Billy Costello defended his WBC crown against Ronnie Shields. During that time, he and his wife had relaxed at home and visited friends. He'd done no exercise, and gained ten pounds. Normally, Victor Valle gives his fighters two weeks off after a bout, but Billy had worked particularly hard preparing for Shields, and the fight—twelve rounds in hundred-degree heat—had been grueling. Billy had used the extra time off to good advantage. Then Victor called and said it was time to go to work again.

The mid-summer air was hot and humid. Just east of 30th Street and Eighth Avenue, on a sidewalk strewn with paper and broken glass, Billy came to a two-story building beside a drab industrial structure. The sign outside read "Gymnasium—boxing lessons."

Gleason's Gym is a fixture in New York. Once there were dozens of places where young fighters learned their trade. No more. Even Stillman's, at one time the most famous gym in America, has closed its doors. Gleason's, Ringside, and the Times Square Boxing Club are now the only major professional gyms left in New York. Each is open six days a week. Monthly dues are $25.00.

Inside Gleason's, fifteen men were at work—two white, four Hispanic, the rest black. The sound of speed bags—a constant "whappity-whappity" like a jackhammer on pavement—filled the air. Two boxing rings, each slightly less than sixteen feet square, dominated the floor. At the far end of the room, three heavy bags dangled from chains, flanked by speed bags against the west wall. Beyond the equipment, a lone shower, a hundred or so lockers, and a single toilet stall were in view. The floor was concrete, painted red, worn by the hops, skips, and shuffles of ten thousand boxers. Six fluorescent lights hung from the ceiling. The walls were light blue to a height of ten feet, then white for ten feet more. Given the blue ring mats, red-white-and-blue ring ropes, and red floor, the gym had a seedy patriotic aura. There were no windows. The smell of sweat, linament, disinfectant, and cheap cigars filled the air.

As Billy entered several fighters turned. "Hi, Billy," one called.

It was always "Billy," not "champ." "Billy's my name," he told people when he won the title. "There's nice things about being champion—having people ask for my autograph, sharing the title with my family and friends. But I don't want nobody treating me different now, because in a couple of years I won't be champ anymore."

As Billy made his way across the floor, Ira Becker, Gleason's owner, approached and extended his hand. Briefly they talked about the Los Angeles Olympics and rumors that Mark Breland (who'd reached the quarter-finals in the boxing competition two nights earlier) would receive $250,000 for his first pro bout. "How does that make you feel?" asked Ira.

A quarter of a million dollars was ten times what Billy had earned for winning the WBC championship against Bruce Curry; more than his total purses for twenty-eight professional fights.

"As long as I get my money," Billy answered, "I don't care what Breland gets."

The conversation done, he climbed the stairs to balcony level. Like the ground floor, the balcony was all spit and little polish. A maze of thin metal lockers; a second shower and toilet stall. The shower was in a particularly decrepit state, with chipped white tiles, a falling ceiling, and sheet-metal floor. Working his way past the lockers, Billy came to a separate room set off from the rest of the balcony, and stepped through the door. Inside Victor Valle stood waiting.

"Let's go, young man. It's three-thirty already."

Normally Billy arrived at the gym at two-thirty. Today he was late because of an interview with Bob Waters of *Newsday*. The interview had been necessary; publicity translates into dollars. Television ratings determine how much a fighter gets paid, and the more publicity he receives the more likely people are to turn on their sets. Mike Jones had arranged for the interview, and had told Victor that Billy would be late. Still, the trainer was worried. By the time Billy changed clothes, taped his hands, and started to work it would be four o'clock. That meant his workout would last until after five, and Gerry Cooney was scheduled to start at four-thirty.

Billy and Gerry hadn't been getting along lately. Fighters are people with worries, jealousies, fears, and pressures like other people. With Billy Costello and Gerry Cooney a rift had developed because of circumstances and the personalities involved. Gerry could be brutal, as the sport required. "The whole thing that takes the heart out of a fighter," he once said, "is to make him feel pain. That's what I want to do, make my opponents feel pain. I want to hurt them. I know it sounds sick, but I see the look in their eyes when I hurt them. I see the fear, and it makes me feel in control. I want to hurt them." Yet beneath it all Gerry was also an extremely sensitive young man, and after losing to Larry Holmes he had fallen into a deep depression.

"After he lost, Gerry wouldn't even talk to me," Mike remembers. "He wouldn't return calls; he wouldn't see me in person; nothing. I started driving out to the pub he owns in Huntington, Long Island, in the hope I could see him, and the few times I did he wouldn't even talk about boxing." Then, finally, Gerry hinted he might return to the ring, and Mike negotiated a million-dollar contract for a fight with John Tate, who had slid far below the crest of the hill as a fighter. "It took me four days to find Gerry," Mike recalls. "When I did, I told him the good news, and he told me no."

Thereafter, Mike decided to leave Gerry alone, but the whispers had begun. . . . "Gerry Cooney wants to be heavyweight champion, but he's afraid to work hard for it and fail.". . . "Gerry has the ability; he has the trainer and the manager; but the desire isn't there.". . . "Cooney never really could fight. His record was built on bums and old men.". . . Many observers doubted that Cooney would fight again, and the state of affairs weighed particularly heavily on Victor Valle. Victor looked on Gerry as a second son; yet Gerry cut himself off from Victor as well, and Victor slipped into a depression of his own. "It got so I was a difficult man to live with," the trainer admits, "always shouting at my wife Lola and Victor Jr. Then, finally, Gerry called and said he was coming back to the gym."

But still Cooney didn't show. "He didn't come for weeks," Victor remembers. "I was telling newspapers that he was coming, and then he wouldn't come. He was making me look like a fool, and I was very hurt. It bothered me that a smart kid like that would stay away so many months just because he didn't know how to accept defeat. A man of twenty-six should have a little more common sense, and I told him so."

Finally in early 1983, Cooney returned to serious training. "To me, boxing is a love," he announced. "I know most people don't understand that. They see where I've been off a long time, and they figure, hey, this guy can't like boxing that much. But I love it." No sooner had training begun, though, than Cooney was forced to undergo surgery to remove bone chips from a knuckle on his left hand. The injury left him idle for the rest of 1983, and criticism turned to sarcasm. "My wife and I have a very good marriage," said one observer. "In the last two years we've had fewer fights than Gerry Cooney.". . . "They're making a movie about Cooney's next opponent," said another. "It's called *The Right Stiff.*" Even Cooney's boosters began to sour. "The biggest problem with Gerry Cooney," said Gil Clancy, "is that when he lost to Larry Holmes a lot of people treated him like he'd won. He had financial security. His picture was in the newspapers all the time. His razor commercial for television still ran. It took away all the hunger and incentive a fighter needs to be great." Said another, "What Gerry really wants is to win the title, and then tell everyone to go fuck themselves, and quit. But you don't become heavyweight champion of the world thinking like that."

In early 1984 Cooney resumed training. A fight was scheduled for July. And again injury forced a postponement. "They say Gerry is pulling out because of a pulled muscle; that his shoulder is only ninety percent," groused Clancy. "I don't know a fighter who ever went into the ring one hundred percent. Emile Griffith was my greatest fighter. If I'd waited for Emile to be one hundred percent, I'd still be waiting for his first fight."

Yet despite it all, despite his not having fought for over two years, Cooney's hold on the media remained extraordinary. "It's fantastic," said Michael Katz. "You get stories—Gerry Cooney hit the heavy bag today, Gerry Cooney skipped rope today. They write about it every time he farts. And the wildest thing is, most fighters have to wait in line and beg for a title shot. Cooney will get one whenever he says he's ready for it."

In short, even without having fought for two years, Gerry Cooney remained larger than life, Babe Ruth in waiting. And even after winning the title, Billy Costello labored in Gerry's shadow. "What happened," says Billy's wife Jane, "is that Billy saw all the attention Gerry got. And he thought that once he beat Bruce Curry to become champion he'd be in the spotlight too. Then Billy didn't get the attention he deserved, and Gerry seemed to resent what little attention Billy did get."

The slights took many forms. Training at the Concord Hotel for his fight against Ronnie Shields, Billy was largely ignored by hotel management, while Gerry was given red-carpet treatment. Reporters who interviewed Billy invariably turned to questions about his more famous stablemate. There's no such thing as a free ride in boxing. No fighter has it easy, but some fighters have it easier than others. "I don't blame Gerry for all the attention and money he's getting," said Billy, "but sometimes I think he should appreciate it more and be more willing to share the glory. Sometimes I think Gerry wants to be the only child, but in this world we all got brothers and sisters."

Then the friction came to a head. Interviewed by Michael Marley of *Inside Boxing*, Billy found himself asked not about himself but again about Gerry. And he told Marley, "Hey, let's face it. Gerry Cooney was the big man then. He was the white guy, the attraction. Now I'm finally getting my chance. I'm the one who won the fight. And even if I never did anything else, I've done something Gerry has never done. I've won the title."

Marley's article appeared in late July, several days after the Shields fight. Thereafter, Gerry stopped talking to Billy. True to form, Billy acknowledged that he had been accurately quoted. "But, number one," he told Victor, "what I said wasn't so bad.

And number two, it's true. I don't know what Gerry's so upset about." Still, at Victor's request Billy sent word to Gerry that he'd like to apologize. Gerry responded that he wasn't interested in talking about it. That left Victor, who trained both men, uncomfortable and unhappy. "Billy is Billy, and Gerry is Gerry," he said. "I don't take sides between them, and I wish they could be friends. The bad feelings pain me." Thereafter, the trainer arranged a gym schedule whereby Billy would work out from three to four and Gerry from four-thirty to five-thirty. Today, though, there would be an overlap of at least a half hour.

The changing room was reserved exclusively for Victor and his fighters, a concession from Gleason's in exchange for the prestige of serving as headquarters for a heavyweight contender and world superlightweight champ. Unlike the rest of the gym, it had industrial carpet and a working fan. A long rubdown table covered with red vinyl, eight thin metal lockers, a cabinet, and four chairs completed the furnishings. Posters of legendary fighters and several montages made from press clippings about Gerry graced the graying plaster walls. A small black-and-white photo of Billy and Victor was taped on a locker adjacent to the door.

Billy slipped out of his street clothes and removed a necklace, the only jewelry he wore. The chain was 14K gold. He'd bought it to go with two tiny gold gloves that had been his prize for winning the 1978 Golden Gloves tournament.

"How's Jane?" Victor asked.

"Real good. She's nice whenever I come home from a fight. That's 'cause she misses me and because I've just been paid."

Victor was dressed in a blue T-shirt and maroon sweatpants with a white stripe down each leg. Billy reached for his socks. He was a creature of habit, steadfast in his quirks. During a meal he always ate the potatoes first, then the vegetable, the meat last. Dressing, he always started with his socks.

"Victor, when does Mike say I'm fighting next?"

"He don't know yet. Maybe in five weeks, September fifteenth."

"It's hard to train if I don't know the date."

"Then train like you're fighting on September fifteenth."

Billy pulled on a pair of red shorts, and began lacing his shoes. Finally, he reached for a black T-shirt with white lettering that read, "Billy Costello—WBC Champ." "Hey, Victor. You know what WBC stands for?"

"Come on, we got work to do."

"W-B-C. William Billy Costello, that's what."

Downstairs, the number of fighters had grown to twenty. Young men with lithe bodies and tightly muscled legs worked beside older once-handsome men whose faces had been misshapened by lumps and scar tissue cutting toward their eyes. Two trainers shouted instructions at a pair of fighters sparring in the ring nearest the door. Several "lifers"—old men who had once been fighters—stood silently watching. Victor reached for a roll of gauze, and began to bandage Billy's hands. When the taping was done the workout started.

Boxing as a sport is remarkably resistant to change. Its gyms are no different today from the gyms of a half-century ago. There are no Nautilus machines, no whirlpool baths. The building, push-yourself, drudgery work has remained unchanged—skipping rope, calisthenics, stretching exercises, hitting the speed and heavy bags. "Shadow box until your shadow gets tired," trainers instruct their charges. "One more sit-up!"

With Victor outside the ropes, Billy climbed into the ring, shook his arms, and began to move in a circular pattern, throwing punches at the air. Often a fighter swings and misses his opponent, and when he does it's important that he know how to bring his arm back without losing balance or leaving himself open to a counter blow.

Next, Victor climbed through the ropes, and positioned himself opposite the fighter as Billy began firing jabs.

"Sharper. Come on, throw the jab!"

With each salvo, Victor offered his head as a target just out of range—a maneuver not without risk. Several years earlier the trainer had been in the ring with Gerry Cooney and unexpectedly lowered his jaw just as Cooney swung. Six thousand dollars of dental work followed.

As Billy and Victor worked, an elderly black man leaned against the ropes and chewed on a toothpick. His fat companion chomped on a cigar that resembled a stale bowel movement. Oblivious to their presence, fighter and trainer continued.

"Back to basics. Throw me a left hook."

Left elbow and arm tucked close to his body, Billy leaned slightly to the side and forward, his weight on his left foot. Then he pivoted, twisting his left hip and shoulder to the right, putting his entire body into the blow.

"Again. Throw it good!"

Next, old tricks—spinning out of corners, avoiding butts. Finally, Billy climbed down from the ring, and Victor began lacing on his gloves. A young fighter approached and waited until the trainer acknowledged his presence.

"Excuse me, Mr. Valle. Every time I throw the jab, my left arm hurts."

"Where's the hurt?"

The fighter pointed to the underside of his forearm about two inches from the elbow.

"It's from blocking punches," Victor told him. "There's a bruise or something. Don't do no sparring today or tomorrow, and you owe me twenty dollars."

"What?"

"You heard me, twenty dollars. I don't give all this knowledge inside my head for nothing. You go to a doctor and he'll charge you fifty dollars for what I just said. Pay me someday when you get rich."

When the gloves were laced, Victor pointed to a large cylindrical bag suspended nearby at body level on a chain. In the background a bell sounded, an automatic timer that rang periodically, simulating three-minute rounds with a one-minute rest period in between.

"Two rounds," Victor instructed. "Wait for the bell."

The heavy bag is a tool for developing punching power and stamina. A fighter must control the bag at all times, circling, using his weight and arms to maneuver its bulk as he would an opponent. At the bell Billy began throwing punches, shaking the bag with each blow. Near the end of the round he missed twice on purpose, following once with a forearm and once with an elbow. Round two was more of the same, his arm muscles bulging like rocks with every blow.

"Overhand right," Victor ordered.

The overhand right is an awkward punch. "I hate it," Billy once told his trainer. "It don't flow like other punches, and it makes me look bad when I miss."

"So don't miss," Victor had answered.

Billy fired a series of overhand rights, and the heavy bag jerked back and forth on its moorings. The punch looked undisciplined, even crude; but well developed and properly timed it was devastating. Several onlookers gathered.

"Time," Victor called as the bell sounded. "Speed bag next. Three rounds."

The teardrop-shaped leather speed bag was suspended at eye level from a platform against the west wall. By moving the bag back and forth, a fighter develops hand-speed and stronger arm and shoulder muscles. Once it was thought that speed work improved hand-eye coordination, but that theory was demolished by Cus D'Amato, who hit a speed bag uninterrupted while blindfolded for a three-minute round.

Gloves off, hands still taped, Billy began to hit the bag. Midway through the first round, Gerry Cooney came down from the locker room, dressed in gym clothes. Neither fighter acknowledged the other, but as the next round began Victor moved away to tape Gerry's hands. Billy finished the round alone, glancing at his trainer from time to time. "Lots of fighters," Victor would say later, "when the trainer walks off, they hit the bag a little slower or a little less hard. I'm no dummy. Even if I'm not watching, I can hear what's going on."

Whatever Billy felt was channeled into hitting the bag harder in the final round.

It was late afternoon, and the number of fighters working out had grown. Five o'clock is the busiest time for fighters' gyms. That's when day laborers get off work and pursue their "second job." With a dozen spectators watching, Gerry climbed into the ring and began a series of therapeutic exercises for his left shoulder. Billy, his speed work done, started jumping rope, 150 jumps per minute, for two rounds. Then he ran through a succession of leg lifts, push-ups, sit-ups, and stretching exercises. At five-fifteen his workout was done.

That night, for the first time in four months, Billy went to the fights at Madison Square Garden.

Once New York was the capital of boxing, and the Garden was its showcase arena. The original Madison Square Garden was an old railroad depot converted by P. T. Barnum into a hall in 1874. The second was built in 1890 by a syndicate under the control of William Vanderbilt. The present Garden is the fourth. Built at a cost of $130 million, it opened in 1968 with seating for 20,000. In its first main events, Joe Frazier knocked out Buster Mathis, and on the same card Nino Benvenuti regained the world middleweight title by outpointing Emile Griffith. Thereafter, the Garden was the site for a number of memorable bouts—most notably the first battle between Muhammad Ali and Joe Frazier—but its decline had begun. Because of antitrust concerns stemming from old legal difficulties, Garden officials were unable to sign quality fighters to option contracts. High state and city taxes drove big fights away from New York, and casinos in Las Vegas and Atlantic City began paying huge site fees to lure name fighters. Television networks refused to broadcast fights from the Garden, since doing so often required blacking out the New York metropolitan area. And perhaps most significantly, the Garden began to deemphasize boxing. "Garden officials will deny that," says John Branca, former chairman of the New York State Athletic Commission. "But the truth is, Madison Square Garden deemphasized the sport the same way the Ivy League deemphasized football. The people in charge really don't seem to care about boxing anymore."

"The people there don't know what they're doing," adds Bob Arum. "It's as simple as that. They're not promoters; they're not imaginative matchmakers." In 1983 Arum himself rented the Garden for a night, and sold it out for a bout between Roberto Duran and Davey Moore. The next year he came close to doing it again with a fight between Marvin Hagler and Mustafa Hamsho. But most fights at Madison Square Garden today are held not in the main arena, but in the adjacent 4,500-seat Felt Forum. Promoted biweekly by Madison Square Garden Boxing (largely for the benefit of the Garden's cable-television network) they feature too many competitive mismatches between fighters who are largely unknown.

"Madison Square Garden," summarizes Bert Sugar, "used to be The Mecca of Boxing. It is now essentially club fights at the Felt Forum. Whenever they have a big fight, it's because they've leased the building to Bob Arum. That's like saying, 'My wife is beautiful, but I can't make her. You fuck her.' "

THE BLACK LIGHTS

Billy arrived at the Felt Forum at 7:20 P.M. The arena resembled a movie set, with only a sparse crowd in attendance. Hot television lights beamed down on the pale-blue ring canvas. Sam Rosen, one of two cable TV commentators, was finishing an interview with Carl Williams, who would be headlining the main event. Off to the side, John Condon, president of Madison Square Garden Boxing, was demonstrating that he is one of the few individuals alive today who can knot a tie perfectly without benefit of a mirror.

Condon loves boxing. A rugged-looking man in his sixties, he has a resonant voice that's been heard for years over the Garden's public address system at a variety of sporting events. He's also Rosen's announcing partner and one of the best boxing color commentators in the business. Whether he administers boxing as well as he broadcasts it is a subject of dispute. Also present was Harold Weston, a former welterweight contender, beaten by Pipino Cuevas and Wilfred Benitez in his only title bouts. Weston, the Garden's matchmaker, had a fairly straightforward job. Condon gave him dates, and Weston filled them with fighters. Each day he received five to ten letters and up to fifty telephone calls from trainers and managers soliciting the opportunity for their fighters to fight.

The crowd was predominantly male and blue collar. Mimeographed sheets had been distributed, offering the names of each fighter, but except for the main event no records were listed. To most of the crowd the names were irrelevant. They would root for the guy in red trunks against the guy in blue, or the guy from New York against the fighter from Virginia. Others would cheer on an ethnic basis. Six of the scheduled bouts matched black against Hispanic fighters. In the other two, both contestants were black. For each four-round bout the fighters would receive $250. Out of that they would pay for equipment, training expenses, a trainer, and manager. Six-round fighters would be paid $350; eight-rounders, $750.

Unnoticed, Billy slipped into a seat two rows behind the press section. Moments later the three judges took positions on different sides of the ring apron. Judges in New York are assigned by the State Athletic Commission, but paid by the promoter on a sliding scale keyed to a night's gate receipts. For eight bouts each judge would receive a total of $75.00.

At seven-thirty a recording of the national anthem was played. Then the first two fighters came down the aisle. Four rounds, bantamweights. Manuel Gago: 117 pounds, red trunks with white trim. Walter Gallman: 118 pounds in blue. Gago was a two-time New York City Golden Gloves champion making his professional debut. Gallman had been knocked out in his only professional appearance.

As the referee gave final instructions, both combatants appeared devoid of emotion except for their eyes. Gago was the aggressor from the opening bell. The match had been made for him to win, and a barrage of punches put Gallman down two minutes into the second round. As the referee's count reached ten, the victor wriggled over his fallen foe, then turned a full somersault beside him. Billy's face turned grim. "I don't like that dancing shit," he said to the man sitting next to him. "The guy who lost feels bad enough. And the guy who won, he thinks he's real tough; wait until the same thing happens to him."

Next up were a pair of junior lightweights—Alberto "The Cobra" Ramos versus Kelvin Louis. Ramos was a prospect—nine and one, the only loss coming on a four-round decision in his first pro fight. Louis, with a record of two wins and two losses, had been imported from Portsmouth, Virginia. If looks were punches, Ramos would be in trouble. Louis had a long ugly scar on his left arm, and a baleful stare that suggested knife tracks. Still, the fight had been weighted in Ramos's favor. He was better trained and better conditioned. Even New York safety standards were in his favor. Under state law, thumbless gloves were mandated for all nontitle fights. The rationale was to guard against detached retinas, but use of the gloves dictated a drastic change in ring tactics. Fighters are taught to use their thumbs to tie up an opponent. In a clinch they hook their thumbs inside an adversary's elbows to twist punches aside or prevent them from being thrown altogether. With thumbless gloves that technique was impossible. And fighters like Louis, used to tying up opponents with their thumbs, found themselves unable to defend the way they knew how.

Midway through round three a left uppercut sent Louis to the canvas. "Get up, Kelvin," a voice cried. "You didn't come all the way from Virginia to get knocked out." Louis rose, but without control of his senses. As he sagged back against the ropes, the referee stepped between the fighters and stopped the fight.

A brief interlude preceded the next bout. A woman in her late teens approached and asked Billy for his autograph. "For my brother," she said. A reporter gravitated back from the press section, puffing on a cigar. No smoking is allowed at the Felt Forum. The crowd complies; the media doesn't. At any given time about a third of the people in the press section are smoking.

"What are you doing with all your money?" the reporter demanded. "You must have millions by now."

"Don't believe it," Billy answered. "Not about any fighter. We got managers; we got trainers; we got sparring partners and doctors. All them people cost money."

"When are you fighting next?"

"I'm not sure. Maybe September fifteenth."

The next bout was another match between a house prospect and an out-of-towner. David Harris, 179 pounds, 8 and 0 with six knockouts. His last bout had been a 52-second triumph over Understanding Allah at the Felt Forum. His opponent, Earl "The Pearl" Fields from Cleveland, claimed a record of five wins and three losses with no knockouts. Ohio, which lacks state regulation of boxing, is notorious for "meat dealers"—managers who sign every fighter in sight and ship them to promoters who want "an opponent who can go six rounds but doesn't have a punch." Harris versus Fields was scheduled for eight rounds.

The pattern of the fight was clear from the start. Harris was a puncher who walked in looking for one big shot. Fields didn't have the power to keep him off. He moved, not by choice but because he had to. Rarely did he throw punches, choosing instead to run and cover up. Twice in the first round, Fields went down from what were ruled slips. "Be first, David," someone in Harris's corner shouted. "You're the boss."

In the second round Fields "slipped" again. Rounds three and four were more of the same, with Fields absorbing punches to the head and body. Harris was beginning to tire, getting hit occasionally with lead rights, and his ferocity was degenerating into wildness, but Fields didn't have the strength to turn the tide. "The right, Earl. Keep using the right," someone shouted from the corner. Fields responded with his eyes as if to say, "It's not that easy."

By round five both fighters were exhausted. Fields in particular looked as though he'd be happier if the fight had been a four-rounder. Harris landed a series of body blows, and Fields lowered his guard. Then Harris fired several shots to the chin, and Fields's hands returned to their upward position. There's an old maxim in boxing—"Kill the body, and the head will die." The corollary to that is, "Kill the head, and the body won't feel so good either." As the round ended, snot was falling from Fields's nose onto the canvas in gobs.

Round six. Harris knocked Fields's mouthpiece out with a vicious right, and followed with more. Fields kept on his feet, but was battered around the ring. "They ought to stop it," Billy murmured. "The guy is hurt. There's no way he can win this fight."

"Put him on ice," someone shouted. "Knock the shit out of him, David."

Round seven. Harris was planting his feet, loading up on every punch. A roundhouse left put Fields on his back. He rolled over, and the look on his face suggested he was trying to decide whether to get up and be knocked down again or simply chuck it. He got up. Harris pursued. At the 57-second mark the referee stopped the fight.

"I wouldn't want to be in his body tomorrow," Billy said, as Fields left the ring to scattered applause. Then his face took on a slightly sour look. "You know something? If that guy tries to get into the Felt Forum next week to watch a fight, they'll charge him ten dollars."

The bouts continued, some fighters entering the ring strong and confident; others frightened and confused. Several didn't know the names of the men who taped their hands. They were club fighters without a future. People milled about, eating hot dogs and drinking beer. Still, the response of the crowd was of secondary concern to the combatants. They were fighting for the win or loss that would appear on their record, for the money, and to hurt their opponent before their opponent hurt them.

Edgar Brito versus Tony Baldwin. Baldwin's record was one and two. Brito had one win, three losses, and a tatoo that said, "amour madre" on his left arm. They fought to a four-round decision for Baldwin.

Cumba Valentine versus Ricky Young was next. Young was another prospect—9 and 0 with five knockouts. Valentine had suffered five losses in six pro fights. At the bell, Young came out circling and jabbing. One minute into the round he threw a straight right. Valentine ducked under it, sat down on the canvas, and stayed down for a count of ten. The punch had missed. Valentine simply quit.

Billy turned and shook his head. "He shouldn't have done that, but it's the Garden's fault for making the fight. Cumba Valentine couldn't beat Ricky Young no matter what he did."

Wade Davis versus Joe Martinez was fight number six. Martinez, with a record of two wins and one loss, had two claims to fame—he'd lost to Mark Breland in the finals of the 1981 New York Golden Gloves, and once Billy Costello had knocked him cold sparring in Gleason's. That was two more claims than Davis possessed. Blood flowed from Davis's nose from the second round on. By the last round he was so far behind on points that one observer suggested he'd have to knock Martinez out to earn a draw. Martinez won on a unanimous decision.

Now the stage was set for the main event—Carl "The Truth" Williams versus Terry Mims. Williams was a legitimate contender: twenty-four years old, six-foot-four, 218 pounds; undefeated in fourteen bouts, with eleven knockouts. In the wide-open heavyweight division he was a prospect in the process of being groomed. Mims, by contrast, was over the hill in a career that never really was. He'd begun boxing in 1977, won his first seven fights, then lost six in a row. According to the *Ring Record Book* he'd won only one fight in the preceding four and a half years.

One of the saddest sights in boxing is to watch a young man beat up an old one—and the great majority of the time, when the two meet, that's what occurs. No one makes the older man fight. He does so of his own free will, bolstered by a creed that says his opponent "is a man like me; if I hit him right, he'll fall." And he does so with the belief that any man who answers the bell for round one has a chance to win. Still, Carl Williams versus Terry Mims seemed to belie those views. The most that could be said for Mims was that it took raw courage for him to get into the ring against a man who was younger, stronger, better, and likely to knock him unconscious. Reality dictated that the line between competition and savage sadism was about to be crossed. Indeed, before the bout Williams had been so unconcerned about the quality of his opponent that he was eating Chinese food. Mims was fighting because he needed money. That was one more excuse than Madison Square Garden had for promoting the bout.

As the fighters met in ring center for the referee's instructions, the disparity in physical condition was clear. Mims's face was scarred, his body sagging. Even his trunks were frayed. Williams—eight years younger, thirty-five pounds heavier—enjoyed every physical edge. As one onlooker put it, even his testicles seemed better muscled. At the bell for round one he came out nonchalantly and fired a jab that sent Mims wobbling back against the ropes. Then for the remainder of the round he toyed with his opponent, circling, jabbing, like a cat playing with a mouse. "Come on, Terry," someone shouted. "He ain't got no fucking S on his chest. Fight back!" Mims continued to retreat, failing to throw a serious blow.

Round two was more of same. Thirty seconds into the round, with Williams continuing to play cat and mouse, the crowd began to boo. In response, the heavyweight fired a left-right combination that felled Mims for a count of five. The downed fighter rolled over to his hands and knees, shook the cobwebs from his head, and rose. One more punch would have ended it, but again Williams began to toy with the jab. "Come on, Terry," the same voice shouted. "He's a fighter, not Superman." Disgusted, the crowd began to chant, "Bullshit! Bullshit!"

In round three Williams chose to terminate the bout, pummeling his opponent into submission with a series of blows.

"It stinks," Billy said when the fight was over. "Two guys with five and twelve records would have been better. With all the hungry fighters out there looking for work, the Garden should do a better job."

"What's the matter?" the reporter with the cigar prodded. "You getting soft?"

"No. I just don't like to see guys beaten up in one-sided fights. I like fights that are close and evenly matched—except mine."

The next morning Billy got up early and ran four miles along Queens Boulevard. Then he showered, ate a light breakfast, and played with his daughter, Christine, while Jane went shopping. At two o'clock he took the subway to Gleason's, arriving at two-thirty. For eighty minutes he repeated the monotonous, sometimes masochistic ritual of the day before. As always, Victor stood by, watching, participating, constantly instructing. Sweat flowed freely. Contrasted with the stifling gym air, the hot humid streets outside seemed sweet-smelling and cool.

At four-fifteen the workout ended.

"No gym work tomorrow or Sunday," Victor told him. "But each day I want you to run four miles."

Billy nodded.

"Mike still don't know if you're fighting in September. He's trying, but the television people say it don't look good."

"When will we know?"

"Sometime next week."

Resigned to the wait, Billy climbed the stairs to Victor's private locker room and began to peel the sweat-drenched clothes from his body. Two teenagers who had come in from the street knocked on the door and asked for his autograph.

"It must feel great being champ," one of them said.

"It's all right," Billy answered. "Sometimes it's less exciting than I thought."

"Then how come you do it?"

"You gotta be kidding, man. I do it for money."

The teenagers left. Billy turned to a friend who had come upstairs, and continued the thought. "This money I'm making; I want it for myself, but I want it more for my wife and baby daughter. I never want them to have to ask favors from nobody. I work hard; I train right; I do everything Victor tells me to do. I'm twenty-eight years old, so I don't got much time left in boxing, but whatever I got left is gonna count. God help me, it's gonna count."

12

As Billy Costello labored in Gleason's Gym, his future was in the hands of Mike Jones.

After the fight against Ronnie Shields, Mike had spent twelve days tending to outside business. In addition to boxing, he maintained broad real-estate interests, which he'd let slide during the weeks preceding the Shields bout. "If I had to depend on boxing for my livelihood," he once said, "I'd go broke, not to mention nuts." Thus, prudence dictated that the latter half of July be devoted to real estate. Then at his wife's urging, he and Stella embarked on their first vacation in five years.

"Some vacation," Stella said when they'd returned to Long Island. "First we spent three days in New Hampshire with Bill Miller, who coordinated the Hagler-Scypion fight for Bob Arum and used to manage Alexis Arguello. Then we went to Maine to visit a boxer Mike might want to manage. After that we enjoyed four lovely days at the race track in Saratoga. It's a good thing I love him."

Mike had also spent a considerable amount of time on the telephone with Duke Durden, Don King's righthand man, trying to schedule a fight for Billy Costello. An Italian promoter named Rudolfo Sabbatini had offered Billy $400,000 to defend his title in Italy against European champion Patrizio Oliva. However, King held options on Billy's next two defenses, and Durden wouldn't (or couldn't) tell Mike how much money King wanted in exchange for one of those options. Finally on August 7, Mike's first day back in New York, Duke called and outlined the terms acceptable to Don King Productions. King wanted a "co-promotion" with Sabbatini, $75,000, and three options as Oliva's co-promoter in the event the Italian won the title. Co-promoting the first fight wasn't a problem, but $75,000 was steep, and Sabbatini was unwilling to concede options on future promotions. Thus, the deal was pretty much dead, but Duke suggested an alternative. King thought it would be "a good idea" if Billy defended the title against Leroy Haley, who had moved into the number-one challenger slot after the Shields defeat. Haley, a former WBC champion, had forty-nine wins, four losses, and two draws. More than coincidentally, Carl King was his manager.

However, any fight for Billy was dependent on television revenue. Home Box Office, which televised major bouts, was out of the picture, since Billy didn't have superstar status. NBC paid less than $100,000 for most of its fights, and the NBC matchmaker, Ferdie Pacheco, had been reluctant in recent months to do business with King. That left ABC and CBS as realistic alternatives, and since Billy's previous title fights had been on CBS, Mike decided to test those waters first.

The initial responsibility at CBS for saying "yes" or "no" to a fight lay with Mort Sharnik. Generally, after consulting with Gil Clancy, Sharnik would forward a recommendation to Terry O'Neil as to whether or not a fight was expected to be competitive. Sharnik, Clancy, O'Neil, Peter Tortorici (vice-president of programming for CBS Sports) and Mel Reddick (director of business affairs for CBS Sports) would then meet in O'Neil's office to decide whether to pursue the fight. Their primary considerations were ratings, whether a fight would last long enough to be profitable in terms of commercials, and what it would cost.

Tuesday night, August 7, Mike telephoned Terry O'Neil at his home in Connecticut. In essence he was begging for a television date. All three networks had loaded their fall schedule with college football, and virtually no slots were open for boxing. ABC was rumored to have two free days in December. CBS had three open dates—September 15, September 29, and November 3. However, September 29 was the probable date for Gerry

Cooney's long-awaited return to the ring, and CBS was internally committed to pursuing that bout. November 3 would most likely be given over to the professional debuts of several American Olympic fighters. That left September 15, with fierce competition among promoters to get it. The next open dates were in January.

Mike's conversation with O'Neil was short and to the point. Billy could be ready by September 15, but the only fight Don King could put together by then was against Leroy Haley. O'Neil's response was less than enthusiastic. He liked Billy, and he liked to broadcast fights from Kingston. Location was important to CBS. The network was trying to get away from casino sites. "A dead crowd makes the fight less exciting for home viewers," O'Neil said. "If you put two boxers in a dismal casino setting, they're more likely to fight a dismal fight." But O'Neil had doubts about Billy Costello versus Leroy Haley. "I know Haley's a former champion," he told Mike. "And I know the WBC has him ranked first in the division, but that ranking is more a tribute to Don King's influence than to Haley. I'm not sure it would be a competitive fight."

Mike spent twenty minutes on the telephone with O'Neil, singing the praises of Leroy Haley. Then he called Duke Durden and asked him to have Don King call CBS. After that he telephoned Carl King's home in Ohio. Haley's manager of record was out, and Mike left a message requesting that Carl call back. "I want him to pressure his father to pressure CBS," Mike told a friend that night. "This isn't a fight that will make Billy rich, but I'm going to push very hard for it. The worst thing possible would be to sit around without a fight until January or February. If a person is good at what he does—and Billy's good—a layoff for any length of time can only hurt."

Wednesday, August 8, Duke Durden called to report that he'd spoken with Mel Reddick, and "Reddick says CBS is considering Costello-Haley and one other fight for September fifteenth."

"Which one?"

Duke didn't know. When the conversation was done Mike telephoned Reddick, who hinted the other bout was a Thomas Hearns fight. Mike wasn't happy. Hearns was a bigger name than Billy, and would probably pull better television ratings. The only question was, would CBS pay Hearns's price?

Thursday Carl King returned Mike's call. "Some manager," Mike groused, when their conversation was done. "Carl didn't even know his fighter was being considered for the fifteenth. But now that he does, he's pretty excited. Maybe he'll light a fire under his father. Don can push CBS a lot harder than Duke can."

For the rest of Thursday, Mike watched Olympic semifinal boxing matches on television. Ten of eleven United States fighters advanced to the finals. The eleventh, lightheavyweight Evander Holyfield, was disqualified on an extremely controversial referee's decision. Of all the Olympic boxers, Holyfield had impressed Mike the most. He'd scored three knockouts against three previous opponents, and been well on his way to a fourth when the semifinal bout was stopped. On impulse, Mike picked up the telephone, dialed information in Atlanta—Holyfield's home city—and asked the operator if any Holyfields were listed. There was one. Mike called. It turned out to be Holyfield's aunt. Mike introduced himself, left his number, and asked that Evander or his representative call back to discuss his professional future.

Friday, August 10, Mike telephoned Mort Sharnik of CBS, who was at the Olympics, to put in a word for Billy: "Essentially, I'm a salesman, and the product I'm trying to sell is Billy Costello." Then, pursuing a rumor on the proposed Thomas Hearns bout, he called Mickey Duff, who managed the number-one super-welterweight contender John Mugabi. Duff confirmed that the alternative fight CBS was considering for September 15 was Hearns versus number-three-ranked Fred Hutchings, but the match couldn't be made unless Mugabi (the mandatory challenger for Hearns's WBC title) stepped aside. In truth, Duff didn't want Mugabi to fight Hearns. He much preferred to pursue the WBA title against weaker opposition, but he was planning to stand tough in the hope of extracting some money from Hearns in return for deferring the mandatory challenge.

With the situation in limbo, Mike turned to other business. First came Wilford Scypion. Once a promising contender, he had broken training repeatedly and squandered his physical resources. For about a month, Mike had been trying to sell his contract, but no deal had been consummated. Meanwhile Wilford was calling repeatedly for money. "What can I say," Mike grumbled after the fourth call, during which he agreed to send Wilford

$175. "I vowed never to send him money again, but he's desperate."

Next Mike put in a call to Bob Dietlmeier's parents in New Jersey. Dietlmeier was a nineteen-year-old heavyweight; tall, good looking, and white. Contractual problems with a previous manager had put the start of his professional career on hold, but the Dietlmeiers were anxious for their son to begin training with Victor Valle as soon as possible. "Some guys," Mike said, "they look fantastic in the gym, but they lose it when it counts. I have a feeling that Bob will be fantastic all the time once he learns the finer points of being a fighter."

Finally Mike turned to Gerry Cooney. Gerry had been scheduled to fight Philip Brown on Home Box Office in late July, but for the third time had pulled out—this time because of a strained shoulder muscle. Now he was back in training, and according to Victor would be ready to fight by September 29. After a series of calls among Dennis Rappaport, Terry O'Neil, Gil Clancy, promoter Sam Glass, Gerry, Victor, and Mike, a deal was struck. Gerry would get the September 29 CBS television date and $250,000. "It's amazing," Mike said. "Billy's a champion; he's at the crossroads of his career; he's an exciting fighter; and I'm begging to get him on TV. Gerry comes back, and he can get any date he wants."

The next day, Mike watched the Olympic boxing finals on television. "I don't think this crop is as good as 1976," he observed when the show was over. Maybe we won nine gold medals, but the Cubans and Russians weren't here. Mark Breland is overrated. There are no Sugar Ray Leonards in the group. The only fighter who really impressed me was Holyfield."

Still, the Olympics presented another worry. With nine American gold-medal winners plus Holyfield and two very good white Canadian fighters—Willie DeWitt and Sean O'Sullivan—television dates would be even scarcer in the months ahead.

Monday, August 13, Gil Clancy called and promised an answer regarding September 15 "by tomorrow night."

Tuesday came and went.

Wednesday Clancy called again to report that a resolution was expected "within twenty-four hours." Mike telephoned Mel Reddick. "Things look dim," Reddick acknowledged. "Hutchings has accepted. Now it's Hearns's choice."

Two hours later another fly appeared in the ointment. "A friend" at CBS advised Mike that Don King Productions had offered two heavyweights—Mike Weaver and James "Bonecrusher" Smith—to CBS for September 15 at a cheaper price than the Costello-Haley fight. Mike was furious. It meant that even if Hearns didn't accept, Billy might be underbid by his own promoter. Several telephone calls later, Mike was on the line with Duke Durden. Duke explained that Don had made the bid "just to be sure another promoter wouldn't get the date" in the event CBS found Costello-Haley "unacceptable." Mike was still furious.

Thursday, August 16, Wilford Scypion called again, as he had been doing incessantly all week. "I'm reformed; I'm changed; I'm broke; I need to fight. Please take me back again." By day's end Mike had agreed to "one last chance." "Wilford's a name," he explained. "I know he can fight. With his head screwed on, he's potentially the best middleweight in the world outside of Marvin Hagler. Managers will be spending millions of dollars in the next few months to sign unproven Olympic amateurs, and I have a known professional commodity who will cost me airfare plus room and board for a couple of weeks."

Next Mike called John Clancy, who agreed to train Scypion on Long Island, away from the distractions of city life. Then he called Victor, as he did every night. "Look at the bright side," Mike counseled. "The fact that we don't have a definite answer on September fifteenth means Hearns hasn't signed yet. There's still hope."

The following morning that hope evaporated. Duke Durden called to report that Hearns and Hutchings had reached an agreement with CBS. Hoping the information was wrong, Mike telephoned Terry O'Neil and Mel Reddick. Neither man was available; neither returned his call. "I'm upset," Mike said later that night. "CBS is in the business of delivering ratings. They think they can make more money with Tommy Hearns than with Billy Costello, and I understand that. I also understand that you can't go to the networks or King or Arum and say, 'Do me a favor.' The business doesn't work like that. But CBS expects me to be loyal to them, and they're not loyal back. All they'll have with Thomas Hearns is one fight. Then he'll jump to HBO or ABC or Marvin Hagler on closed circuit. Billy Costello was a fighter they could have kept for a long time." Then Mike turned pensive. "You know, Billy is in his prime now. Up until this point in his career, each year that passed represented an increase in skills. But it won't be long now before each year represents erosion. This is Billy's livelihood, his future. He doesn't have that much time left."

13

Billy was at home when Mike Jones called to tell him that the September date had been lost. All Mike could say was, "Stay in training. It doesn't look good for the next few months, but I'll do my best." Saturday and Sunday there was roadwork as usual, with Billy running four miles each day along Queens Boulevard. Monday he called in sick with a cold. Tuesday, August 21, he went back to work. "Once you're a champion, you want to be a good champion," he told Victor. "But the title don't mean nothing if you can't make money from it." Wednesday after Billy's workout a CBS camera crew arrived to tape an interview with Gerry. Even though Cooney's fight with Philip Brown was five weeks off, the network was already pushing it hard. Billy watched as the interview was taped. When the camera crew was done, several reporters, also in the gym to see Gerry, began firing questions. Billy turned and started upstairs.

"Keep punching," one of the reporters called after him.

"Keep writing," Billy answered.

Thursday and Friday were regular workouts. Saturday, August 25, Mike called with more news. Final contracts for the Cooney-Brown fight had been signed, and the promoters were setting up a training camp for Gerry in Eugene, Oregon. Gerry, his personal entourage, and Victor would be going there shortly. Since Victor was also Billy's trainer, Billy would have to come along. That meant more time away from Jane and Christine, in a place Billy really didn't want to go.

Monday, August 27, Billy worked out at Gleason's again. When he was done, Gerry stepped into the ring for his first sparring session since early July. Bob Dietlmeier was the opponent. "Go easy," Victor instructed his fighter. "He's very young."

Cooney came out, jabbing, moving forward. Dietlmeier moved laterally, retreating, jabbing occasionally, but more interested in not getting killed. Once in the second round he tried to catch Cooney with a sneak right. The punch glanced off the side of Cooney's head, and immediately the larger man drilled a hard left hook to Dietlmeier's body in retaliation. "Easy, dammit Gerry," Victor shouted. "Go easy."

"He's a mountain," Dietlmeier said when the two-round session was over.

Next Cooney sparred with Joe Cristle, a cruiserweight from Ireland. One minute into the first round, a sharp jab bloodied Cristle's nose. "Head down," Victor shouted at Gerry as the round progressed. "You're holding it up like a goddamn lantern in a storm. . . . Step to the right and hook. . . . Use the jab. . . . Listen to me, goddammit. When you was born, I was born already, so I'm a little ways ahead of you."

After the workout Cooney went upstairs to shower and change clothes. Victor spent several minutes with Dietlmeier and Cristle, critiquing their performance, then motioned to a young fighter who was standing nearby. The fighter, an amateur, had been sent by a friend who wanted Victor to train him. "All right," Victor instructed. "Get in the ring and shadow box for a round." The fighter complied. As the round progressed Victor turned to Cristle. "Watch this fellow," the trainer said. "He only throws punches. He don't do nothing on defense with his hands. And his punches, they're all to the head, nothing to the body."

At the end of three minutes, Victor called the fighter aside and told him to stay in the amateurs a while longer. "Go after a Golden Gloves crown." Then he went upstairs to change clothes, marveling at how a boxer could contemplate turning pro with so few skills. "You're never gonna get a fighter perfect," he grumbled. "But this young fellow, he had too far to go. Thirty years ago he wouldn't even have been allowed in the Golden Gloves."

"You're old-fashioned," someone suggested.

"You're damn right I'm old-fashioned. Everything is changing now. Men are carrying hair dryers and going to beauty parlors. The women have hair that's shorter than the men, and they dye it orange, purple, and blue. All that don't bother me. But I'm old-fashioned when it comes to putting somebody who don't know how to defend himself to box in a ring."

For the remainder of the week, Billy and Gerry worked out on separate schedules. Saturday, September 1, Billy, Mike, and Victor flew to Oregon. Two days later Gerry and several members of his personal entourage followed. For two weeks Billy worked in Eugene. Then on September 16 he came home. "Mike and Victor said I could," he told Jane on his return. "Things out there were kind of tense between me and Gerry. There's no fight for me scheduled, and Victor said I could train at Gleason's on my own."

Unspoken was the knowledge that a fighter who works too hard too often for fights that don't happen can burn himself out. Billy was in his prime. Time was slipping by, and Mike couldn't get a fight for him.

Meanwhile, as Billy's future was in limbo, Mike had been pulled in a dozen directions. Wilford Scypion was coming in from Texas to begin training at the Police Boys Club in West Hempstead, New York. CBS was asking if Mike and Gerry would fly to Dallas for a halftime interview at an upcoming football game to promote the broadcast of Cooney's impending bout. Negotiations were still underway to determine the fight site, with Las Vegas, Corpus Christi, and Anchorage, Alaska, the leading contenders. And in the midst of everything, the very day that CBS said "no" to Billy for September 15, Mike received a telephone call from Evander Holyfield, the Olympian he coveted.

"Have you signed with a manager yet?"

"No, sir," Holyfield answered.

"When can we meet?"

"Tomorrow, the day after. It don't matter."

The next day, Mike and Stella ("I always like to put my best foot forward, so I bring Stella") flew to Atlanta and settled in a suite at the Marriott Hotel. The following night, Sunday, August 18, they met with Holyfield and his business representative, Ken

Sanders. The fact that they were meeting at all indicated that Holyfield was available. Even in the amateurs certain fighters "belong" to particular professional managers and promoters. It was common knowledge that after the Olympics, Mark Breland would sign with Shelly Finkel. Other Olympic hopefuls were similarly slated.

Sanders owned a profitable Buick dealership in Morrow, Georgia. He'd met Holyfield a year earlier, and assisted the fighter financially during the Olympic trials. Holyfield, black, one of eight children, whose previous employment had consisted of pumping gas into airplanes and working as a lifeguard, sat silent for most of the meeting as Mike and Sanders discussed his future.

"I'm not about to get into a bidding war," Mike told them. "I know Evander has other offers, and I'm sure some people will pay a lot more up front than I will, but long-term potential is more important than immediate dollars. No one in boxing gives away money. Paying Evander a fortune now means a promoter or manager will want to make it back quickly, and that might not be in Evander's best interests. Olympic exposure spares a fighter years of working his way toward the top as a gate attraction. I know that. But sometimes, in terms of opponents, it's best to bring a fighter along slowly. My record with Gerry Cooney and Howard Davis speaks for itself. They both made a lot of money. Billy Costello is another of my fighters. He's a world champion. What I have to offer can't be measured in terms of upfront dollars."

Sanders responded that a long line of managers and promoters had expressed interest in Holyfield, and that bonus offers had run as high as $500,000. What was Mike willing to offer?

Mike answered that he would deal within the parameters of $200,000 to $250,000 as a combination bonus and first-fight figure, plus whatever purses Evander earned on his own thereafter. Contract length was not discussed. The meeting lasted two hours. Sanders closed by saying that he had appointments with many more managers, and would get back to Mike in the near future.

"I think there's something very special about Evander Holyfield, both as a person and a fighter," Mike told Stella that night. "I'd like to be associated with him."

The next day Mike flew back to New York and, after conferring with promoter Lou Falcigno about Holyfield's marketability, refocused his attention on Billy Costello. The key question now was whether CBS would be willing to give Billy the last remaining open 1984 date, November 3. Meanwhile Duke Durden promised to explore the possibility of doing business with NBC and ABC. "I suppose that's something I should have pushed him to do sooner," Mike said ruefully. "But CBS televised Billy's previous title fights, and I wanted to show loyalty to them."

On Thursday, August 23, Mike had dinner with Mickey Duff, the British manager and promoter who was a potential pipeline to NBC's Ferdie Pacheco. Afterward the two men went to Madison Square Garden to watch the fight between James Broad and Eddie Gregg. Broad and Gregg were heavyweights. Both were ranked by the World Boxing Council, and Mike saw them as possible future opponents for Gerry Cooney.

It was the fight of the year for the Felt Forum. All 89 regular press seats were full, and the Garden had added another row to accommodate the overflow. Celebrity fighters were sprinkled throughout the crowd—Mark Breland, Hector Camacho, Carl Williams, Davey Moore.

The first bout featured junior-middleweights Mike Martinez and Jose Fuentes. Neither was particularly adept defensively, and as the rounds progressed Martinez seemed to be taking punches like they were valuable items on sale. Fuentes won on a fourth-round knockout.

Next up were two more junior middleweights—Troy Darrell and Dennis Fain. Darrell was 12 and 0, with eleven knockouts. Fain, a journeyman fighter from Akron, Ohio, claimed a record of 11 and 9. The bout ended when Fain stayed on his stool and refused to come out for the fourth round.

A featherweight match-up between Juan Muriel and Benny Perez followed. Neither man showed much intensity. Neither wanted to test the other for fear of being tested himself. The bout ended in a decision for Muriel, after which the crowd readied for a scheduled twelve-round contest between Angel Cruz and Ricky Young for the "New York State Junior Welterweight Championship." Young was 10 and 0, his most recent victory coming against Cumba Valentine at the Felt Forum two weeks earlier. Cruz, fighting out of Bethlehem, Pennsylvania, was 16 and 5 with one draw in a career that spanned seven years. No one seemed able to explain satisfactorily why a fighter from Pennsylvania was fighting for the "New York State Championship," but no one seemed to care.

The fight started slowly with both men pacing themselves. Young had never gone beyond eight rounds; Cruz had fought ten rounds seven times. As the bout progressed, Young began finding small openings between his opponent's gloves, and put his punches through with fairly good power. Then he tired, and Cruz came on. Clearly, Young had the more promising future, but Cruz was better and more experienced for now. "Hey, you judges," someone shouted when the bout was done. "Don't steal it. The PR won fair and square." The judges' decision was unanimous for Cruz.

Shortly after nine-thirty the heavyweights came on stage. James Broad wasn't a great fighter, but he was pretty good. Six-foot-three, 246 pounds, he looked perpetually out of shape, but a record of 15 and 1 against fair opposition spoke for his skills. In another era he probably wouldn't have been ranked anywhere near the top ten, but 1984 was a bad time for heavyweight aficionados. His opponent, Eddie Gregg, had compiled a record of 20 and 0 with seventeen knockouts and one draw. Gregg stood six-foot-five and weighed 212 pounds. This was his first fight against a quality opponent, and since he was thirty years old, possibly his last major chance. Both Gregg and Broad were black.

Round one began with Broad advancing behind a ponderous left jab. Gregg looked tentative, and moved backward, which precluded him from setting his feet to throw solid blows. "In his gut, Eddie," a fan shouted. "In his fat gut." Still, Gregg continued to retreat, seemingly afraid to let his punches go. Round two was more of the same, with Broad landing several hard shots to the head in the last minute. In round three Broad picked up the pace, getting off first with his jab and everything else. Midway through the round, a hard right staggered Gregg, who moved for a moment as if one leg were shorter than the other. "You'll think I'm crazy," Mickey Duff told Mike when the round was over, "but I think Eddie Gregg will win this fight. Broad is tired. His mouth is wide open."

"Put your money where your mouth is."

After brief negotiation, Duff placed $500 against Mike's $1,750 on the outcome of the fight.

Round four also belonged to Broad. Weight is a weapon. Properly used, it puts more power in punches, drags an opponent down, and bolsters resistance to blows. Using his 246 pounds to full advantage, Broad again staggered his foe. Then ponderously, inexorably, he advanced, cutting off the ring by moving forward at an angle to intersect the escape routes of his retreating foe.

Round five saw Gregg rally, moving, jabbing. Still he was reluctant to throw the right when the opportunity presented itself. Round six was even.

"I'll take two-to-one odds now," Duff announced. Mike bet another $1,000, making his total stake $2,750 against Duff's $1,000.

Through most of round seven, Gregg did a pretty good job of pushing Broad around the ring, but he was using up energy. In round eight Broad came out and simply took Gregg apart. A series of right hands turned the lighter man's legs to jelly and the ring lights to a river of molten silver. Gregg, in trouble, sagged back against the ropes, doing everything possible to stay on his feet, but Broad's punches were coming through unhindered. Forty-eight seconds into the round, referee Tony Perez stopped the fight.

"I chopped him down," an ebullient James Broad told reporters in his dressing room afterward. "I planned to take him out in six, but he disagreed with my plan so I made it eight. World title coming up!"

Meanwhile in a dressing room across the hall, Eddie Gregg slumped on a bench and cried. When a fighter wins he's surrounded by well-wishers. When a fighter loses he's very much alone. People kind of look at him and say nothing. Even his own people wish they weren't there. As Gregg stared disconsolately at the floor, one of his cornermen, George Washington, stood over him. "This is your career," Washington said softly. "It's something you want to do. The man beat you fair and square. What you have to do now is take this loss and use it to make you fight harder."

Gregg didn't answer. Dr. Edwin Campbell, medical director for the New York State Athletic Commission, entered the room and advanced to the fighter's side.

"How are you?"

"A little groggy," Gregg answered.

Blood was flowing from a cut beneath the fighter's lower lip. "I'll send someone in to stitch that up," Campbell said. Then he left, and Gregg turned to Washington.

"I didn't get knocked down, did I?"

"Never. You stayed on your feet."

"I worked hard for this fight. I just didn't have it. My jab wasn't working. I didn't feel no strength. I don't know what happened. I tried to reach down, but nothing was there."

A commission doctor came in and began stitching Gregg's wound.

"You had him," Washington told the fighter. "In the fifth round, and again in the seventh, you had him. And each time, you stepped back to take a picture. You can't do that. It gave him confidence."

The commission doctor finished his task. Then, still not making eye contact with anyone, Gregg spoke again. "This fight meant a lot to me. A top-ten ranking, big money, maybe a title shot down the road. I could have been somebody important in boxing. Now—"

Washington interrupted: "Eddie, nothing we say is gonna change it. The greatest fighters in the world get knocked out. So take a shower, get dressed, and let's go home."

14

Mike Jones sat on a bench in Gleason's Gym and watched several fighters working out nearby. Several days had passed since an incident that was little noticed by the media but spoke volumes. Wilford Scypion had been fighting Murray Sutherland, with Mike and John Clancy in Scypion's corner. As the bout progressed, Wilford tired badly, and early in the tenth round Sutherland began to land punishing blows. Scypion's guard came down, and Mike leapt into the ring to stop the fight. What was remarkable was the way he stopped it. He didn't throw a towel in. He didn't yell for the referee to stop it. He wasn't climbing through the ropes when the action was halted. Mike actually bolted into the ring and physically came between the fighters, saving Wilford from consciousness-sapping blows.

"Why did you do it?" Mike was asked afterward.

"Because it was right."

Billy and Jane Costello had watched the fight on television. "It made me feel good," Jane said later. "I've been with Billy long enough to know what boxing is about. God forbid he should ever need that kind of help. But if he does, it's good to know that Mike and Victor are in his corner."

A manager's job is to protect his fighters. But a manager's job is also to get his fighters fights. In August 1984, Mike was trying desperately to achieve the latter, but there simply wasn't anything open on television. Meanwhile, the rest of the world was going on, and again his energies were divided.

On August 25, two days after the Broad-Gregg fight, Mike and Gerry Cooney flew to Dallas for a halftime interview on CBS. Before the game, Gerry was introduced to football greats Terry Bradshaw and Roger Staubach. The prospect of talking on prime-time television with millions of people watching made him nervous.

"What should I say?" he asked Mike.

"Just be yourself. Be sincere."

The interview with John Madden of CBS went smoothly. Gerry said he was returning to the ring, not for money but to win the heavyweight championship. Then he and Mike watched the second half of the game from the private box of Dallas Cowboys' owner Bum Boyle. The next day they flew back to New York, where Mike received a telephone call from Evander Holyfield's business representative, Ken Sanders.

"We've talked to about twenty managers and promoters," Sanders reported, "and narrowed the list to seven. You're still in the running."

Monday, August 27, Mike telephoned Terry O'Neil at CBS and said he was expecting feelers from NBC on Billy, but wanted to stay with CBS because they'd given Billy his network start. What should he do?

"Get the right opponent," O'Neil answered. "If Mort Sharnik and Gil Clancy okay it, there's one date open between now and New Year's, November 3."

For the next four days, Mike tried unsuccessfully to reach Don King and Duke Durden who were in Las Vegas for the upcoming Tim Witherspoon versus Pinklon Thomas heavyweight championship fight. Sharnik and Clancy were also in Vegas. It would be relatively simple for the four men to sit down and agree on an opponent for Billy, but Mike was unable to reach King. "I've got a world champion," he complained to Stella on Thursday night. "I've left emergency messages for Don and Duke, and neither calls back. I've had them paged at the hotel, and they don't answer. I don't call Don King for nonsense. I don't leave emergency messages to ask what he ate for dinner. When Don King needed me to sign up Holmes and Cooney, I returned his calls, and you'd better believe he called me plenty. Wherever

THE BLACK LIGHTS

I was, at a health club in Queens, at McDonald's in the Bronx, he found me, and I was always polite. Now he won't even return my calls, and because of options my hands are tied."

Friday night, August 31, Mike watched the bout between Witherspoon and Thomas. It was indicative of boxing's muddled state that the sport had three "heavyweight champs." Larry Holmes was the publicly acknowledged ruler, but political squabbles had led the WBC and WBA to crown their own monarchs. Boxing needs a standard bearer, and the heavyweight champion is best equipped to play that role. Having three heavyweight titleholders was like having three kings of England. Not surprisingly, Don King had options that enabled him to control all three crowns.

Tim Witherspoon, the WBC champ, was managed by Carl King. Pinklon Thomas, the challenger, was new to the Don King Productions fold. "I tried to stay away from King," Thomas had said before the fight. "You can't do it. It's like staying away from taxes. Sooner or later he'll get you." Thomas was undefeated in 25 bouts, with only a disputed draw against Gerrie Coetzee marring his record. "Dan Duva gave me seventy-five thousand dollars for a promotional contract," Thomas explained. "I was undefeated, ranked number two in the world, but none of the other heavyweights would fight me. Finally I went to Duva and told him, 'You can't take me no further, let me go.' He said okay—for a hundred thousand dollars. Then I went to Don King, and Don told me, 'No problem, we'll work it out.' I signed with Don, and gave him a four-year contract as my exclusive promoter. He gave a hundred thousand dollars to Duva, and a hundred thousand dollars to me as a bonus for signing. That was six months ago, and already I'm fighting for the title."

The heavyweight championship of the world once stood for something besides dollars. It was an awe-inspiring throne that belonged to the one man in the world capable of beating all the others. "When you become heavyweight champion," Rocky Marciano once said, "something comes between you and other people, even your family. Everybody stands back a little, not because of anything you do but because of what you are."

Times have changed. Tim Witherspoon and Pinklon Thomas were competent fighters, hardly stars. Thomas had only two weapons—a punishing left jab and an awkward right—but he employed them intelligently, winning a twelve-round decision over Witherspoon in a lackluster fight. "Pinklon Thomas won the heavyweight championship of the world because Tim Witherspoon didn't know how to slip a jab," Mike Jones observed that night. "What does that tell you about the future if Gerry Cooney ever gets back on track?"

The next day, September 1, Mike flew to Oregon. Sunday through Wednesday, he telephoned Don King daily with no response. "I just don't know what to do," Mike told a friend Wednesday night. "Billy's twenty-eight years old. He's at the peak of his career, but time goes by. Maybe Don's trying to get two of his heavyweights the TV date. Maybe something else is afoot. I don't like it." Thursday Duke Durden finally called back, but reported only that CBS was considering several fights and Don would "get on the case." Friday Mike spoke again with Terry O'Neil. "CBS is keeping Billy from fighting," Mike said.

O'Neil's response was short and to the point: "Billy Costello can fight any Tuesday night he wants at the Tropicana Hotel in Atlantic City. We're not stopping him. But for a fighter to expect he'll always be on network TV for a couple of hundred thousand dollars just because we had him once or twice is an unreasonable expectation."

Saturday, September 8, Mike flew back to New York for some business dealings. Sunday he spoke by telephone with Mort Sharnik and Gil Clancy, who expressed concern that Leroy Haley (the only opponent Don King was offering for Billy) might not be competitive. Monday, Mel Reddick of CBS called to report that Sharnik and Clancy had viewed tapes of Haley's last two bouts and he was acceptable as an opponent, but that other fights were being considered. Mike called Don King Productions immediately, but both Duke Durden and King were out of town, and by day's end neither had called back. As if to confirm that this wasn't Mike's week, that night he learned through press reports that Evander Holyfield had signed with Dan Duva as his promoter and Duva's associate, Shelly Finkel, as co-manager. The other co-manager was to be Ken Sanders, who had cut himself an 18.3 percent piece of the action.

"I'm not as driven as I used to be," Mike said when the news was announced. "I could have gone to the networks and found out what they were willing to pay for Holyfield, which is what Duva and Finkel must have done. I could have picked up a partner for outside cash, or offered Sanders a piece of the pie. There's lots of things I could have done that might have landed the fighter, but I have to be more concerned with the fighters I have already."

By Wednesday, September 12, Don King still hadn't called back. Mike telephoned Gil Clancy at CBS to see if there'd been any negotiations at that end. Clancy said no, and volunteered the information that budget problems were an added consideration. Costello versus Haley would be a relatively expensive fight. Bob Arum was offering former WBA junior middleweight champ Davey Moore against Louis Acaries at a reduced price. Thursday, Mike flew back to Oregon. "Fight managers travel so much we get ground lag," he said. Arriving in Oregon, he learned that NBC had just signed a Don King Productions fight between WBC lightweight champ Edwin Rosario and challenger Jose Luis Ramirez for the same November 3 date. Now Mike had a new worry. Would CBS be willing to broadcast a Don King championship fight in the same time slot as another Don King championship fight on a competing network?

Another week passed. Thomas Hearns knocked out Fred Hutchings in the third round of their one-sided September 15 fight. A representative of Adidas sent Mike four pairs of boxing shoes as a gift for Billy. Boxing equipment is expensive. Professional gloves cost between $70 and $120; headguards, $100; heavy bags up to $400. Unlike athletes in other sports, boxers, except for superstars, are rarely paid for endorsing a product, but because of the visibility that comes with a champion's use, items are sometimes given away for free.

The shoes were the wrong size. Mike returned them, then told Billy about it.

"Why'd you give those shoes back?" Billy demanded.

"Billy, I just told you, they were the wrong size."

"That don't matter. I could have sold those shoes for good money."

On Wednesday, September 19, Duke Durden telephoned to report that things at CBS appeared bleak. "Several competing fights are in the running," he told Mike, "and it looks from here like the numbers are against us." Still, Duke continued, there was another possibility. Don King Productions had just concluded a deal with Home Box Office to televise the heavyweight championship bout between Larry Holmes and James "Bonecrusher" Smith on November 9. "If we don't get November third, Don will take money out of his own pocket to put Billy on as part of an HBO doubleheader."

Mike was skeptical. "Rarely have I known Don King to take money out of his own pocket," he told Victor that night. "Plus, Don King has no more control over the allocation of air time on HBO than he does on CBS." Life was a nuisance, the two men concluded. However, despite the confusion, one thing was evident. Time was the enemy. The longer the wait, the more likely it was that CBS would come up with a match it considered more attractive than Billy Costello versus Leroy Haley. Then, in one lightning moment, the reason for the delay became clear.

The press conference had been called for eleven A.M. in Ballroom A of the Grand Hyatt Hotel in Manhattan. Its purpose was to announce the signing of Larry Holmes versus James "Bonecrusher" Smith for a fight billed as "Countdown To Glory." Ten tables with seats for a hundred guests were interspersed with lights and TV cameras. A raised dais with seats for twelve overlooked the scene. By eleven-fifteen, ninety reporters, boxing dignitaries, and camp followers were present. Each had been handed a glossy white folder with a shiny Don King Productions logo embossed in gold on the front. Inside the folder, along with various publicity handouts, was a photo of King himself and the words, "People are my most important asset. Faith in the Supreme Being, trust, credibility and performance are the things that have brought me to the top."

At eleven-twenty, dressed in a black tuxedo and ruffled white shirt, wearing two diamond-and-gold necklaces, two heavy gold bracelets, and three diamond rings, Don King entered the room. It was an electric moment—the appearance of a personality whose face had been in the press and on television thousands of times, reinforced in this case by the man's sheer bulk. King was enormous. Dressed in a conservative suit, light-blue shirt, and striped tie, Larry Holmes followed. For ten minutes the two men mingled with reporters. Then at eleven-thirty a stream of waiters brought the Hyatt's best buffet brunch into the room—eggs benedict, bacon, sausage, quiche, pastries, melon, raspberries, strawberries, tropical fruits, assorted cheeses, and whipped cream. Finally, several minutes after noon, King stepped to the microphone and began:

"Ladies and gentlemen, we call this fight The Countdown To Glory because Larry Holmes—the greatest champion of his era—is out to break the legendary record of the late great Rocky Marciano, who retired as an undefeated heavyweight champion after winning forty-nine fights in a row." Mixing quotes from Shakespeare and assorted philosophers, King spoke for twenty minutes, focusing his attention after a while on the challenger, James "Bonecrusher" Smith: "Look at him! Look at that wild look in his eyes. Just before we came in, I heard him out in the hall mumbling, 'Fee fi fo fum, I smell the blood of a champion.' "

Smith, a likable, soft-spoken black man with receding hair, who was being offered as a sacrificial lamb for Holmes, seemed embarrassed by the poetry. When finally given the opportunity to speak, he confined his remarks to thirty seconds: "I'm not good at making speeches. My goal is to win the heavyweight championship of the world, so I want to thank Don King and Larry Holmes for giving me this opportunity to fight for the title."

Then King introduced the other people seated on the dais. Eddie Futch, Holmes's trainer; Robert Lee, commissioner of the International Boxing Federation, which had sanctioned the fight; Ray Arcel, who would be in Holmes's corner; David Bey, a Don King–promoted heavyweight expected to fight Holmes shortly; Steve Nelson and Allen Kornberg, Smith's co-managers; Emile Griffith, Smith's trainer; a representative of the Riviera Hotel in Las Vegas, where the fight would be held; and Pia Zadora, who had large breasts and no apparent connection with the fight.

At one o'clock Larry Holmes was introduced. A native of Cuthbert, Georgia, one of twelve children born to John and Flossie Holmes, he'd grown up in Easton, Pennsylvania, and won the heavyweight championship in 1978. Thereafter, Holmes had dominated his division in his time, which is all that can be asked of a fighter. Beyond that, though, Holmes had been an exemplary role model. Married, with three daughters and a son, he'd done his job quietly and well. There were no articles in the newspaper about Larry Holmes and drugs, Larry Holmes driving without a license, Larry Holmes and other women or guns.

"On November third I'll be thirty-five years old," Holmes began, addressing the crowd. "At first my goal was to make some money, move out of the ghetto to a nice home, and own a car. Then it was to be heavyweight champion of the world. After that I wanted to own businesses. Now I want to break Rocky Marciano's record, and there's five fights to go. People will always look at me and ask could I have beaten Joe Louis, could I have beaten Sonny Liston, could I have beaten Rocky Marciano? I can't answer those questions, but if I can beat Rocky Marciano's record, that will show people that I was unbeatable in my time."

When Holmes was finished, the reporters' questions began.

How did he feel about the fact that the WBC and WBA recognized other champions?

"Letters don't mean nothing. I'm not the IBF or the WBC or the WBA heavyweight champion. I'm the *world* heavyweight champion. Since I won the WBC title, there've been six champions on the WBA side. Since I gave up the WBC title, they've had two more so-called champs. Until someone beats me or I retire, I'm the one."

Did he really think James "Bonecrusher" Smith was a worthy foe?

"James Smith has won fourteen fights, twelve by knockout. He's a world-class fighter."

Why was he fighting for Don King when, a year ago, he'd called King a thief and swore never to fight for him again?

"There's a lot of promoters out there promising they'll do things for you," Holmes answered. "Don King is the only one who makes things happen."

"That's right," King added. "Every now and then your teeth bite your tongue, but you don't throw them away."

At one-thirty the press conference came to an end. King stayed behind for another half-hour to mingle with stragglers, then readied to leave himself.

"One last question," someone asked. "Will Billy Costello be on the Holmes-Smith undercard?"

King's face turned grim.

"Ain't no reason for Costello to be on the undercard," he said in a voice as cold as snow. "There's a November third date open at CBS, and Costello's only problem in getting it is Gerry Cooney. They don't got no budget problem at CBS. There ain't no question about what they want to do. The big white boy is fighting on September twenty-ninth, and if he does well, if he don't get hurt, the people at CBS want to use him again. That's all. Well, let me tell you something. Costello's manager has a responsibility to see that don't happen. Gerry Cooney has pulled out of fifty fights. He ain't fought since June of 1982. If he don't fight two months in a row, it won't surprise nobody. Look, man, you got a world champion, Billy Costello, who can have that November third date on CBS. If he don't get it, and his stablemate does, you tell me, who's fucking who."

* * *

On Saturday, September 29, Gerry Cooney stepped into the ring against Philip Brown in Anchorage, Alaska, to resume his quest for the heavyweight championship of the world.

"We have a new theme for Gerry," Dennis Rappaport had said before the fight. "Patriotism. Gerry is very proud of being an American." As if to prove the point, the fight's promoters distributed four thousand American flags to be waived on camera by the crowd. Cooney himself entered the ring wearing white trunks with red and blue star-spangled trim. His robe was red, white, and blue, with the name "Gerry Cooney" inscribed beside an American flag.

Cooney's opponent, Philip Brown, had been well chosen. It was no contest. America's fighter looked like the United States invading Grenada. Brown, in full retreat from the start, was knocked out in the fourth round. Only one thing didn't go as planned.

Mike Jones was absent from Gerry's corner.

"Gerry isn't talking to me right now," Mike said on returning to New York when the fight was over. "It's a mutual thing, really. When Billy left Oregon and came back to New York, Gerry kept talking about him; how he didn't want him around; that he wanted Billy out of his camp. Billy's not blameless in this thing. As far as Billy's comments to the press are concerned, Gerry's resentment is completely justified, but when I tried to make peace, Gerry wouldn't talk to me. Then Gerry learned there was a November third date open at CBS. Gerry doesn't need that date. For Gerry Cooney the networks would make a new date, but all of a sudden, before he'd even fought Philip Brown, he was planning his next fight. What can I do? My hands are tied. I can't tell the networks what to buy. The easiest thing in the world would be for me to tell CBS that Gerry can't be ready by November third, but I have a managerial responsibility to Gerry as well as Billy. And now Gerry's mad at me because he says I'm always taking Billy's side. What can I tell you. In some ways, I'm very fond of Gerry. We've been together a long time. I'm very hurt by it all."

On Monday, October 1, two days after the Cooney-Brown fight, CBS made its move: "We want Gerry!" That night a list of seven prospective opponents was submitted to the Cooney camp—Greg Page, Michael Dokes, Mitch Green, Tony Tubbs, Tony Tucker, James Broad, and Carl "The Truth" Williams. Then the remarkable happened.

"Sure I said no to all seven guys CBS wanted for Gerry," Victor Valle would say later. "But I don't got the final decision. For each one I needed Mike or Dennis to agree that the opponent wasn't right."

Late Monday the Cooney camp submitted an alternate list—Jeff Sims, Mike Jamison, and Lucien Rodriguez. None was acceptable to the network. By Tuesday night, October 2, the Cooney deal was dead.

Then came three days of interminable waiting. On Wednesday, October 3, CBS sought to package Michael Spinks versus Carlos DeLeon for the WBC cruiserweight title, but the deal fell through. "They were offering beer money for a champagne fight," Spinks's promoter, Butch Lewis, said. Thursday Bob Arum resurfaced with a double offer—WBA welterweight champ Donald Curry versus Louis Acaries, and WBA junior welterweight champ Gene Hatcher against Ubaldo Sacco. That same day, Dan Duva entered the fray—WBA lightweight champ Livingston Bramble versus Jorge Alvarado, and Hector Camacho against Darrell Tysen.

"What happens now?" Mike was asked.

"We pray and we wait."

THE BLACK LIGHTS

On Friday, October 5, shortly before noon, Mike's telephone rang and the waiting came to an end.

"How you doing, Mike?"

"Not bad, Duke. How about you? What's new?"

There was a long pause as Duke Durden played out the drama.

"Billy Costello against Leroy Haley. November third on CBS. We got it."

15

Once again Don King had delivered. With every major promoter in boxing vying for the November 3 date on CBS, he'd reached into his bag and pulled out another trick. The network wanted a doubleheader? Fine! King held options on WBC junior featherweight champ Jaime Garza, undefeated in forty fights with thirty-eight knockouts. Don King Productions simply offered Garza versus number-one challenger Juan Meza to CBS in addition to Costello-Haley. As far as King was concerned, the network could have as many title fights as it wanted.

Meanwhile, with the fight a reality, Victor Valle and Billy Costello focused their attention on Leroy Haley. Born in Garland, Arkansas, thirty-two years old, Haley was the fourth of eleven children. In 1966 his parents moved to Las Vegas, leaving him behind with his great-grandmother until four years later, when he followed west. In 1971 Haley began boxing. In 1973 he turned pro, losing only once in his first forty fights. Still, his career languished until 1982, when he signed with Carl King as his manager. Six months later, Haley was fighting for the WBC super-lightweight crown. Under King's guidance he had fought for the title five times, losing twice and winning three times. Both losses were to Bruce Curry; each could be traced to a broken hand. In their first bout, the hand was broken in round three; in the second, round five. Now, after rehabilitation, Haley was free of pain, and ready to fight again. On Sunday, October 7, he flew to Don King's camp in Orwell, Ohio, to begin final preparations for Billy Costello. "I owe my success to Don King and his family," Haley told a reporter. "I plan to win this fight. I won't let them down."

Meanwhile, as Leroy Haley was setting up camp in Ohio, Billy and Jane had sex for the last time before the fight. Most fighters abstain from sex in the days leading up to a bout. The prevailing logic, once expressed by Sonny Liston, is "fucking takes the aggression out of a fighter." From a clinical point of view that may or may not be so. But if a fighter thinks something is true, simply by virtue of his believing, it often becomes a reality. "Without sex," says Angelo Dundee, "a fighter gets mean, angry, anxious to fight. Keep a fighter away from women, keep him in camp pounding bags, punching fighters day in, day out, and when he gets in the ring he's ready to take it all out on his opponent." Before the Shields fight, Billy had gone without sex for five weeks. This time it would be four.

Monday, October 8, Billy began the regimen he would follow for the next ten days:

10:00 A.M.	wake up
10:30 A.M.	run
11:30 A.M.	shower
Noon	juice and fruit
12:30 P.M.	read newspapers and magazines
1:30 P.M.	leave home
2:30 –4:30 P.M.	Gleason's Gym
5:30 P.M.	laundry
6:30 P.M.	dinner
7:30 P.M.	watch television
11:00 P.M.	evening news
Midnight	bed

The first two days' workouts at Gleason's were light—shadow boxing, reflex drills, heavy and speed bag work, jumping rope, and calisthenics. About ten minutes each day were devoted to practicing a move designed specifically ˆor Leroy Haley. The challenger was well conditioned, expert aι adapting to an opponent's style, and able to take a good punch. Still, Victor had studied films of Haley's past few fights and noticed a possibly fatal flaw. "What I want you to do," he told Billy, "is jab, and instead of bringing the jab back, use it to brush Haley's right hand aside. Then follow through with a right of your own." Monday and Tuesday, Billy repeated the maneuver dozens of times.

"He's learning now better than ever," Victor said when the second workout was done. "Whenever I teach a fighter something new, I look for the reaction—not whether he says he likes it, but what it says in his eyes. When I teach something now to Billy, I can see the enjoyment. His mind is open. Everything I tell him, he soaks up like a sponge."

On Wednesday, October 10, serious sparring began. Once the November 3 date was confirmed, Mike Jones had put in a call to Johnny Bos. "The Wizard of Bos," as he liked to be known, was part promoter, part matchmaker, part manager, and mostly a man who fit between the cracks of what everybody else in boxing does. Six feet three inches tall, in excess of 260 pounds, generally unshaven with shaggy dirty-blond hair, Bos kept files on most people in boxing, and his information was pretty good. Mike had consulted with him extensively in choosing opponents for Billy's early years, and he still relied on Bos to furnish sparring partners. Now two candidates were ready to be tested.

When Billy arrived at the gym on Wednesday, Victor Valle was in the locker room recounting the vagaries of life for his son Victor, Jr. "I knew Jimmy Carter when he was poor," the trainer was saying. "So poor he had to borrow money from me to eat and ride the subways."

Billy was incredulous. "You knew Jimmy Carter?"

"Of course I knew Jimmy Carter."

"Victor, you're bullshitting me."

"What for do I want to do that?" the trainer answered. "I—wait a minute. I'm not talking about the peanut vendor, you dummy. I'm talking about Jimmy Carter the fighter who was lightweight champion thirty years ago."

Billy undressed and smeared his body with a white petroleum jelly called Albolene ("It warms me up, makes me feel looser"). Meanwhile Victor continued to reminisce, voyaging deeper into the past: "President Roosevelt gave inspiration to me and all of America. When I was poor it was the President of the United States who gave me hope because, back then, we had a President who cared. Let me tell you, I learned a lot from those days. Don't spend unwisely; don't throw things away too fast. If a shirt is torn, sew it. If you don't like a jacket no more, save it anyhow. Because of The Depression and my father dying, there's always the fear I might lose what I got. Sometimes my wife says I should spend more, but I'm happier knowing I have what I have in case bad weather comes again."

Downstairs on the gym floor, the sparring partners were waiting. One was Tony Arneaud, 154 pounds, 27 years old. Arneaud had been born in Trinidad, and came to Brooklyn with his family at age nine. He was part African, part French, with Portuguese blood mixed in; stocky with thick legs and a bulldog neck, brownish-pink skin, and a touch of red in his tightly curled brown hair. "I never spent much time in school," Arneaud said later, explaining his decision to become a fighter. "I was a street kid. I started boxing because I love to fight. It's not even a career for me so much as I love it. If the money comes, fine; but that's not what's important."

Most likely the money would never come. While Arneaud claimed he had never been knocked off his feet in the gym or a bout, his record showed five wins, two losses, and a draw in eight fights. Five days a week he loaded trucks for a furniture store in Brooklyn at $7.00 an hour.

The other sparring partner, Pedro Montero, was a lighter, more experienced professional from the Dominican Republic. He claimed a record of 17–7–2, but also claimed to be 23 years old and looked at least ten years older. Montero, like Arneaud, was scheduled to spar three rounds with Billy. Both men were auditioning to become $60-a-day sparring partners.

Billy began the workout with two minutes of shadow boxing and stretching exercises. Then with Victor's help he laced a protective belt around his hips to shield the groin area from low blows. Next came a pair of fourteen-ounce gloves and a leather headguard. Some trainers don't like headgear. They feel it encourages a false sense of security in a fighter. However, headguards also cushion blows and reduce the chance of a fighter sustaining cuts, and thus are commonly used.

The sparring began with three rounds against Tony Arneaud.

Neither man would pull his punches unless the other was stunned. And unless Billy was seriously hurt, he'd have to fight his way out of any trouble on his own.

Right from the start it was clear that Arneaud was "a catcher"—a fighter who came in like the charge of the light brigade regardless of an opponent's firepower. Extremely aggressive, he moved straight ahead, jabbing, then following with a straight right hand. That was what he had, and he did it again and again. Mostly Billy circled and jabbed. Then Arneaud landed a hard right, and Billy retaliated with two hooks to the body. "Watch his head," Victor cautioned the champion between rounds. "When he comes in, push the head down so you don't get butted. Jab, circle, make him look foolish. But the main thing is, watch the head, because when he comes in his head is low."

Rounds two and three were more of the same, with Arneaud crowding Billy, trying to smother his punches and bull him around. Several times Billy spun his opponent into the ropes and punished him with uppercuts, but the challenger kept working for every minute of every round. Hard punches and hard work were the only way to keep him off. "Good job," Billy told him when they touched gloves at the final bell.

Next came three rounds with Pedro Montero. Montero was a cutie, a professional survivor. He saw his task as not to get hit, and toward that end he danced and ran as though he were trying to win the Nobel Peace Prize For Boxing. Several times in the first round, Billy landed solid hooks to the body that shook Montero's entire frame. Billy's right wasn't landing. It always seemed in the spot where Montero's head had been a fraction of a second before, but the left hook was a dominating blow. Round two was a repeat of round one. In the final round, Billy's sixth of the day, the champion tired slightly but remained in command. When the session was over, Victor took Montero aside and told him that Billy was just too strong for him. Montero agreed. They would not work together again.

For Tony Arneaud the verdict was brighter. "I don't expect him to last too long," Victor told Billy. "The body shots will wear him down, but for now he's a good partner. He tries like hell, and he makes you work hard." Soon after, Arneaud was given the good news. For the next few days, at least, he'd be sparring with a world champion. The job would pay $60.00 on days they sparred three rounds or less, $75.00 on days they sparred more. Johnny Bos would send another sparring partner whenever Mike Jones called.

The next day Billy sparred five rounds with Arneaud, and went through a series of rigorous calisthenics and stretching exercises. Friday the pace slowed. Billy's arms were sore from two days of blocking and throwing punches. Also, as he explained to Victor, "The baby woke me up singing and shit at three o'clock this morning."

"Is she sick?" Victor queried.

"No. She wanted juice, so I gave her some. Then all she wanted to do was play. Every time I put her back in the crib, she started to cry."

"All right," the trainer told him. "This afternoon we do only three rounds."

Again Arneaud was aggressive. Again Billy had to work hard to keep him off.

"I know I wasn't right today," the champion said when their workout was done. "I was pushing my punches. The power and snap weren't there, but it was good experience. If I'm not right on the day of a fight, I still got to be there."

Saturday, October 13, Billy and Arneaud went five more rounds. This time Billy's punches were crisp, and he was moving well. For the first time, Arneaud seemed badly outclassed, vulnerable to clean shots at will. Despite the blows and a flow of blood from his lower lip, he refused to go down. Still, by day's end, he was leaning rather than bulling forward. Billy's punches had taken their toll.

"You did a good job," Victor told the sparring partner when the day was done. "Now we got to find somebody who moves a little more like Leroy Haley. Someday, maybe for another fight, we'll use you again."

Over the course of four days, Tony Arneaud had sparred sixteen rounds—that came to $270. Upstairs in the locker room, Victor handed him five fifty-dollar bills and one twenty. "Keep your hands up," Billy told the fighter as they said goodbye.

There were three weeks left. Discounting Sundays and a day of travel, that meant sixteen more workouts before the Haley fight. "You know something," Billy said to Victor when Arneaud had gone. "That guy probably thinks two hundred and seventy dollars is a lot of money, but it's not. Once you're married and have a child, you learn how expensive things are. I count my money. Jane and I eat home a lot instead of going out for dinner. We don't spend much on clothes and jewelry, but sometimes it still worries me what things cost. People ask, and I tell them I want to retire with one million dollars when I'm thirty years old. But one punch in the wrong place and I wouldn't even be champion anymore."

The tingling of nerves had begun.

Once the November 3 date on CBS was
secure, Mike Jones took a rare weekend off. Saturday, October
6, he and his family celebrated Yom Kippur. Sunday they went
to visit his father, who had been incapacitated by a stroke several
years earlier, and was living at a veterans' home in New Jersey.
Then boxing moved back to the forefront. Throughout the week
of October 8, Mike, Dennis Rappaport, and promoter Sam Glass
met to investigate the possibility of buying their own television
time and syndicating Gerry Cooney's next fight. That way they
could choose their own opponent, "someone right for Gerry at
this stage of his career." Then Mike and Stella journeyed to
Montreal for the annual World Boxing Council convention.

On its surface, workshops, official votes and committee reports predominated the WBC convention. The real business,
however, was transacted in backrooms, hotel lounges, and bars.
"I'm here to cover my ass," promoter Butch Lewis announced
on arriving in Montreal. "If a man doesn't show, there's no telling
what might happen to him and his fighters.". . . "The world is
full of people who will shove an umbrella up your ass," observed
Rich Giachetti, also in attendance. "But some of the people here
will shove it up and then open it just for fun."

The most visible presence at the convention was Jose Sulaiman. "I am here to serve boxing," the WBC president told reporters before the showcase began. Part of Sulaiman's genius was
that each of the five hundred people at the convention would

think Jose looked on him as a special friend. Speaking carefully, choosing his words like a man taking only green jelly beans from a multicolored jar, Sulaiman would dominate the convention from beginning to end. "Who does the most to help boxing?" he asked rhetorically. "I will tell you, it is the boxers. And after the boxers, the boxers. And after all the boxers, nobody. I am but a humble servant of boxing."

The first meeting of the convention began on Wednesday, October 17, at 9:30 A.M. in Room B of the Regency Hyatt Hotel. A U-shaped dais at one end of the room seated each member of the WBC Executive Council. The flags of 104 member nations draped the room. Welcoming remarks were extended by a representative of the mayor of Montreal, followed by tedious speeches by representatives of all seven WBC continental federations. Three hundred people were present. Each speech was simultaneously translated into French, English, and Spanish over headphones provided free of charge. Dressed in a gray jogging suit with red trim, Don King sat quietly in the back of the room. This was Sulaiman's show, and King would maintain a low profile.

After all the welcoming remarks, a huge screen was lowered and a slide show, ostensibly designed to trace the history of boxing, began. The artistic format involved photographs interspersed with music from "Man of LaMancha," "Rocky," and "Chariots of Fire." However, it soon became clear that the presentation was largely a paean to Jose Sulaiman. There were pictures of Jose with Muhammad Ali, Jose with his family, Jose with Alexis Arguello, Jose with Carlos Monzon. Sulaiman's achievements as president of the World Boxing Council were catalogued in detail, and his words rang throughout the hall. Meanwhile, the musical background changed to a recording of Frank Sinatra singing "My Way." It was all quite inspirational, particularly when one considered the fact that through it all Jose stood at the lectern, his head erect, silhouetted in a dim light for all to see in the flesh as well as on the screen. As the last strains of Frank Sinatra's voice slipped away, Rich Giachetti leaned over to Mike and whispered, "You'd better believe, Jose does it his way."

When the slide show was done the audience rose in a standing ovation. Sulaiman stood erect with an appropriately dignified smile, and spoke only after the last drops of applause had died away:

Honorable gentlemen of the Presidium; honorable members of the Executive Council; honorable friends. When I received the honor of being elected President of the World Boxing Council, I found the magnitude of the responsibility difficult to understand. But still, my first decision was to begin an era of change and reform. Many of you know how difficult it has been for me to carry my position of President of the World Boxing Council. It seems that some people, regardless of what we do, even come to the point of gross slander to discredit us. I assure you all that I have kept my actions free of embarrassment, that my commitment to you and my love for boxing has been the innate strength that has kept me from ever answering mud with mud. To those that I may have upset by my mistakes, and to boxing itself, I extend my apologies as I have never meant anything but to assist all who seriously promote the sport, to open the doors to all, always within the strictest principles of integrity, fairness and equality.

For twenty minutes the speech went on, closing with reference to the enemies of boxing and "our boxing family":

There are those who are irresponsibly trying to ban boxing. They do not understand that there are many people born in the humblest of beds whom society rejects and the influences which drag them to suffer a miserable starving life. They do not understand that it is boxing which is one of the few sports which extends a friendly hand to lead them to a life of high achievement to make them conquer the highest goals and become heroes of their nations and the world. We in the WBC will fight to the limits of our endurance to protect the future for the sake of the poor people of the world and for the sake of the many millions of fans who love the sport. The world needs boxing. Boxers need boxing. Nations support boxing. The public wants boxing, and we are all here because of boxing. There are no better friends than our boxing friends. There is no better family than our boxing family. A family of drama, courage, suffering and sacrifice but, in the end, a family that is always united.

After lunch the convention continued with a series of medical presentations. In recent years, medical technology has allowed neurologists to identify three key anatomical features indicative of chronic brain damage in boxers.

The first of these is "cortical atrophy." As a boxer's brain bounces off the inside of his skull, neurons on the brain's surface begin to erode, and tissue is lost. This leads to a second condition—enlargement of the ventricles (cavities in the middle of the brain), which expand to fill the space created by the loss of tissue around them. A third, more critical condition that sometimes results is "cavum septum pellucidum"—a hole in the membrane separating the ventricles that develops as a consequence of concussive forces deep within the brain.

Boxing and the medical profession have been at odds for years. Many fight people dispute findings that link boxing to chronic brain damage. Others accept the findings, but argue, "Boxing increases the chance of brain damage; cigarette smoking increases the chance of lung cancer. Of the two, cigarette smoking kills infinitely more people each year." However, as the World Boxing Council met to discuss medical issues in Montreal, an ominous pall had fallen over the dialogue. One month earlier, Muhammad Ali had checked into Columbia Presbyterian Medical Center in New York for a series of diagnostic tests and treatment of his deteriorating physical condition. "I never have any pain," Ali told reporters the day after tests began. "I'm just drowsy all the time, and there seems to be a slur in my speech. It bothers me that people don't understand me. I go to bed and sleep eight, ten hours, but two hours after I get up, I'm tired and drowsy again."

Other reports were more chilling. "You hear stories about Ali," Billy Costello said. "About how he goes to the bathroom on himself all the time."

In truth, Ali's decline had been well catalogued for years. As early as 1976, Dr. Ferdie Pacheco, Ali's personal physician, had advised him to retire from boxing. "You could see brain injury coming up," said Pacheco. "He took some mammoth beatings. There were the fights with Frazier, Foreman, and Norton, to say nothing of all the sparring with Larry Holmes and Michael Dokes." Still, Ali continued in the ring for five more years. Several months before his last fight, against Trevor Berbick in the Bahamas, he underwent a CAT scan at New York University Medical Center. Later, Dr. Ira Casson, a neurologist at Long Island Jewish Medical Center, reviewed the X-rays and said, "I wouldn't read this as normal. I don't see how you can say in a thirty-nine-year-old man that these ventricles aren't too big. His third ventricle's big. His lateral ventricles are big. He has a cavum septum pellucidum."

Shortly after his loss to Berbick, Ali visited England. Interviewed on BBC radio, he slurred his words to the point of incomprehensibility, and a second interview was canceled. "It was very sad," said a BBC spokesman, "that so much of what history's most celebrated fighter said was unintelligible."

"You can actually see Ali trying to talk," observed his longtime supporter Howard Cosell. "You can see him groping for words that are no longer there." Later, in August 1984, Ali would attend the Olympic boxing competition in Los Angeles. Cosell was the ABC network commentator. "Ali's people begged me to put him on the air," Cosell remembers. "I wouldn't do it. I love him too much to embarrass him like that. The man is a vegetable compared to what he once was."

With Jose Sulaiman presiding, the WBC convention delegates sat through an afternoon of medical presentations. Meanwhile, business of a different sort was being conducted in the hotel lounge. Don King, Mickey Duff, and dozens of other managers and promoters were milling around. Michael Spinks, who held both the WBC and WBA lightheavyweight crowns, had been brought to Montreal by his promoter, Butch Lewis. Now Spinks was reminiscing about how he'd consolidated the title in a unification bout against Dwight Muhammad Qawi. "There's no way I thought I'd come out of it without my face all bruised and bloodied," Spinks said. "Both times when Qawi fought Matthew Saad Muhammad, I stayed home, put on trunks and gloves, and boxed with them while I watched the fight on television. I was fighting for Saad. I was rooting for Saad. Both times I took a beating. When Qawi fought me, I couldn't believe it. I thought he wanted the championship bad, maybe even more than me. Night after night, for weeks before the fight, I'd lie in bed and see him coming out at the bell, tearing into me. Every night I was on the ropes. Every night it was the fight of my life. And then when the fight came, Qawi lay back. He never did what he could have done; he never went all out to beat me."

As Spinks spoke, Rich Giachetti stood across the lounge, casting glances at Don King. A large, bulky man with a long scar on his cheek and curly black hair, Giachetti began training fighters at age nineteen. Now forty-four, he had trained and managed Larry Holmes from Holmes's first pro fight until losing him to Don King after the fighter had become heavyweight champion of the world. "When Larry Holmes walked away from me," Giachetti was saying, "it was like your wife divorcing you when you still love her. I sacrificed for Larry. I fed him. Out on the road, I slept in the same room with him. I spent more time with him than I spent with my own family. It took three years for me to even begin to get over his leaving."

Working his way through the crowd, Mike spoke briefly with Butch Lewis about a possible title fight against Michael Spinks for French lightheavyweight Jean Emebe. "Emebe lives in Europe, but I represent him in the United States," Mike explained to the promoter. "You can promote the fight. I'll give you all the options you want."

"Get me five hundred thousand dollars in TV money for January or February, and it's yours," Lewis answered.

Next Mike buttonholed Don King about a still-unresolved matter. CBS had given Billy Costello and Leroy Haley the November 3 date. It had promised King $400,000 for television rights to the package, but no dollar figure for Billy had been set. Most likely the amount would be $150,000, the minimum figure specified for option number two under the Costello-Curry fight contract. Still, Mike wanted the matter put to bed.

"Later," King told him. "I'm busy now."

For the rest of the afternoon, Mike mixed with members of the WBC Ratings Committee, hoping to increase their respect for the pugilistic abilities of Wilford Scypion and Gerry Cooney. Then he and Stella went to the first of two WBC banquets that would be held during the week.

The second convention session began the following morning.

As the first order of business, Jose Sulaiman announced the formation of a committee to improve the image of boxing. Several more medical reports followed, with Sulaiman in control of the proceedings. Under WBC rules, anyone present could speak from the floor, but only the Executive Council voted. Clearly, Sulaiman dominated that council, albeit with a flair for the diplomatic. "That is a good idea," he told one questioner, who failed to get the message that the president was tired of discussing a particular point. "We will form a committee and very carefully study your thoughts."

Several onlookers noted the presence of Gilberto Mendoza, president of the rival World Boxing Association, in the convention hall. Rumor had it that Sulaiman and Mendoza were concerned about the fledgling International Boxing Federation, and might somehow join forces to prevent its growth. The fact that the IBF was headquartered in New Jersey, and most boxing revenue flowed from the United States, added fuel to the rumor fire.

Midway through the morning session, Sulaiman presented an award "for service to boxing" to Marvin Kohn, who had been a deputy commissioner for the New York State Athletic Commission for 33 years. Then in the first of the day's major events, Don King was honored with a plaque to commemorate his tenth anniversary as a promoter.

King loves the spotlight. Jose Sulaiman himself once said of his friend, "When Don King promotes Michael Jackson, he wants to overshadow even Michael Jackson." Thus the promoter could not let the moment pass without a mini-oration. Dressed in a conservative gray suit, King strode to the microphone and told the convention floor, "First of all, let me say how humble and grateful I am to receive this award from our distinguished president, Jose Sulaiman. There are some moments in a man's life when everything comes together in a way that makes it all worthwhile. When you took it upon yourselves to award me this honor, I thought the whole thing through. I see myself as a hard-working man. I do the best that I can like everyone else who cares about what he does. I love boxing, so I'm a salesman for boxing. I love the WBC, so I'm a salesman for the WBC. And I love Jose Sulaiman. He's a man who gives of himself for the betterment of boxing, the betterment of society, and the betterment of mankind."

During the remainder of his speech, King quoted John Donne and Thomas Alva Edison, closing with more accolades for Jose Sulaiman. Then Sulaiman introduced WBC heavyweight champion Pinklon Thomas, and the convention experienced one of its few genuinely moving moments. Thomas was a former heroin addict, with all the fringe activity that addiction entails. "Two things helped me out of it," he told his listeners. "One was my wife. She stayed by me through it all. And the other was boxing. Those two things gave me something to hold onto when I wanted to get out of drugs. People talk about banning boxing, and I don't like it. Boxing brought me out of a hole and made me a worthwhile person. Without it I'd be selling heroin, dead, or in jail."

With Thomas's speech the convention had reached its dramatic high point, and when he was done Sulaiman announced that he would be a candidate for reelection as president for a third four-year term. No other candidates were nominated. The entire procedure from announcement of candidacy through re-election took ninety seconds. Then, his face flush with emotion, Sulaiman stepped to the microphone and spoke again: "I am the son of a very humble Lebanese, who left his country many years ago. He came to Mexico, and worked his whole life to give a better world to his children." The speech went on and on until a final flourish: "I commit myself to fight to the end of my strength to serve the sport that I love. I commit myself to fight to the end of my strength in the defense of boxing."

Thursday's afternoon session featured a workshop on thumbless gloves, and a report on the WBC Sports Medicine Foundation of which Jose Sulaiman was president. Meanwhile, for Mike Jones the most important developments were taking place in a hotel room on the twenty-third floor. Don King had flown back to New York, leaving Mike and Duke Durden to negotiate the size of Billy's purse for November 3. The two men met in Duke's room at 5:00 P.M.

Mike liked Duke, a tall, powerfully built black man with a neatly trimmed graying Afro. Durden had a reputation as being pretty straight (which in boxing meant he was shaped like an "S" instead of an "8"). He and Mike had always gotten along.

"I'm gonna put all my figures on the table," Duke said at

the start of negotiations. "That way you can see what we got, and we'll be fair to everybody. Our total revenue on this fight is $445,000. That's $400,000 from CBS, $40,000 as an estimated live gate, and $5,000 from foreign television rights. Out of that, without paying Billy, we have expenses of $245,000. That's $40,000 for TV production costs; $40,000 for airfare, hotel, meals, judges, and things like that; $30,000 for Leroy Haley, $30,000 for Juan Meza, $85,000 for Jaime Garza, and $20,000 for preliminary fighters. Subtract one from the other and you've got $200,000 to be divided between Billy Costello and Don King Productions."

Mike asked for $175,000.

"Haley's an old man," Duke wailed. "You only got $140,000 for Shields, and Shields was tough."

"Haley's tough too. He's the number-one contender, and Billy is more valuable now than before the Shields fight."

For over an hour the two men went back and forth. Mike was unyielding.

"If we can't reach an agreement," Duke said, "we might have to call the show off."

"If it's off, it's off; but I suggest we go over the figures again, since neither of us wants to cancel the fight."

After reviewing the numbers, both men still held firm. Mike at $175,000, Duke at "something less than Shields."

"This fight is a losing proposition for us," Duke said. "By the time Don pays overhead there'll be nothing left. If you don't believe me, call CBS. They'll tell you the total package is $400,000."

"That won't be necessary. I trust you."

One reason for Mike's trust was that several days earlier he had called CBS himself to get the figure.

Finally Mike gave ground: "Look, there's a $150,000 minimum for this fight in the contract we signed when Billy fought Curry. I can't go back to Billy with less than that."

"Maybe Haley is tough," Duke conceded.

By 7:30 P.M. the contract was signed. Billy would get $150,000— $10,000 more than his purse for the Shields fight; $5,000 more than Haley, Garza, and Meza combined. In addition, he would receive 50 percent of any gross live gate over $50,000, fifteen free tickets, and the concession rights to T-shirts, hats, and other fight memorabilia. Duke also agreed to put Wilford Scypion and

Billy's younger brother Vinnie on the undercard for $3,500 and $1,000 respectively.

"I figured I'd only get $150,000," Mike told Billy when they spoke by telephone that night. "But I was feeling Duke out to see if I could get more, and he was feeling me out to see if I'd take less. You can make good money with Don King. You just have to have what he wants, and be careful."

Billy's response was practical. "If I'm getting fifty percent of the live gate over fifty thousand dollars, everyone's paying to get into that fight. You're paying; Victor's paying. Hell, I'm even gonna make Leroy Haley pay to get in."

Friday's convention session was away from the hotel in a large room on the second floor of Montreal's Le Palais Des Congres. The subject was ratings. Nothing would be more intensely lobbied in Montreal.

Ratings are a fighter's future. A top-ten rating means a boxer is eligible to fight for a WBC title. A number-one rating guarantees a title shot within one year. Every manager and promoter at the convention was trying to maneuver the ratings to benefit his fighters—an exercise that could be carried out in one of two ways. First, there was the Ratings Committee. Under the Chairmanship of Bob Busse, the twelve-man group had been meeting behind closed doors throughout the week to establish a top ten for each weight division. And throughout the week, managers and promoters had been buttonholing committee members to plead their cause. If that didn't work, there was a second route. The committee's decision could be appealed in open session on the convention floor, and overturned by majority vote of the WBC Executive Council.

Friday's meeting began with Busse reading a list of the top-ten heavyweights in order of rank. Gerry Cooney was not among them. In truth, Cooney didn't need a rating. He was able to command big television dollars without one. Still, top ten would be nice, and Dennis Rappaport rose to move that Gerry be ranked number ten. Briefly he outlined Cooney's status as a former number-one contender, the "unfortunate injuries" he'd suffered, and his recent victory over Philip Brown. Before Busse could answer, Jose Sulaiman responded, "To me, this is a good idea. I think that Gerry Cooney should be number ten."

A vote of the Executive Council was taken. Tony Tubbs was dropped from ten to eleven, and Gerry Cooney installed as number ten.

Next, George Kantor, a British promoter, moved to put Lucien Rodriguez in the top ten. The motion was denied. Then came the lightheavyweights. Dennis Rappaport moved to raise Eddie Davis from number two to number one challenger for the title. Denied. Rich Giachetti moved to raise Marvin Johnson from number four to number one. Denied. The pattern was clear. On all votes, when Jose Sulaiman spoke in favor of a motion, it prevailed. Otherwise it was denied.

Mike Jones moved to put Wilford Scypion in the middleweight top ten. Jose sat silent. Denied. Efforts to place Louis Acaries and Darnell Knox in the superwelterweight top ten were turned aside. The welterweights followed. A motion was made to put Simon Brown in the top ten. Busse began to respond.

"I would like to be honest," Sulaiman interrupted. "I have strong objections to Nino LaRocca. I don't think he should be in the top ten."

LaRocca was an Italian fighter with a 60 and 2 record and promotional ties to Bob Arum, Don King's major nemesis. By an Executive Council vote of 14 to 5 with three abstentions, LaRocca was removed from the top ten, and Simon Brown was upgraded. Busse stood silent, doing a slow burn. He and Sulaiman looked like a husband and wife unwilling to talk or even make eye contact with one another.

In a similar vein the session went on.

That afternoon, Mike telephoned Victor Valle, as he did every day when a fight was pending. This time, their conversation concerned a training site for Billy's last two weeks before the Haley bout. Neither man wanted Billy at home. The distractions of being with Jane and Christine would make it difficult to develop the cutting psychological edge necessary for a major fight. For Shields and Curry, Billy had trained at the Concord Hotel, getting free room and board in exchange for publicity value. Now the Concord was full and unable to make room for Billy, Victor, and several sparring partners. For the better part of the afternoon Mike telephoned resorts and publicity agents. Kutsher's, Grossinger's, Great Gorge, resorts in the Poconos and Adirondacks, all gave the same response. It was autumn leaf season. Conventions were in full swing. No one with gym facilities was willing to offer a free ride. That meant that the best place to work was probably Gleason's, but Mike wanted his fighter away from home. Working through CBS, which had a 30 percent corporate discount, he reserved a room for Billy at the Park Lane Hotel on Central Park South in Manhattan for $145 a day. Then, that night, after another convention banquet, he watched the Marvin Hagler versus Mustafa Hamsho middleweight title fight on television. Hagler, from Brockton, Massachusetts, was among the best fighters of his era. Hamsho, born in Syria but living in New York, was a plodder whom Hagler had knocked out three years before. "If I was Irish or Italian," Hamsho once said, "I'd be the biggest thing in New York; but instead, I'm Arabic Muslim. I come to the United States, and the Arabs raise the price of oil. I challenge for the middleweight championship, and the Syrians, my people, are involved in Lebanon. Always, fucking politics makes problems for me."

Friday night, Hagler caused more problems, knocking Hamsho out in the third round.

Saturday's WBC convention session (the last) was also held at Le Palais Des Congres, and started with an instructional film on boxing. Then Executive Council votes were taken for various WBC awards. Thomas Hearns was named Fighter of the Year; Pinklon Thomas, Exemplary Fighter of the Year. A June 1, 1984, flyweight title bout between Gabriel Bernal and Antoine Montero was declared Fight of the Year.

At noon the first open fireworks began. Jose Sulaiman liked presentations and reports. He did not like controversy within his domain, but three controversies had been lurking beneath the surface since the convention began. Now, like it or not, he had to deal with them.

The first dilemma concerned Dwight Muhammad Qawi, the number-one challenger for Michael Spinks's lightheavyweight crown. One week before their scheduled September 7 rematch in Las Vegas, Qawi had withdrawn from the bout, claiming a shoulder injury. A Nevada State Athletic Commission physician then recommended that certain tests be performed to determine the veracity of his claim, but Qawi refused. Later his own physician reported that the fighter was suffering from bursitis of the left shoulder. Not satisfied, the North American Boxing Federation, one of the WBC's member federations, was seeking to suspend Qawi and remove him from the rankings pending a complete medical examination. Rounding out the situation was the fact that, at the time of his walkout, Qawi was in a chaotic psychological state. Four weeks earlier, his brother had shot their father to death. Then three weeks after that, the fighter's seventeen-year-old wife had walked out on him, taking their only child.

Sulaiman made short shrift of the suspension motion. "Dwight Muhammad Qawi is not my friend," he told the convention, "but he is a boxer. I urge you to have compassion for him. I will not support the suspension of Qawi. I am a human being, and I have compassion for the boxer."

By an overwhelming vote of the Executive Council, Qawi retained his number-one ranking.

Next up was a battle over promotional rights to an upcoming title fight between Wilfredo Gomez and Azumah Nelson. The dispute pitted a Puerto Rican promotional company against Don King Productions, and as the Latin promoter pleaded his cause, Sulaiman became exasperated. "We have already had a hearing on these points you now make." ("A hearing," Rich Giachetti observed, "is when you beg Jose to listen to you for a minute in the hotel lobby.") The matter was expeditiously decided. Then came the most explosive issue to be faced by the convention, one that would not as easily go away.

In boxing's early years, championship fights had lasted until one of the combatants was unable to continue any longer. Then bouts of fixed duration came into vogue, and for about fifty years fifteen rounds was considered the true test of a champion. However, on January 10, 1983, after "polling" the WBC Executive Council, Jose Sulaiman had announced that all WBC title fights would be limited to twelve rounds.

The immediate catalyst for Sulaiman's decision was public furor over the much-criticized bouts between Larry Holmes and Randall Cobb, Alexis Arguello and Aaron Pryor, and Ray Mancini versus Duk Koo Kim. Viewing the late-round carnage, Sulaiman had done what he thought was best for boxers and best for boxing. "We didn't make this decision because we found out among boxers," the WBC President said. "No boxer in his prime can make a medical decision because his macho feelings go against it. We took a deep investigation with all the doctors of the Medical Committee of the WBC and we consulted with many very prestigious doctors in sports medicine in the United States. We concluded that one of the most important factors for serious injuries is fatigue, and who could deny that a boxer has got to be weaker as rounds go on. Over the twelfth round," Sulaiman continued, "this is a dangerous line. We go to the Ali-Frazier fight in Manila. After the twelfth round it was savage. They were finished. They couldn't fight anymore. You see Arguello being knocked out in the fourteenth round. It is true, we can take all the precautions in the world and still something might happen, but this is a precaution we must take for the safety of the boxer."

The twelve-round limit sparked bitter debate in boxing circles. Mickey Duff, often at odds with Sulaiman, supported the change. "Twelve rounds, fifteen rounds; either way, the better fighter will win," Duff concluded. "Besides, rounds thirteen through fifteen often prove nothing except which man has more stamina, and stamina is only one facet of boxing."

However, opponents of the change were livid. *Ring Magazine* published a study showing that of 439 deaths documented in professional boxing since 1919, only four had occurred in rounds thirteen through fifteen. Traditionalists cried that a twelve-round limit would have changed the history of boxing. Billy Conn would have beaten Joe Louis; Jersey Joe Walcott would have decisioned Rocky Marciano; Sugar Ray Leonard would have lost to Thomas Hearns. One critic of Sulaiman asked rhetorically, "Should the marathon be reduced from twenty-six to twenty miles because that's where the wall is?"

The controversy came to a head in the person of world middleweight champion Marvin Hagler. In 1980 Hagler had won both the WBA and WBC crowns. Thereafter he'd defended his title successfully ten times. However, with the twelve-round WBC rule in effect, Hagler continued to schedule his fights for fifteen rounds. Sulaiman was amenable to a compromise whereby the champion alternated between twelve- and fifteen-round bouts, the latter being the official distance sanctioned by the WBA. However, Hagler held firm. Sulaiman did not appreciate the challenge to his authority. It may or may not have mattered that Hagler's sixteen preceding fights had been promoted by Don

King's archrival, Bob Arum. In any event, Jose Sulaiman had set forth an ultimatum. If Marvin Hagler stepped into the ring against Mustafa Hamsho in a fight scheduled for fifteen rounds, he would be stripped of his title. Hagler had done so last night. Now it was Sulaiman's turn.

The issue had been saved until the last hour of the last session when convention delegates with other commitments had left for home. "It is one o'clock," Sulaiman announced, looking at his watch. "We have promised to vacate the room at this hour, so regrettably I must cut short the conversation."

With virtually no debate, the premier fighter in the world was stripped of his crown.*

"I felt badly for Hagler," Mike Jones said later. "In boxing you learn not to laugh at the other guy's misfortune because, the way the business works, next week it could be you. Still, I had more important things to worry about when the convention was over. There were only two weeks left to get Billy ready for Leroy Haley, and things in New York were beginning to get a little complicated."

---

* Several months later, Hagler agreed to abide by the twelve-round rule for a fight against Thomas Hearns, and his title was restored.

17

For Billy Costello the days until fight time were winding down. Sunday, October 21 (the day after the WBC convention ended), he ran six miles in Central Park. Then he showered, changed clothes at the Park Lane Hotel, and went home to visit Jane and Christine.

Training is psychological as well as physical. It requires a rough serrated cutting edge that can't be developed in the surroundings of home. "Early in Billy's career," Jane remembers, "he was irritable on the day of a fight. Now, every fight means so much that he's on edge for weeks before. I miss him when he's gone, but at least I know Christine and I aren't holding him back. Separation is one of the ways we share the burden of his being a fighter."

For most of Sunday, Billy played with Christine. Then he and Jane watched the second televised debate between Ronald Reagan and Walter Mondale. "My mind's made up," Billy said when it was over. "If any pollsters call, you tell them that Billy Costello is voting for Mondale." Then he took the subway back to the hotel and watched television for the rest of the evening. "One of the hardest things about training," he told Mike on the telephone before going to bed, "is being away from Jane and the baby. It's like being in jail."

Monday's workout was light. Afterward Billy stopped at a laundromat near Gleason's to wash his gym clothes. "I don't like the way they do them at the hotel," he explained to Victor. "And besides, everything at the hotel costs too much. You gotta pay four dollars just for a Coke."

Tuesday, October 23, with the fight eleven days off, hard sparring resumed. In Mike's absence two new sparring partners had joined the fold. One was Bruce Williams—soft-spoken, black, 27 years old. The fifth of fourteen children, Williams had dropped out of school in twelfth grade "to take a job that might not have been there once I'd finished school." Thereafter he'd pursued an amateur career, winning two state Golden Gloves titles and a national AAU crown. His record as a pro was 16 and 1, with one draw. The loss was a fifth-round knockout by Harry Arroyo; the draw, an early bout against Livingston Bramble. Both Arroyo and Bramble had since become world champions. "I don't know what got me into boxing," Williams said when asked. "When I was young, I was real small, but I was quick and fast. One day, just for the hell of it, I went to the gym. It was something to do; it kept me from getting bored, and I was good at it. I was fourteen at the time. Now, sometimes I say to myself, 'Damn, why couldn't I have been a singer or an actor?' But this is my job."

Bruce Williams was a fighter with legitimate hopes for the future. He wasn't a heavy puncher (four knockouts in eighteen bouts), but he was a quality boxer and expert counterpuncher. Sparring with Billy would give him experience and get him in shape for a scheduled November fight of his own. More important, the job paid $350 a week plus room and board.

The other sparring partner was David Odem, also black, 25 years old. Odem had an amateur record of 17 and 11, and was 14–5–2 as a pro. He had been knocked out twice. The highlight of his career was a disputed loss to former WBA lightweight champ Hilmer Kenty. "Of the fights I lost," Odem told Victor, "I really only lost three. The other two were bad decisions." Quiet and affable, Odem knew his role: "I'm here to get Billy in shape, to give him good honest work. I won't hold back. For the champ to get his money's worth, every day I go into the ring I have to be looking for an opening, a good punch, a way to knock him down. That's the only way I can enjoy it, and the only way I'm any use to him. But I know my place; it's his show, not my turn."

In their hearts, Bruce Williams and David Odem weren't sparring for $50 a day. They were fighting for the chance someday to make millions in the ring. "I'm committed to boxing," Odem said. "For me there's really no place else to go."

When Billy arrived at Gleason's on Tuesday afternoon, Mike Jones was already there. From now until fight time, they would be together at least part of every day. Also present was Jeff Boyle.

Some champions travel with a large entourage of sycophants and hangers-on. In the days immediately preceding his fights, Billy traveled with a friend. Billy and Jeff had met in 1981 while Jeff was a student at Ulster County Community College. In 1982 he'd started going to Billy's fights, and hadn't missed one since. For the next eleven days, Jeff would be Billy's constant companion, catering to his moods, trying to keep him "up" for the fight. Outside of Mike and Victor, he would be the most important person in Billy's camp.

Upstairs in the locker room, Billy changed into his gym clothes—bright red shorts, blue shoes, a purple sweatshirt, and a white T-shirt that read "Little Italy Pizzeria and Restaurant." ("I never wear black. Black shoes, black trunks, they remind me of funerals.") Then he went downstairs, where Victor was waiting.

"Haley's gonna run from you," the trainer instructed. "You're gonna have to cut the ring off and give lots of feints to bring him in. That's what I want you to practice today."

David Odem was the first opponent. Rather than come right at Billy, for most of the first round he waited, throwing occasional counterpunches. Both men's eyes were wide with concentration. Billy was blocking punches well with his forearms, but his own punches were long. Too often Odem beat him to the punch. The first ninety seconds of round two was more of the same. Then Billy advanced behind hooks to the body, pinned Odem against the ropes, and began to wear him down. Victor stood on the ring apron, shouting instructions, observing what was going on. "When I shout something to Billy during a fight," he explained later, "I don't necessarily mean to do it now. I mean do it whenever the opening is there."

For round three Victor substituted Bruce Williams, a fresh

opponent to make Billy work harder. Williams was more aggressive than Odem, and landed several hard body shots followed by a solid righthand. Billy's punches were still long. His rhythm wasn't there. Round four was a repeat of the third, with Williams landing solid rights. "That shouldn't happen," Victor muttered. "The right hand has all that distance to travel. Billy should see it coming for miles."

Odem was back for round five, refreshed, more aggressive, landing jabs and moving well. Two minutes into the round he caught Billy off balance with a straight right that sent the champion halfway through the ropes. A follow-up would have put him out of the ring and onto the floor, but Odem stepped back and waited until Billy was upright before resuming the assault. Round six wasn't much better for the champion.

"I'm not happy," Victor said when the workout was done. "Billy went six rounds today, and lost four of them. Some fighters, they always look bad in the gym, but that's not Billy's style. Everyone's entitled to an off day, but today Billy didn't look like a world champion."

The next afternoon Billy went four more rounds with Odem. Round one began where the previous workout had ended, with Odem landing double and triple jabs. Once again Billy's punches were long. Then, as on the day before, the champion began landing hooks to the body in the second round. Odem bent low, dodging, weaving, trying to frustrate his opponent, but Billy was gathering steam. A right uppercut pierced Odem's gloves. Two jabs and an overhand right sent him backward, bringing a flow of blood from a split upper lip. It was Billy's round.

In round three both fighters began to unload. Odem's punches were faster; Billy's harder. The final three minutes of their four-round session saw the sparring partner in a survival mode. "It was a fair workout," Victor said upstairs in the locker room afterward. Odem hit Billy clean too many times. He just didn't have the power to hurt him. Haley's got power, and Haley don't get tired after two rounds."

That night Billy and Mike had dinner at The Conservatory restaurant in the Mayflower Hotel. Mike had been at the gym, and had seen the obvious. He knew Billy had been "off" for consecutive afternoons. The purple discoloration beneath the champion's right eye was testimony to that failing. Billy had been cut only twice in his career—once from a butt, once from punches—and there weren't many times his face had been bruised. This was one of them. Mike's job, as he saw it, was to get Billy to relax, get him in a cheerful mood.

"Boy, you have it easy," Mike began. "In the old days, fighters had to go up to the mountains, chop wood, and live the hard life when they were in training. Now, here you are, in the Park Lane Hotel, surrounded by luxury. You just pick up the telephone and call the chambermaid if your room isn't fixed right."

Billy's answer was noncommittal, and Mike switched to a different topic.

"Yesterday I bought myself one of those computer chess challengers. I was up last night until two o'clock, and the son-of-a-bitch beat me five times. What's more, whenever it wins it lights up and a bell rings like it's laughing at me."

The waiter came, and both men ordered. Mike had put Billy on a diet of 20 percent protein and 80 percent carbohydrates. Until the fight Billy would be eating chicken, fish, pasta, vegetables, and fruit.

"I'm gonna beat that computer. By the time you whip Leroy Haley, I'll have checkmated its ass."

The meal was quiet. Billy was in a reflective mood, dwelling on the impending fight. "It's hard being champ," he said, beginning to open up. "I can never sit back and really enjoy it. There's always a challenger ready for the fight of his life because I have what he wants. Sometimes people try to use the fact that I'm a fighter to humble me. That means there's an extra burden to express myself right and keep my image up. And then there's all sorts of other shit to worry about. Leroy Haley's got connections. He's Don King's fighter. That means, if it's a close fight, they could steal the decision from me. The job is tough."

The next day, Billy again arrived at the gym at two-thirty. Several wellwishers were at the door. "I wrote a poem for you," one announced. This is it:

> Billy Costello is training daily
> He'll knock the shit out of Leroy Haley

A tall, thin fighter just out of the shower was standing in the locker area, sprinkling baby powder on his male organ: "Hey, man, see all this cocaine I got on my dick. It makes it hard."

Billy climbed the stairs to the private locker room, and changed into his gym clothes. Then Victor taped a piece of cotton over the swelling beneath his right eye. "Four rounds today," the trainer told him. "All with Bruce Williams. He fights more like Haley than the other guy."

Downstairs, Williams and David Odem were comparing thoughts on "get-rich-quick bounties." To encourage intense workouts, some champions put a price on their head. When Larry Holmes was training to fight Gerry Cooney, he made a standing offer of $10,000 to any sparring partner who could knock him down. No one collected. Then the conversation shifted. "They're talking about matching me with Bret Summers," Odem said. "He's undefeated; 20 and 0. I'd be an underdog, I know that. But I can beat Summers; I've seen him fight. Let's say I beat Summers, score an exciting knockout, and the fight's on cable TV. After that maybe I'd get a network fight. For Summers they'd pay two or three thousand. For network TV it would be ten or twenty; more against someone like Ray Mancini. I can beat a lot of those guys in the top ten; I know I can; and I can fight lightweight or superlightweight, either way. So let's say I win that fight too. Next I could be fighting for the world title. I'd be in shape; I'd fight a good fight. Who knows what might happen?"

Billy appeared, and Bruce Williams excused himself to loosen up. Several CBS cameramen arrived with announcer Tim Ryan to tape an interview for airing just before the Haley fight. Then the sparring started. Four rounds, all the same. Bruce Williams was moving better, jabbing better, landing better than Billy.

"Don't move back, damn it," Victor shouted. "Every time he jabs, your head's moving back instead of to the side. If you're standing on a railroad tracks and a train's coming, you don't move back. You step aside."

Billy's punches were harder, but they weren't landing nearly as often as Williams's. He was pressing too hard, loading up for the big blow that never came.

"I'm gonna tell you like I told you a thousand times," Victor instructed. "You can spend all day looking to land the big punch, and it won't come. The big punches happen by themselves if you're fighting right."

All four rounds belonged to Williams.

"What happened?" Tim Ryan asked Victor in the locker room afterward. "Billy didn't look good."

"He was tired," the trainer answered. "I've been working him a little too hard lately."

"Nine days before a fight a champion shouldn't be tired."

"That's a lot of bullshit. There's no son of a gun in the world who don't get tired."

Ryan left unconvinced. After he'd gone, Victor gave Billy a long rubdown with a mixture of alcohol, Omega oil, eucalyptus oil, and baby oil. "What do you weigh now?"

"One-forty," Billy answered. "I weighed myself at the hotel this morning."

"All right. That's the weight you got to come in at for the fight. Take tomorrow off. Rest up. I'll see you again on Saturday."

Friday morning Billy slept late, then took the subway out to Queens to visit with Jane and Christine. He came back to the Park Lane Hotel around seven P.M., precisely the time Mike Jones got on the telephone with Don King.

"We got a problem," King said.

"What kind of problem?"

"Haley's hurt. The fight's in trouble."

18

"I'm telling you what I know, man. Haley's hand is hurt. Duke flew out to Ohio, and is bringing him to New York to see a doctor tonight."

With those words from Don King, Mike Jones entered into three days of chaos. Immediately following the conversation he telephoned Dr. Edwin Campbell of the New York State Athletic Commission. Campbell knew nothing about the injury, nor did any of Mike's other contacts. Saturday morning Campbell called back to report that Haley had arrived in New York the previous night and been examined at the Westbury Hotel by Dr. Frank Folk of the commission, with inconclusive results.

Gil Clancy of CBS telephoned. "Mike, I've heard rumors. What's happening?"

Mike told him what he knew. Then several hours later he spoke directly with Folk, who outlined the parameters of the problem. On Monday, October 15, twelve days earlier, Haley had experienced pain in his right hand, and minor swelling around the second and third carpal areas. Despite treatment by a chiropractor, the pain continued and spread to his upper arm. An injection of Butazolidin decreased the swelling, but full training was never resumed. "There's no fracture," Folk explained. "He complains of tenderness. I suggested therapy, and he refused."

"What happens now?"

"Dr. Campbell will examine the fighter on Monday morning.

If Haley is found fit to fight, either he fights or he'll be suspended. If he's not fit, the fight is off."

More frantic telephone calls followed; first to Victor Valle, then to Don King.

"It looks bad," King reported. "It's the same hand Haley broke twice against Bruce Curry. What we'll probably have to do is find a substitute."

"Like who?"

"Maybe CBS would take Saoul Mamby."

Mamby was the last opponent Mike wanted. A former champion and veteran of 55 pro fights, he had a ring style that was all wrong for Billy: jab, hold, box, run. Mamby was a master at feinting, slipping punches, and frustrating his opponents; and he took a punch as well as anyone in the division. In 55 pro fights, Mamby had never been knocked off his feet.

"No way," Mike told the promoter. "I don't want Mamby. Styles make fights. Everything Billy has worked for the last five years could go down the drain."

More telephone calls followed. Victor again, Dr. Campbell. Midway through the afternoon, Mike went through a list of the top-ranked WBC superlightweights one name at a time. There were two prerequisites for a substitute—acceptability to CBS, and someone Billy could prepare for properly in a week. Hidekazu Akai of Japan was a possibility; all the others were likely to be rejected by the network or were all wrong for Billy on short notice. Moreover, there was no guarantee that any of them could be ready to fight in one week.

One person Mike didn't call was Billy Costello. If the fight was on, there was no point in screwing up Billy's head. And if it was off, Billy would find out soon enough. Until Monday everything would be on hold. Still, Mike wondered if a conspiracy was afoot.

Managers have been known to do strange things to get fights for their fighters. Mike himself was no stranger to the trade. Twenty months earlier, Frank Fletcher had been in line for a shot at Marvin Hagler's middleweight title. Mike wanted the bout for Wilford Scypion, and to get it he spread rumors about his own fighter. "Wilford got knocked down in the gym three times this week; his legs are shot; there might be drugs; all he wants is one last payday before he retires." Fletcher's camp reached for the bait, and scheduled a fight against Scypion as a tune-up for Hagler. Scypion beat Fletcher decisively, gaining the championship bout for himself.

"Carl King manages Saoul Mamby," Mike told Victor when they talked on the telephone for the third time in as many hours. "Don King is Mamby's exclusive promoter. Maybe Haley is really hurt, or maybe King figures that Mamby has a better chance to beat Billy, and this is all a Don King plot."

That night, with visions of conspiracy dancing in his head, Mike went out for dinner with Stella and another couple. "Sometimes life gets very confusing," he said as they walked. "I love boxing, I love the challenge. But more and more, I have trouble with the lack of control over my own destiny. Rankings are arbitrary. Too many times I can't get fights when my fighters deserve them. Sometimes I go through so much just to get Billy or Gerry into the ring that the fight itself seems anticlimactic."

The couples separated, the two men walking twenty yards ahead of the women.

"At least real estate is stable," Mike continued, gazing toward a modern high-rise a block ahead. "You own a building, and it's always there. You don't have to worry about it getting knocked out or breaking its hand. It's always in the same place. . . ." His voice trailed off, then picked up again. "In boxing everybody's priorities become distorted. It's all-consuming. Sometimes I think it takes too much out of me. I'm married to the most wonderful woman in the world, and I'm away from home all the time. When the kids were growing up, I felt guilty every time I had to get up and go. Sometimes even now I'll be on the phone with a lawyer negotiating a multimillion-dollar real-estate deal; another call comes in, and I have to put the lawyer on hold to discuss a six-round preliminary fight. I don't know. Maybe there isn't any answer."

The next day, Sunday, October 28, Mike, Billy, and Jeff Boyle were picked up by a CBS limousine and taken to the Giants-Redskins football game at the New Jersey Meadowlands. CBS was broadcasting the contest, and wanted a halftime interview with Billy to promote the Haley fight.

"How's this for luxury?" Mike asked as the limousine made its way through the Lincoln Tunnel. "A color TV, a bar, all in the back seat."

"First bar I've been near in six months," Billy said.

The remark might have been true. Even apart from the demands of training, Billy carefully guarded his image. One night at the Concord Hotel, during preparation for the Shields fight, he'd been looking for Mike. "I think he's in the cocktail lounge," someone said.

"No way I'm going in there," Billy had answered. "Next thing you know, people will say they saw Billy Costello in the lounge chasing girls and having a drink."

Just before kickoff time, the limousine arrived at Meadowlands stadium, where Mike, Billy, and Jeff were ushered into a waiting room on the mezzanine level. From there they watched the game until midway through the second quarter, when Mike gestured for Billy to step outside.

"What's up?"

"I'll tell you in a minute."

The two men retired to a corridor where they could speak alone.

"Billy, there's something I have to tell you. And the only reason I'm telling you now is, if the subject comes up during the interview, I don't want you to be embarrassed by not knowing about it. There's a rumor that Haley wants the fight called off."

Billy's face looked like he'd been shot. "What do you mean, call the fight off?"

"Just that."

The roar of the crowd punctuated Mike's tale of events.

"For the moment there's nothing we can do about it," he said as he finished.

"That's terrible. I've been training for this fight for three months. I've made my weight. I already got the money added up—what I'm gonna spend, what I'm gonna put in the bank. I've just about killed myself getting ready for this fight."

"I know. And there's nothing I can tell you besides do the interview like the fight's going to happen. But in case the subject comes up, I wanted you to know."

The interview with John Madden lasted seventy seconds. Billy talked about how he was looking forward to the fight, and that it would be good to have his home town of Kingston behind him. Then he, Jeff, and Mike drove back to New York.

"It won't be long," Mike said just before the limousine stopped at the Park Lane Hotel. "We should have an answer after Dr. Campbell examines Haley tomorrow."

No examination took place. Early the next morning, Monday, October 29, Don King Productions advised the New York State Athletic Commission that Leroy Haley had returned home to Las Vegas and would not fight. The twelve hours that followed were among the most emotionally demanding of Mike's life.

During the preceding week, Mike, Dennis Rappaport, and Sam Glass had put together a syndicate to broadcast Gerry Cooney's next fight. The opponent would be George Chaplin, a journeyman heavyweight who had lost five of his last twelve bouts. To make the promotion more attractive to advertisers and local television stations, a WBC featherweight championship bout between Wilfredo Gomez and Azumah Nelson had been added as a co-feature, and a press conference to announce the bouts had been called for 11:00 A.M. at Gallagher's Steak House. By the appointed hour a hundred media representatives, state officials, and hangers-on were present. Most were on hand for the heavyweight announcement, but several were there for other reasons. Gil Clancy had been sent over by CBS to find out whether the network still had a Billy Costello fight. John Branca, chairman of the New York State Athletic Commission, was trying to save Billy's bout for New York State. Carl King would be in attendance, ostensibly as Azumah Nelson's manager.

At precisely eleven A.M. Carl King entered the room—with Saoul Mamby beside him. All eyes turned. Lean, handsome, with soft eyes and light brown skin, Mamby looked fit and trim. A gold chain dangled around his neck. Dressed in brown slacks and a cream-colored shirt, he sat silently as Carl King explained what was happening.

"Leroy Haley hurt his hand about two weeks ago," King told the assemblage. "It's an inflammation around the break he suffered in his fight with Bruce Curry a year ago. The day after the injury he soaked it, and didn't do nothing in the gym. Then he tried sparring, but the hand got tender again."

"Why didn't you tell anyone before now?" a reporter demanded.

"Because Leroy wanted the fight to go on. He's a brave man. It wasn't until late last week that he became resigned to the fact that he couldn't fight. Friday night he flew to New York and was examined at the Westbury Hotel around midnight by Dr. Folk. Saturday Dr. Folk saw him again, and said it would be three to four weeks before he could even start sparring."

Then it was Mamby's turn. "Carl called me last night and told me to pick him up at the airport this morning," the fighter explained. "I didn't know anything about it until then. But I'm in good condition; I'm ready to fight; I'm ranked number seven in the world by the WBC. The easiest thing would be for me to substitute for Haley, and let the fight go on."

It was a stroke of genius, masterfully staged with dozens of reporters watching. Before Mike could respond, Gerry Cooney arrived and the press conference began. One by one, there were short speeches by Sam Glass, George Chaplin, Wilfredo Gomez, and Azumah Nelson. Then Mike, Dennis Rappaport, and Victor Valle spoke, followed by Cooney himself. Meanwhile around the room small groups were caucusing—Gil Clancy, John Branca, Carl King, Marvin Kohn.

When the press conference ended, Clancy took Mike aside. "CBS will accept Mamby," he said.

"I don't want him," Mike answered. "He makes his opponents look bad."

"Mike, I'm going back to CBS. Come on over, and we'll talk about it."

"Give me a few minutes. I want to talk to Victor."

Clancy left. Mike waited until the reporters had moved away, then went over to Billy's trainer.

"What do you think?"

"I don't like it," Victor answered. "Mamby's style is all wrong for Billy. Maybe the injury to Haley was real, but everything else is a fake. Don King has been planning to give us Mamby."

"Billy can beat him."

"Billy can beat him, and Billy could get beat. The biggest mistake a trainer can make is to think his fighter is unbeatable."

An honest give-and-take of views was taking place. If Mike said, "Victor, this is what we have to do," Victor would do it. But Mike respected Victor's opinion, and would be reluctant to overrule it. At one-thirty, leaving the trainer behind, he walked over to CBS headquarters at Sixth Avenue and 52nd Street, and went up to Terry O'Neil's office on the thirtieth floor. O'Neil, Peter Tortorici, Tim Ryan, and Gil Clancy were present. O'Neil took the lead in the conversation: "The question now is how do we save the fight. CBS has two-and-a-half hours of air time to fill, and Garza-Meza alone won't do it. We like Billy. We see the Billy Costello story as the story of a fighter who got his chance late in life and made the most of it. He's supported by a terrific community up in Kingston that watched him grow and is thrilled by his accomplishments. Small-town success stories are rare in boxing. We want Billy on the air, and we'd like him to fight Saoul Mamby."

"Mamby's the wrong style," Mike responded. "Billy hasn't had time to prepare for him properly. He could make Billy look bad the entire fight."

"It's not our job to convince you that your fighter can't look bad or lose a fight. CBS has a show to put on, and we like to deal with fight camps that cooperate."

The dialogue was growing more tense.

"What does that mean?" Mike demanded.

"It means that someday you're going to come back to us with a big-money Billy Costello fight, and we're going to say, 'No. Why should we pay big money for a guy who wouldn't fight Saoul Mamby?' One of the differences between a champion and an ordinary fighter is a champion can adjust to all kinds of styles."

The meeting ended at two o'clock. Mike went to a vacant office and telephoned Victor, who was at Gleason's with Billy: "Victor, they got me in the steam room here."

Victor repeated his objections to Mamby. Mike retreated to Clancy's office, where the two men were joined by Tim Ryan. The situation was uncomfortable for both network officials. CBS didn't like to be in the position of pushing to make a particular match. It preferred to pick and choose among what was offered by promoters, but because of circumstances, a more active posture was required.

"Mamby's an old man," Clancy implored. "Billy will knock him out. It's a fight CBS wouldn't even take if it wasn't on short notice."

"Mamby is trouble," Mike answered. "He makes people look bad."

"I know he makes people look bad, but what kind of champion will Billy be if he doesn't take an old man on short notice?"

"A thirty-seven-year-old man won this year's Olympic Marathon," Mike countered.

Michael Burks, who would be producing the fight for CBS, entered the room and asked about the status of the bout. If Billy Costello wasn't fighting, the show would be moved from Kingston to Las Vegas. Burks wanted to know where his equipment should be shipped.

"Promoters are already calling with alternative bouts," Ryan added.

Meanwhile Clancy had reached for a copy of the *Ring Record Book*, and looked up Mamby. "For chrissake, Mike. This guy hasn't beaten anyone who counts since Monroe Brooks two years ago."

"He knocked someone out in Kingston this July on the undercard of Ronnie Shields against Billy."

"Kevin Austin. That's who he knocked out, and it took him ten rounds to do it. Thumbing through the pages, Clancy turned to Austin's ring record. "Look at this! Kevin Austin, a journeyman fighter with a five hundred record, and he had Saoul Mamby in trouble. Mike, Mamby is shot. You're thinking about the Saoul Mamby of two years ago."

A not very subtle by-play was underway. Clancy was tearing down Mamby to encourage Mike to take the fight. His job, apart from any personal opinions he might have had, was to save the show for CBS.

At three o'clock Mort Sharnik called, and urged Mike to accept Mamby. When the conversation was done, Mike phoned in to his telephone answering machine. More pressure. There was a message from Ted Beitschman, the boxing editor at *Sports Illustrated,* asking for credentials to cover the fight. *Sports Illustrated* represented Billy's first chance ever for national print exposure.

"Mike," Clancy asked wearily. "Is there anybody in the top ten you will fight?"

One by one, Mike studied the names on a list of top ten WBC-rated fighters.

"Mamby, Gary Hinton, and Ronnie Shields are the only ones we won't take."

Clancy was growing more exasperated. "Mike, you gotta be reasonable. The other seven are all from outside the United States. It's Monday afternoon. The fight is Saturday. Akai is in Japan. Oliva's in Italy. Billy Famous is in Nigeria. Do you really think we can find some guy in Nigeria, get a tape to make sure he can fight, bring him over here, and have him ready to fight by Saturday at five o'clock?"

At 3:50 P.M., Ryan, Clancy, and Mike returned to Terry O'Neil's office. "If Billy Costello goes through with this fight," O'Neil said, "it will enhance his chances of fighting again on CBS. The converse is also true."

Again Mike repeated his objections to Mamby.

The meeting ended at four o'clock.

"Come on," Clancy said to Mike. "Let's go over to Don King's office and see if we can work this thing out."

Don King Productions was headquartered in a five-story townhouse at 32 East 69th Street. Owing to the crazy-quilt pattern of midtown traffic, Mike and Gil didn't arrive there until four-thirty.

The cab ride gave Mike a chance to reflect on his traveling companion. Clancy had been in boxing since 1947. Among the champions he'd trained were Emile Griffith, George Foreman, Rodrigo Valdez, and Ken Buchanan. He'd also served as matchmaker at Madison Square Garden, before taking his job as a color commentator for CBS. "I personally think that every young man in the United States should put on a pair of boxing gloves and learn how to box," Clancy once said. "Too many people today, young and old, are afraid of a challenge."

Don King was out of the office but "expected back shortly" when his visitors arrived. The corridor walls and townhouse stairwell were lined with photographs. Don King with Hubert Humphrey; Don King with Muhammad Ali; Don King with Jackie Gleason; Don King with Frank Sinatra; Don King with Joe Louis; Don King with Howard Cosell. Literally hundreds of portraits. At Clancy's suggestion, the two men journeyed to a second floor office where King's collection of tapes was stored, and sat down to study Mamby's 1983 fight against Leroy Haley. Mike watched three rounds, then turned to Clancy. "I don't want to see anymore. We're not trained to fight this guy. His style is all wrong for Billy."

Clancy shrugged. "If it was my fighter, he'd fight him."

An aide came in to announce that Don King had arrived, and the two men took the elevator to King's fourth-floor office. The room looked as though it had been furnished by Hollywood central casting. Red carpet, plush leather sofas, a formica desk and glass-topped conference table with two huge American flags standing in the background. The wall opposite the door was primarily windows. An adjacent wall bore sixty plaques awarded to King by various civic and boxing organizations. Opposite that was a fully mirrored wall. Three color televisions stood on a wall unit to one side of the door. A fully stocked bar was on the other. The ceiling was also mirrored. Only one autographed photograph graced the walls—a picture of two men with the inscription, "To Don King, Best wishes, Hugh Hefner." Behind the desk, at floor level so they weren't visible from most parts of the room, six television screens attached to closed-circuit cameras monitored the rest of the townhouse.

Don King was seated at the desk, dressed in brown slacks, a white shirt with faint brown stripes, and a brown silk tie. His face looked tired. Rumor had it that the promoter was suffering from diabetes and high blood pressure. And perhaps more troubling, he was the target of an ongoing investigation by the Organized Crime Task Force of the United States Attorney's Office for the Southern District of New York. In public King joked about the situation. "Investigation is my middle name," he said. "My plight is to be investigated from the day I was born until the day I die." But in private King was far less flippant about the matter. Indeed, in a recent civil lawsuit he had refused to answer questions other than his name and address, and had taken the Fifth Amendment 364 times.*

As Mike and Clancy entered, Don King looked up from his desk. "What a life," he muttered. "Once I was poor and hungry. Now I got money to spend and no time to eat." Then, he gestured toward Mike. "Gil, I just can't believe this guy. Nine months ago Mike Jones was chasing me all over the country, begging to fight Bruce Curry for twenty-five thousand dollars. Now I'm chasing him, begging him to take a hundred and fifty thousand."

"I know how you feel," Mike said, "but I have to go by my instincts. Billy just isn't prepared for Mamby."

"Hell, Mamby ain't prepared for Costello. If your man turns this fight down, people be talking about him the same way they talk about Gerry Cooney. Costello will never live it down. They'll say he don't fight nobody."

"Styles make fights."

"Yeah, Mike, I know. But the way you work, you always find problems with styles. This opponent's too fat. This one's too slow. This one's too tall. This one's too wiry. Hell, when you say the words 'world champion' that means you fight everybody. If your man don't fight this thirty-seven-year-old opponent, he should retire."

Don King was warming up. His words were coming incredibly fast, yet each one was rich and resonant, enunciated with the ring of a carnival barker.

"Mike," Clancy interrupted. "You're depriving Billy of his right to become a great fighter. And you're depriving him of a pretty good payday too."

"But he'll still be champion."

"A diminished champion."

"Mike," King said, picking up the assault. "I hate to see you make this mistake. I got too much respect and admiration for you. Up until now, Billy Costello has been a worthy cham-

---

* On December 13, 1984, six weeks after his October 29 meeting with Mike Jones and Gil Clancy, King and an aide were indicted by a federal grand jury on twenty-three counts of income tax evasion, filing false and fraudulent income tax returns, and conspiracy with regard to the concealment of over $1 million in unreported income. After a lengthy trial, he was acquitted but the aide was found guilty and imprisoned.

pion, but if you turn this fight down he'll no longer be worthy. A coward dies a thousand deaths; a brave man dies but once."

Don King was known for pulling out all the stops to get what he wanted. In 1977 George Foreman had retired from boxing to preach the Gospel for a small church in Texas. With the heavyweight ranks growing thin, one day Foreman received a breathless telephone call from Don King.

"George, I just had this vision."

"What did you see, Don?"

"It was like a dream, George. It looked like Mr. Hayward Moore [a friend of Foreman's who had just died]. He was leading you and me together, and you were back in boxing, entering the ring with a cross on your robe and trunks."

"Don," Foreman had answered. "You don't put the cross on your robe. You put it on your heart."

Now Don King was putting the pressure on Mike. Clancy's loyalty was to CBS. King, obviously, was concerned with his own interests. Mike's job was to protect Billy. At six o'clock he excused himself and telephoned Victor at Gleason's Gym. Once again Victor said "no" to Mamby. When Mike returned, King was on the telephone. "Just a minute," the promoter said. "Here he is." Then he handed the receiver to Mike.

The voice at the other end belonged to Jose Sulaiman.

"Mike, I do not understand why you will not fight Saoul Mamby. For the good of boxing, I urge you to accept this fight."

The screws were being tightened.

"Jose, I just don't think it's the right fight for my fighter."

Don King picked up on another receiver. "Jose, this man is hurting boxing. And I love boxing."

Mike wouldn't budge. Finally King changed the subject for a moment, telling Sulaiman that he had received the tape of an interview aired recently on CNN in which he'd effusively praised the WBC president. Sulaiman expressed interest in hearing the tape, and King called his stepson Carl into the room, instructing him to hold the telephone receiver to a television set while the entire interview was played. Partway through the tape, which lasted thirty minutes, another King aide came into the room with a tape of Mamby's 1983 loss to Ronnie Shields. Again Mike retired to the second-floor video room. Mamby looked less impressive than on the earlier tape. His legs seemed weak. After three rounds, Mike picked up the telephone, and called Victor.

"Victor, come over to 32 East 69th Street. I want you to look at a tape with me."

Victor replied that he was in the middle of training Gerry Cooney, and would need at least an hour to get there. Mike told King and Clancy that he was going across the street to the Westbury Hotel for a drink. When he returned, Victor still hadn't arrived. Meanwhile King's staff had unearthed a tape of Mamby's most recent fight, against Kevin Austin the preceding July. Mike watched it. Mamby's legs looked strong again.

Victor arrived at 6:45 P.M., and Mike took him out onto the street where they could talk without fear of eavesdropping devices.

"How did Billy look today in the gym?"

"Very good. He boxed four rounds with Bruce Williams, and won all of them."

"Billy could be the first person ever to knock out Mamby."

"Mike, I don't like the style for Billy; not on short notice. To fight Mamby there's too many things Billy has got to do different."

"The pressure is on. CBS, Don King, the WBC—they're all pressing."

"But none of them care about Billy."

At seven o'clock, King and Clancy went across the street for a beer at a bar called Confetti's. When they returned, Mike and Victor were on the second floor watching a tape of Shields versus Mamby. Clancy telephoned CBS for a status report. The network had decided if necessary to substitute Mark Holmes versus Odell Hadley, and broadcast it with Garza-Meza from Las Vegas.

At seven-thirty Mike reentered Don King's office. Everybody was tired.

There was an ugly edge to King's voice. "Are you ready to fight?"

"I've watched the tapes," Mike answered. "I've consulted again with Victor. We don't want this fight. Billy signed to fight Leroy Haley, not Saoul Mamby. We want to fight. We'll fight all the big names—Pryor, Mancini, Hatcher, Oliva—but not Mamby. That's it."

"Who do you think you are, motherfucker?"

"Pardon?"

"Who do you think you are, motherfucker? You can pull that shit with Gerry Cooney because he's big and he's white, but not with Billy Costello, man. Not with Costello."

"Look, Don—"

"You're a liar, man. You know that." King's voice was rising. "Nine months ago you was begging me for a shot at Curry. You was crawling and begging and you said, 'Give us a chance at Curry and we'll fight anybody after that.' Well, you're a fucking chickenshit coward, and your fighter is too."

"Don, there's a lot of brave managers out there who don't do what's best for their fighters."

A Shakespearean rage was building. "Fuck you, man. Fuck you. You don't care shit about your fighter. You're just playing ego games, sucking the blood out of your fighter's heart. You're gonna be a fat rich white boy living out on Long Island, and your fighter will be hungry. If you think Billy Costello is fighting for me again after this, man, give it up."

"Don, if that's the way you feel, release us from the options, and we'll find someone else to promote Billy."

In one motion, Don King picked the telephone off his desk and slammed it down. Papers flew. The receiver spun off and twisted wildly, dangling in midair.

"You ain't worried about your fighter looking bad," King shrieked. "You're worried about losing. You're a coward, man, and your fighter is too; a chickenshit coward."

"Billy Costello's not afraid of anybody."

"Fuck you, man. Fuck you. Get out of my office. Don't want to see you again. But I'll get you, motherfucker. It's just a matter of time, that's all. It's just a matter of time."

The weather outside was unseasonably warm for the end of October. Mike walked the twelve blocks to the Park Lane Hotel, and took the elevator to 3814. Billy was dressed in a plaid shirt and jeans. The room looked out over southern Manhattan.

For several minutes Mike recounted what had happened. "Maybe I was wrong," he said at the finish. "I don't know. I did what I thought was best for you."

Billy sat silently, the emotions of the moment written on his face.

"Are you disappointed?"

"Yeah, but you're the manager. You make the deals. All I do is fight."

"You're still champ."

"It don't feel like it."

The two men talked for another twenty minutes. Then Mike rose to leave.

"Hey, Mike," Billy said softly. "You know something. It's all bullshit."

* * *

That night shortly before midnight, the telephone rang in Room 3814 of the Park Lane Hotel. Billy Costello reached across the bed, past the ornate headboard covered with silk damask, and picked up the receiver.

"Billy, this is Mike. I'd like you to do a favor for me."

"What is it?"

"This Saturday I want you to go up to Kingston and kick Saoul Mamby's ass."

PART

4

Billy Costello punches hard, but he's mechanical and repetitious. He loops his right; he doesn't follow up on his own feints; and he's way too slow getting into position to punch with leverage. I'm in good shape. I've never been knocked off my feet. I'm the best counterpuncher Costello has ever faced. I'm a scientific fighter, and science will outclass brute strength every time. I've been in nine title fights, so I know what I have to do to win. There's no way that Billy Costello can beat me.

—Saoul Mamby

"It was a hard decision, probably the hardest decision involving Billy's career that I'll ever have to make."

On the morning of October 30, Mike Jones summed up the events of the previous night. After leaving Billy at the Park Lane Hotel, Mike had gone for a walk, then a drink. "If you can't live with something like this, you don't belong in boxing," he'd told himself. Still, inside there was a gnawing feeling that he'd made a mistake. "I kept thinking about Billy going back to his one-bedroom apartment in Queens with no money and no TV date. He'd trained three months for this fight, and it would be three months more before another date opened up. Don King's ranting and raving didn't move me, particularly since he stayed safely behind his desk while he was doing it. But I kept thinking about how everything would look to the networks and the public. Billy's credibility was at stake. I don't claim I'm the greatest manager in the world, but I'm a good manager. My fighters haven't won ninety-five percent of their fights by my making mistakes. This time, I decided, I had made a mistake."

Shortly before midnight, Mike telephoned Billy and asked him to fight. Then he tried reaching Don King, but the promoter had left New York for an appearance in Washington, D.C. Finally at 1:00 A.M., Mike located Peyton Sher, King's on-site coordinator in Kingston, and Connie Harper, vice-president of Don King Productions in New York. At 3:00 A.M. he telephoned Jose Sulaiman, who was on business in London where, because of the time differential, it was eight o'clock. Finally at 8:00 A.M. New York time, Mike called Gil Clancy at home on Long Island. The inevitability of Saoul Mamby had come to pass.

Tuesday afternoon, Billy arrived at Gleason's at two o'clock. Victor and Mike were already there. Victor, in particular, showed none of his normal ebullience. Leroy Haley was a walk-right-in, rough-and-tumble opponent. Fighting Saoul Mamby demanded major adjustments.

As Billy dressed for the workout, Mike sought out David Odem and told him he was released. The departure of Leroy Haley required a new sparring partner closer in style to Mamby. Bruce Williams would be retained as a back-up. The new number-one sparring partner would be Ricky Young. Tall, quick, 23 years old, Young was one of the fighters being developed by the Felt Forum. Earlier in the year he had sparred with Mamby for several weeks, and more than a little of the former champion had rubbed off on him.

Meanwhile, Billy had finished dressing and was getting a new set of instructions from his trainer. "You can't wait for Mamby," Victor cautioned. "If you do, he won't never come to you. Also, you got to remember, every time he throws the jab he's gonna lean in to you. That's when you unload the right. The rest of the time, hit him with double hooks to the body. Be rough. Control him."

Billy sparred three rounds with Ricky Young and three with Bruce Williams, looking "fair" in Victor's estimation. Then, after a rubdown, he did his laundry, went back to the hotel for a nap, and ate dinner with Mike. For most of the meal his thoughts were on the man he would face four days hence.

One of five children, the son of a bus driver, Saoul Mamby was born in the Bronx and graduated from Bronx Vocational High School in 1965. That same year he started fighting as an amateur, turning professional four years later after a stint in Vietnam. "I was in Nam for one year, six days, and four hours," he remembers. "Did I see combat? Yeah, enough—and boxing is easier." During the early years of his career Mamby had worked at odd jobs—a stockclerk, washing windows on skyscrapers. "I drove a gypsy cab for a while, but it got too dangerous so I quit." Meanwhile, his career languished until he met Don King.

"My manager Paul Mitrano had died," Mamby recalls, "and Don King asked to see me. We met and he asked me to sign a promotional contract, which I did, and a managerial contract with his son Carl, which I refused. So now I had a promoter but no fights. During a ten-month period all I got was a walk-out fight against Norman Goins—and remember, I was a fighter who'd gone the distance with Antonio Cervantes and Roberto Duran. Finally in 1979 I signed with Carl King as my manager. I'd never met him in my life. In fact, outside of seeing him at my fights, I don't think we've ever been together [prior to the October 29 press conference]. And right away after I signed with Carl King, I was offered Marion Thomas in New York and Tom Tarantino in Atlantic City—both easy fights. One month after the Tarantino fight I was in Seoul, Korea, fighting Sang-Hyun Kim for the world title."

Mamby won the crown with a fourteenth-round knockout of Kim, and successfully defended his championship five times. Then on June 26, 1982, he defended the title against Leroy Haley.

"Just before the fight," Mamby remembers, "Carl King came into the dressing room and told me he couldn't work my corner. I asked why, and he mumbled something about rules and regulations or some kind of obligation. The fight went on. I lost a decision. And after the decision was announced—here I am, I've just lost my title—I look across the ring, and there's Carl King hugging Haley. I looked over there and said, 'What the fuck is going on?' Then I realized that Carl King might have been my manager, but he was also managing Haley. Why is Carl King still my manager? His daddy is the main man. Business is business."

Inside the ring, Mamby was a master at generalship and pacing, throwing punches from all angles, which made them harder to block. "He's not a heavy puncher," Victor Valle had told Billy, "but he hits hard enough to get your attention, and he tires you out. He hits you with a lot of little punches, and over ten or twelve rounds, the damage adds up." But the most impressive thing about Mamby was his defense. He seemed to have an intuitive sense of when punches were coming, and an uncanny ability to make opponents miss by fractions of an inch. In five hundred rounds of boxing, no one—not even Roberto Duran—had knocked him off his feet.

"When I was just getting started in boxing," Billy told Mike over dinner Tuesday night, "Saoul Mamby was my idol. He'd train at Gleason's the same time as me, and sometimes I'd just stand there and watch. He was the master. Lots of times I used to ride home with him on the subway. I'd get off at 59th Street, and he'd go on uptown to the Bronx. Once we sparred together. He beat me pretty good."

Wednesday, October 31, Billy rose at eight o'clock, did his roadwork in Central Park, and weighed himself in the hotel bathroom—139 pounds, a full pound under the championship limit. After a breakfast of cereal, he watched television with Jeff Boyle. Then he took the subway to Gleason's.

Some fighters spar up until the day of a fight; others stop several days earlier. Each trainer must evaluate when his fighter is ready, when he's as good as he can get. With the fight against Mamby three days away, Victor had decided that today would be Billy's last sparring session. And it would be all-out; four rounds against Ricky Young, with both men instructed to hold nothing back.

As Billy and Young entered the ring, most activity on the gym floor halted. This was the champion's final sparring session, and a crowd gathered at the edge of the ring anticipating true combat.

Throughout the first round, Billy was off. Young, a counterpuncher like Mamby, relied on a quick stiff jab to control the entire three minutes.

In round two the punching power of both men increased, but Billy's punches were long and he was falling into his old habit of pulling back from punches rather than slipping them. "Don't do that, goddammit," Victor shouted. "You'll never get in on Mamby like that." Several times Billy landed hard shots, but each time he seemed tentative and failed to follow up, giving Young time to regain his balance. "Move in when you hit him," Victor pleaded. "Move in, dammit!"

Round three. The sparring had become a war. Ricky Young was hungry and going for the kill, anxious to prove himself, advancing behind his jab, snapping Billy's head back. Billy landed several hooks to the body, slowing Young down, but the challenger kept coming. Fifteen seconds before the bell, a left uppercut staggered Young. Gathering his strength, he sought to retaliate with a left hook to the body, but it was too low and too slow. Instantaneously Billy fired a straight right that landed with concussive power flush on the challenger's jaw. Young crumpled to the canvas, and rose unsteadily at a count of eight, dazed, unable to continue.

"We're all feeling better now," Victor said in the locker room a half hour later. "Bruce Williams, David Odem, Ricky Young, all those guys—they can stay with Billy for three or four rounds but not for twelve. Part of being champion is knowing that somewhere during the fight you're gonna get your opponent."

Ricky Young, the left side of his jaw grotesquely swollen, came into the room to wish Billy well against Mamby.

"What happened?" someone asked the younger fighter.

"I guess I got a little cocky," Young answered. "But I learned something. You can make mistakes against preliminary fighters. You can't make them against a champion."

"What are you going to do now?"

"Take a shower; go home; lie on the bed awhile; and tell myself either I want to come back tomorrow or I don't. It's one or the other. There's only two choices. I'll be back."

Young left.

"He's a good boy," said Victor. "And he learned a good lesson this afternoon. You can hit a guy all night and he's laughing at you. Then suddenly you hit him right, and he isn't laughing no more. When Billy is on, he can make the other guy change his mind fast about being a fighter."

The knockdown had been Billy's first in over two months of training, and it couldn't have come at a better moment. Mamby had experience and style. Billy had youth and power. Their fight held out the promise of a classic confrontation between boxer and puncher, but today's session meant that Billy would go in with a psychological high.

"That last punch was something," Mike said when the locker

room had emptied. "With all the confusion and everything else that's gone on lately, it might be the most important punch that Billy has ever thrown."

The following day, Thursday, November 1, was Billy's last at Gleason's. The session consisted of calisthenics, speed bag work, and jumping rope. Then Billy went back to the hotel with Jeff, and began to pack for their drive to Kingston. Meanwhile Mike went ahead in his own car to make certain everything was in order at the fight site.

It was a 90-mile drive to Kingston. Mike arrived at the Holiday Inn, which was fight headquarters for Don King Productions, at 6:15 P.M. Waiting for Billy, he had two beers at the bar, then played Ping-Pong with a reporter.

The inn was busy, with representatives of the New York State Athletic Commission, CBS, and miscellaneous fighters checking in. Unlike training camps, which are fairly dull and designed for work, the atmosphere was one of drama and excitement. Overseeing it all was Peyton Sher, the on-site coordinator for Don King Productions.

Sixty-one years old, a resident of Overland Park, Kansas, Sher had moved from the insurance business to boxing in the 1970s, and served as a manager, promoter, and booking agent ever since. Large and avuncular with a pleasant manner and full head of gray hair, he worked for King on an average of six shows per year.

Promoting a fight is a lot like producing a movie. There are thousands of pieces to put together. Sher's job had begun as soon as the match was made. Arrangements for hotel rooms, transportation, press conferences, and weigh-ins fell within his domain. He had to print and sell tickets, set up dressing rooms, install electrical outlets for television cables, telephones, and typewriters, and hire ushers, ticket-takers, security guards, and concessioneers. Equipment was also a problem. Fighters don't bring their own corner stools to a fight, so Sher provided them, along with buckets, water bottles, and the like. It was also his job to see that seats and the ring itself were set up in the arena.

Sher had arrived in Kingston twelve days before the fight, and wasn't happy with the fight site. Unlike many hotels that served as fight headquarters, the Holiday Inn refused to "comp" rooms, so Don King Productions had to pay for them. Moreover, there were competing political factions in Kingston—each one hoping to capitalize on Billy Costello's popularity—and if one group worked on a particular aspect of the promotion, the other wouldn't. There was no major airport nearby, creating the added problem of how to get WBC junior featherweight champ Jaime Garza, Juan Meza, and their respective entourages from JFK Airport to Kingston. "After all," Sher reasoned, "you can't tell Garza to take a bus." All of those problems, Sher concluded, existed because of CBS. The network had wanted a happening—a fight where tickets were sold in the town barbershop instead of being given away to casino high rollers; a sold-out town hall with people screaming for the home-town boy made good. Sher hoped his next fight would be in Atlantic City or Las Vegas.

Billy, Victor, and Jeff Boyle arrived at the Holiday Inn at 10:00 P.M. Checking in, they were handed a Don King Productions memorandum advising that they were entitled to free rooms plus a food allowance of $25 per person per day. All other expenses— tips, telephone calls, etc.—would be borne by the fighter's camp. They went upstairs; Victor to room 413, Billy and Jeff to 417. Mike had already checked into 415, between them.

Billy unpacked and turned on the television to watch the news. Victor and Mike came by for a brief visit, then left to go to bed. "Try to get a good sleep," Victor instructed. "Tomorrow night you might not sleep so good."

Billy watched television until the news was over, then turned off the set. The room was well lit, clean, and airy. A small wooden nighttable, two chairs, a bureau, and two double beds were the only furnishings. "I wish it was over," he told Jeff. "Before a fight I always wish it was over."

"You'll kick his ass."

"That's what Mike says." Still dressed, Billy lay back on his bed. "I tell myself that I'll outpunch Mamby; and if I can't outpunch him, I'll outbox him; and if I can't outbox him, I'll outslick him. Somehow I'll find a way to win. But then I say, suppose I don't. All my life I've worked to get where I am today. After all these years, finally I can take care of Jane and Christine the way they deserve. And now Saoul Mamby wants to take everything away from me. Fuck Saoul Mamby."

20

For a fighter, the thirty-six hours before a championship bout are a mixture of edginess and boredom. Billy woke up Friday morning at nine o'clock. At nine-thirty he went out and ran three miles along the streets of Kingston. Then, back at the hotel, he weighed himself. The scale he'd brought from New York registered 137 pounds, safely below the 140 pound limit. For breakfast he ate pancakes, eggs, and three glasses of orange juice. Afterward he went back upstairs to his room.

On the surface it was a quiet morning. Beneath the surface, emotions were bubbling. For the next few hours Billy relaxed on his bed, reading the newspaper, watching television quiz shows, and talking with Mike. Several bags of fruit lay on the dresser. The window looked out over an automobile junkyard and Esopus Creek.

"Hey, Mike. Listen to what Mamby said." Pointing to a paragraph in the local newspaper, Billy began to read aloud. "A true world champion fights people all over the world, not just in his home town. I'm going to give Billy Costello a boxing lesson on Saturday."

"He'll eat those words," Mike answered.

Jim Cozza, a friend from high school, came by to wish Billy luck. At one o'clock, Victor Valle and Jeff Boyle joined the group, and Mike went downstairs for lunch. Billy switched channels to a television soap opera. Several more friends from Kingston High School came by the room to pay respects.

"You remember that song I wrote for you?" Victor asked during a lull in the conversation.

One of Victor's pleasures was composing songs in honor of his fighters. Billy's song, written before he'd won the title, fit loosely to the tune of "Hi Lili Hi Lo."

"Yeah, that was a good song. It's not something Michael Jackson would sing, but it's good."

Without prompting, Victor began to croon:

> Billy Costello is coming up
> Hooray, hooray, hurrah
> Billy Costello is coming up
> Hooray, hooray, hurrah
> He can punch with his left and right
> And knock you flat on your back
> Billy Costello is after the crown
> Lookout, lookout, my friend
> Billy Costello will be the champ
> Someday not far away.

As the last strains faded, Mike returned from lunch and introduced himself to Billy's high-school friends. "Your name sounds familiar," he told one of them. "Were you with Billy in the supermarket on that famous night?"

"No, sir. I had a date."

The next hour passed quietly. At three o'clock, Billy, Mike, Victor, and Jeff left the hotel for a light workout at the Ulster County Community Action Center, a converted schoolhouse built in 1867. On the second floor, in a makeshift gym, Billy changed into his gym clothes, and hit the speed bag for three minutes. There were no calisthenics, no jumping rope. It was a day for storing energy and violence. Physically and psychologically, Victor felt that Billy was at his peak. Nourishing his ring instincts was the only task left. Six minutes of reflex drills followed the speed bag work. Then trainer and fighter retreated to a corner, away from listeners, for a tête-à-tête.

Weapons alone don't win wars. Rather, the manner in which they're deployed determines effectiveness. So too, boxers must deploy their weapons in response to an opponent's weaknesses and strengths. Some trainers send their fighters into battle with detailed instructions. Others opt for a less comprehensive plan of attack. "My philosophy is not to give a fighter too much," Victor Valle once remarked. "Sometimes, you tell a fighter too many things, and if the other guy does the unexpected, it mixes him up. That's why I plan my fighters for two rounds only. Then, when I see what's happening, I tell them what to do next."

Now, Victor's instructions to Billy were straightforward and to the point: "Against Mamby you got to fight three minutes of every round. Don't pose like you do sometimes, waiting for the other guy to stop, because Mamby won't stop. He'll hit and run. He's gonna move all night, jabbing and circling to pile up points. He'll try like hell and never give up. Everything he does, he'll do to break your concentration. Don't fight his fight."

Billy nodded.

"To get inside," Victor continued, "you got two choices. You can wait for Mamby's jab, and slip to the side. Or you can wait for the jab, and counter with uppercuts or a straight right. Every time you get inside, I want you to rough him up. When the referee says to break, take only one step back. Under the rules that's all you gotta take. Then come right back. When Mamby moves side to side, keep putting on pressure. Don't stand still. Don't throw wild punches, because no one hits Mamby with wild punches. And no matter what happens, don't pull back. Against this guy you go forward the whole fight."

Word had spread that Billy was in the Community Action Center. By the time the workout was over, twenty onlookers had gathered. Most of them clustered around the fighter as he changed back into his street clothes. Several pressed forward with scraps of paper, asking for autographs.

Meanwhile across town in the Kingston Midtown Neighborhood Center where the fight would be held, a small army of technicians was at work. Sheets of black plastic had been placed over windows to maximize the effect of television lights. Makeshift camera scaffolding towered above rivers of cable on the hardwood floor. Folding wood chairs would be set up shortly. For the moment only the ring was in place. Standing in the midst of what appeared to be barely controlled turmoil was a small bearded man named Dave Fox, who coordinated television production for Don King–promoted fights. It was Fox's responsibility to oversee all technical work and interface with Michael Burks of CBS. Twenty-five freelance technicians and ten CBS employees were at their disposal.

Off to the side Sugar Ray Leonard stood eating a hot dog, conferring with Gil Clancy. Together with Tim Ryan they would provide commentary for the CBS broadcast. Clancy and Leonard were dressed in color-coordinated jogging outfits. They were waiting for boxing gloves so they could tape a prefight segment that would explain what Saoul Mamby had to do to beat Billy Costello. The gloves arrived, and the two men climbed into the ring. For the actual fight CBS would utilize five cameras, but now only one was in use. With Clancy playing the role of Costello, and Leonard imitating Mamby, they demonstrated how the challenger could win, acting out their scenario on the robin's-egg-blue canvas with the Don King logo on top.

Meanwhile back at the hotel, Carl King and Mamby had checked in, and the cocktail lounge was filled to overflowing. Two hookers sat at the bar, plying their trade without success. Several cornermen and sparring partners traded insults and jokes.

"What's long and hard on a black man?"

"I don't know."

"Third grade."

"All right, motherfucker. What's thirteen inches long and white?"

"I give up. What?"

"Nothing."

At 7:00 P.M. the WBC "rules meeting" began in a conference room on the ground floor of the Holiday Inn. No fighters were present. Mike and Victor were there on Billy's behalf. Also in attendance were Bill Prezant, who would be the chief second in Mamby's corner; Benny Georgino and Jimmy Montoya, who managed Jaime Garza and Juan Meza respectively; Mort Sharnik, Tim Ryan, and Gil Clancy of CBS; Peyton Sher for Don King Productions; and Marvin Kohn, Pete Della, and Edwin Campbell of the New York State Athletic Commission.

Dr. Romero Garcia, the WBC representative in charge of the fight, began the session by introducing the referee and judges. Under New York State law the appointment of ring officials fell within the domain of the State Athletic Commission. However, under WBC rules, Jose Sulaiman was empowered to make the appointments, and the bout needed WBC sanction to be advertised by CBS as a championship match. Ergo, WBC rules governed.

The referee would be Tony Perez—50 years old, a veteran official with 46 world title fights to his credit. Perez made his living as a whisky salesman, and had the reputation of "letting the fighters fight." Mike and Victor were pleased with his selection. A referee can make an enormous difference in the conduct of a fight. He alone decides the extent to which fighters will be allowed to maul and brawl on the inside, and to the extent it mattered, Perez fit Billy's style.

Arlen "Spider" Bynum—49 years old, a Texas attorney, and chairman of the WBC's Ring Officials Committee—was the first judge. Stuart Kirschenbaum—39, chairman of the Michigan Athletic Board of Control—was the second. Lou Filippo—a 58-year-old supervisor in production control for Cal-Doran Metalurgical Services—would be the third. In the event the bout went the distance, these three men would hold the ultimate power.

Pursuant to WBC rules, the fight would be scored on a "ten-point-must" basis. The winner of each round would receive ten points, the loser nine or less. For even rounds, each fighter would be awarded ten points. Technically, the judges' decision would be based on an evaluation of ring generalship, effective aggression, number of blows struck, damage done, and defense. But judging is an interpretive art, and controversial decisions, like cigar smoke, were a part of boxing. Mike wanted a knockout.

Much to the dismay of everyone, Romero Garcia insisted on reading the WBC rules governing championship fights aloud from beginning to end. There followed a half-hour rendition of 39 paragraphs, covering everything from beards on fighters to how hands should be taped. The only moment of conflict occurred when Prezant announced that Mamby would be wearing light-blue trunks. In a championship bout, choice of color belongs to the champ, and Billy had opted for dark blue. Mort Sharnik of CBS rose to object, saying that the network wanted Mamby in white so the contrast would be greater. Prezant relented.

The meeting adjourned at eight o'clock, with the announcement that the prefight weigh-in would be held at 7:00 A.M. That would give the first preliminary fighters, who went on at three o'clock, eight hours to replenish their systems. Billy's fight would start at five o'clock sharp. If either Billy or Saoul Mamby weighed more than 140 pounds at 7:00 A.M., he would be given two hours to "make weight." Then if a fighter was still overweight, the bout would go on. But if an overweight champion won, the title would be declared vacant.

A few minutes after eight P.M., Mike went to the dining room to eat dinner with Victor. "My gut feeling," he told the trainer, "is that the officials are honest. They're good people; I trust Jose Sulaiman to run an honest fight. Still, whenever you're in against a Don King fighter, you have to be little paranoid."

"What would you do if they robbed Billy on a decision?"

"I'd go absolutely, completely, one hundred percent berserk. If Billy gets robbed, I couldn't be held legally responsible for my actions."

Meanwhile, upstairs in Room 417, Billy was relaxing on his bed after a light dinner, talking with Jeff. As the hours passed he would become more demanding. No one would speak of tension. Like fear of defeat, it would go unmentioned unless the fighter himself brought up the subject. "Tread carefully" would be the guideline for the night.

A knock on the door interrupted the conversation. Jeff opened it, and found himself face to face with ten children of varying age, sex, and color, asking for autographs.

"Let 'em in," Billy said. For the next few minutes he signed his name and shook hands with each of the children. Then they left, and Mike came by with Victor and William Nack of *Sports Illustrated*. Despite the emotions of the moment, Nack was welcome. *Sports Illustrated* had over 2,500,000 subscribers, and was highly influential in determining which fights its readers watched on television. Ratings meant dollars. The interview with Nack lasted twenty minutes. The session was interrupted twice by knocks on the door and more requests for autographs from groups of children.

"Mamby seems like a nice guy," one of the children said.

"Yeah," Billy answered. "Except, if he gets you in trouble, he forgets to be nice."

After Nack left the conversation turned quiet. Everyone knew how much of himself Billy had invested in the fight, and in one way or another everyone was worried. For Mike there was concern that too many distractions had robbed Billy of emotional energy in the week leading up to the fight. For Victor there was apprehension as to whether the tools and fight plan he'd given his fighter were adequate to win. One of boxing's truisms holds, "They'll all go if you hit them right." What if Mamby landed the punch that turned the fight? "That's the problem with competition," Victor told himself. "You have a winner and a loser. These are human beings. Funny things can happen."

At 10:00 P.M. a State Athletic Commission representative came by the room to report that the offical scale to be used for the weigh-in had been set up on the ground floor.

"Go downstairs to check your weight," Victor instructed his fighter.

With Jeff at his side, Billy left. Minutes later, he returned with a grim look on his face. "We got a problem," he said.

"What kind of problem?"

"The scale downstairs says 143." Visably shaken, Billy went into the bathroom, stripped down naked, and stepped onto the scale he'd brought from New York. The needle registered 139. Then he stepped off and back on again—142.

"Where'd you get that piece of shit?" Mike demanded.

"At the hotel. I figured for all the money they charged, the scale would work."

"You found a bathroom scale in the hotel, and that's what you've been using to weigh yourself?"

"For the last week, yes."

A crisis had been reached. Billy had nine hours to lose three pounds or forfeit his title. Victor went into the bathroom and turned the shower hot water on full blast. Billy waited until steam filled the area, then closed the door after Victor had left. Ten, minutes later he emerged from the bathroom. "It's not hot enough," he said. Still naked, he stood silent while Victor covered his body with Albolene. Then trainer and fighter went downstairs to the hotel sauna, where Billy jumped rope and ran through a series of light calisthenics for fifteen minutes. At 10:50 P.M. he went back to the offical scale—141½.

"You gotta run," Victor told him.

The danger was obvious. Too much exercise would weaken Billy for the fight, but the excess weight had to be lost. Back in his room Billy donned jogging clothes, then went downstairs with Victor, Jr., who had been summoned by his father. The two men drove to a secluded area where Billy ran for two miles. At 11:20 P.M. the official scale read 141. "All right," Victor told the fighter. "The last pound will come off by itself tonight."

Upstairs again, the trainer spread three towels across the bed and ordered Billy to lie on his back.

"What for?"

"I'm gonna give you a rubdown to loosen your muscles and help you relax."

"How much do you weigh, Victor?"

"What are you, crazy or something? It don't matter what I weigh. I'm not fighting tomorrow. But I'll tell you something. I can see from this, someday you'll be fat like me. And when that happens, I'll go to your house, and say to you, 'Hello, fatso.' "

At midnight, Mike and Victor went to bed. Everyone had to be up in seven hours for the weigh-in. At twelve-thirty Billy decided he wanted some gum. His throat was parched from the evening's work, and drinking water would put weight back on again. Jeff went down to the hotel desk and spent ten minutes persuading the night manager to open the restaurant, go behind the cashier's counter, and take out a pack of Wrigley's spearmint gum. Knowing he wouldn't be able to sleep, Billy watched television until 1:30 A.M., then turned off the set and lay in the dark with his eyes open, thinking about the fight.

"The night before a fight is when it hits me," he said later. "When I'm trying to go to sleep. In the back of my mind I keep thinking maybe the other guy has something I can't handle. I worry about getting thumbed in the eye, butted, or cut by a lucky punch. A thumb would be worst. You can't see punches coming from the side if your eye is shut. Your balance is off. Just walking down the street with one eye shut makes you dizzy. Imagine someone trying to punch you in the head when you're dizzy like that."

The minutes ticked by. Two o'clock . . . two-thirty. . . . "In the history books I'm a world champion," Billy told himself. "No one can ever take that away from me. Twenty-eight times I've gone one-on-one, and no one could beat me."

Three o'clock. . . . "If I lose, there'll be all those people laughing at me, saying they knew Billy Costello was never any good. Boxing is something. It can make you a hero and wash you up, all before you're thirty. It's crazy, it drives you nuts. . . . I can beat Mamby. I'm gonna beat Mamby. I gotta think that way. Otherwise there's no reason to fight."

Sometime close to 3:30 A.M., Billy Costello drifted off to sleep.

21

Time is perpetually ticking away for a fighter. His career is short. Opportunities are few. He has a limited number of weeks to prepare for each bout. And then, suddenly, on the day of a fight, time is inverted. Its pace becomes unbearably slow, and everyone whose life is wrapped up with the fighter questions how many more times the waiting can be endured. Everyone who cares about the fighter suffers a queasy feeling in the pit of the stomach, and begins to wonder whether there will come a time when the strain of waiting will overwhelm them all.

On the day of the fight, Saturday, November 3, Billy woke up at 5:30 A.M. For half an hour he lay in bed with his eyes open, then roused Jeff and turned on the television to watch "Wild Kingdom." At six-thirty a retired Kingston cop named Pat Colbert came by the room. Nine years earlier, Colbert had taken Billy's confession and placed him under arrest when he went to the police station to turn himself in after robbing the supermarket. Now, knowing that a fighter needs replenishment after a weigh-in, Colbert had brought three quarts of his wife's homemade chicken noodle soup.

Victor knocked on the door at 6:50 A.M. Mike—his hair uncombed, badly in need of cutting, and standing on end—arrived two minutes later. "You look like a white Don King," the trainer told him.

Victor was tired. Like Billy, he had spent most of the night awake, imagining Saoul Mamby jabbing, moving, dancing in the ring. "Did you get any sleep?" he asked his fighter.

"A couple of hours."

"Any good dreams?"

"Yeah, I was dreaming about a big glass of water."

Next to the bed lay several shriveled lemons that Billy had sucked on during the night.

Dressing quickly, Billy pulled on a pair of faded blue jeans, sneakers, and a yellow T-shirt with "Gerry Cooney" inscribed in green letters on the front. Then flanked by Mike and Victor he went downstairs for the weigh-in. At 7:00 A.M. sharp they entered Gallery A, which was crowded with preliminary fighters, CBS personnel, and New York State Athletic Commission officials. A dozen townspeople, most of them wearing Billy Costello sweatshirts, looked on.

Ten minutes later, dressed in a cobalt-blue jogging suit, Saoul Mamby entered the room. Two men were with him. One was Al Smith—a wizened black man, 80 years old, wearing a peaked cap, a red-and-black checked jacket, and oversized jeans. Smith had worked Mamby's corner for years. The other was Bill Prezant, employed full-time as a cornerman, trainer, and cut man by Don King. Over a 45-year career, Prezant had worked 5,000 fights and been in the corner for a host of champions including Larry Holmes, Michael Dokes, Aaron Pryor, Alexis Arguello, Carlos Ortiz, and Roberto Duran. A good cornerman motivates his fighter, explains why he got hit, formulates strategy, and stems the flow of blood when necessary. Prezant was a professional on all scores.

At 7:11 A.M., Billy stepped to the scale. Every ounce of superfluous fat had been removed from his body. As the onlookers pushed closer, he removed his shirt, sneakers, jeans, and underwear. Then he stepped onto the scale. Romero Garcia, the WBC representative, adjusted the weights. Victor and Mike held their breath . . . 140 pounds; perfect weight. Mamby followed, weighing in at 139¼.

Billy put his clothes back on, and went through a side door into the adjoining Gallery B. There Mike handed him the first quart-container of chicken noodle soup. Lifting it to his lips, Billy drank slowly until the entire quart was gone. Several children stood by. "Good luck, Mr. Costello," one of them said.

Billy drank another half-quart of soup, then returned to Gallery A, where Victor was examining four pairs of Everlast gloves. Each fighter would designate two pairs (a primary and a back-up) for use in the fight.

"Try these on," the trainer said, handing a pair to Billy.

The fighter did as instructed.

"How do they feel?"

"Good."

Using a felt-tipped pen, Victor inscribed his initials, followed by "xxx" on the inside lining of each glove. Then, on a second pair, he wrote "VV xxx #2." Al Smith and Saoul Mamby duplicated the process, and the four sets of gloves were handed to a commission inspector for safekeeping. Then Billy went back to Gallery B for a brief physical administered by Edwin Campbell, medical director of the New York State Athletic Commission.

"How do you feel?" Dr. Campbell asked.

"Fine."

"Sometimes I think the most brutal thing about boxing are these seven o'clock weigh-ins."

Billy nodded.

The conversation continued as Campbell made the necessary checks. "I see where several states are licensing women to box," the doctor said. "I hate that. It sets a bad example. It's unfeminine and dangerous. Of course, I like the lady wrestlers."

One chair away, Saoul Mamby sat patiently, waiting for his own physical. Several reporters hovered nearby.

"Are you ready for Costello?" one of them asked.

"I'm always ready," Mamby answered. "Whenever I train for a fight, I make my opponent out to be as good as possible. I visualize a strong, fast, smart opponent. I build him up in my mind as much as I can. That way, when the fight comes, if he has those qualities I'm ready. And if he doesn't, I'm ahead of the game."

"Will fighting in Costello's hometown bother you?"

"No way. I won the title in Korea. I defended successfully in Indonesia and Nigeria. I've fought all over the world in the other guy's backyard. I've been in arenas where the only people cheering for me were the men in my corner. I'm gonna win this fight."

At 7:50 A.M., Billy went to the hotel dining room for breakfast with Mike, Victor, Victor, Jr., and Mike's wife, Stella, who had arrived the previous night. After ordering scrambled eggs, pancakes, bacon, toast, and juice, he decided he wasn't hungry, drank the juice and left the rest. Then he went upstairs to his room, lay down on the bed, and called his wife. Jane would be at the fight; Billy's mother wouldn't. "I want my son to get what he wants out of boxing and then get out," Dolores Costello once said. "When a fight is over, I watch the tape because it makes Billy happy, but I don't like it."

"I don't go to church much, but I believe in God," Billy had said after winning the title. "And my mother is so into God and prays so much before every fight, sometimes I think that's what brings me through."

At nine o'clock, Billy finished talking with Jane and left the receiver off the hook. Jeff hung a "do not disturb" sign on the door, and the two men talked for an hour. Then Billy fell asleep. Shortly before noon, Mike knocked on the door and woke the fighter up.

"Lunch in twenty minutes," he announced.

Still dressed in jeans and the Gerry Cooney T-shirt, Billy got out of bed and turned on the television. The cremation of India's martyred Prime Minister, Indira Gandhi, videotaped earlier in the day, was taking place. "Man," he said, staring at the screen, "it's a fucked-up world when everyone goes around killing people. I only want one child. This world is so crazy, I don't want to worry about bringing more children into it."

At twelve-fifteen, Billy and Jeff went downstairs for lunch. "They burned her right on TV," Billy told Mike, recounting the morning's events. "Can you believe that?"

A stream of wellwishers came by to pay respects. Billy ate lightly—rice, boiled shrimp, fruit salad, and tea. Then he returned upstairs and lay down on the bed. The tension was mounting. "Do you know what it's like," he told Jeff. "Every time, before a big fight, it's like right before I got married. I want to do it, but I'm nervous."

At one-fifteen, Mike and Victor left the hotel and drove to the arena with Billy's younger brother Vinnie, who would be fighting in the afternoon's first bout. Vinnie was something of an enigma as a fighter. One day in the gym he'd look like a million dollars; the next day he'd be off. He had all the moves, but was unable to consistently put them together.

"Your fight is at five o'clock," Victor told Billy just before he left. "Get to the dressing room around three-thirty."

After Victor and Mike had gone, Billy turned the television on again, and began watching the football game between Syracuse and Pittsburgh. At 1:35 P.M. he decided that he and Jeff should take a walk. Outside it was a perfect autumn day; the kind of weather made for college football homecomings. The sky was blue. Touches of orange, red, yellow, and brown hung from the mostly bare trees. The two men walked for forty minutes, with Jeff working to keep the conversation going. Occasional passers-by would stop, stare, and call out, "Hi, Billy," or "Good luck, champ."

"It feels strange, walking around like this, where I grew up," Billy said. "This is my home town. There are lots of memories."

At two-fifteen they returned to the hotel. Syracuse was leading Pittsburgh 13–0 late in the third quarter. Billy retied both his shoe laces, then switched channels to CBS, where Wisconsin was ahead of Iowa 10 to 3. The minutes moved slowly. Time was the enemy.

"As long as I win," Billy said, "that's all I care about."

Two-thirty. . . .

Two-forty. . . .

Iowa scored to tie the game at ten apiece.

Jeff thumbed through the pages of a local newspaper.

Several times Billy wiped the perspiration from his palms on the side of his jeans.

Two-fifty. . . .

Two-fifty-five. . . .

At three o'clock, Billy looked at his watch and got up from the bed. "Let's go to work," he said.

Jeff drove, easing the white Chrysler LeBaron out of the Holiday Inn parking lot onto Washington Avenue. Down Washington, left onto Hurley. They followed Hurley to a point where it fed into Clinton, past a huge billboard with red, white, and blue letters that read:

WELCOME TO KINGSTON
HOME OF BILLY COSTELLO
WBC SUPERLIGHTWEIGHT CHAMP

Left onto Albany, right onto Broadway. At 3:15 P.M. they arrived at the red-brick Midtown Neighborhood Center.

The first preliminary bout was underway—Vinnie Costello versus Ricky Lehman of Tuscon, Arizona. Despite a ticket scale of $100, $50, $40, $30, $20, the arena was jammed. Billy walked past the stands, unnoticed at first, toward the stage at the far end of the hall. Then the crowd took note of his presence, and warm applause sounded as he climbed the stairs, disappeared behind the stage curtain, and made his way to the dressing room with Jeff beside him.

"Youth lounge; Monday-Friday; 2:30–4:30," read the letters painted on the dressing room door. Inside, a CBS technician, Dr. Edwin Campbell, a New York State Athletic Commission inspector, and Billy's brother Tony were waiting. The room was twenty-six feet long and half as wide, with industrial orange carpet, a worn olive sofa, and eight folding metal chairs. Three of the walls were painted white; the fourth, blue with a bright rainbow mural. An "Asteroids" video game stood against the far wall.

Dr. Campbell handed Billy a small plastic cup for the required prefight urine sample. Billy took it to the men's room and returned soon after, the chore done. A small television monitor set against the south wall showed the progress of Vinnie's fight against Ricky Lehman, now in the fourth round. Billy sat on one of the folding chairs and watched impassively as the battle unfolded. The fight was close, with Vinnie holding his own. There was no sound on the monitor, but the roar of the crowd sounded through the dressing room walls. Then the bout ended, and the ring announcer's voice heralded the score—a unanimous decision for Vinnie Costello.

"Put on a tape," Billy ordered.

Jeff reached for the casette machine he'd brought with him and turned it on. At three-forty, flanked by Mike and Victor, Vinnie entered the room. The skin above his left eye had been sliced open. Wordlessly, he slumped on a chair next to his brother, breathing hard.

"You okay?" Billy asked.

Vinnie nodded. "He was a tough bastard, real tough."

Victor came over and examined Vinnie's eye. "It don't need stitches," the trainer said. "A butterfly bandage will do the job."

At 3:43 P.M., Billy stripped down to his Gerry Cooney T-shirt, and pulled on a pair of blue and white briefs, white socks, and blue boxing shoes. Two minutes later the WBC superbantamweight championship bout between Jaime Garza and Juan Meza began. Garza, undefeated in 40 fights, with 38 knockouts, was the heavy favorite. Meza, the challenger, had lost six times. Once again Billy turned toward the television monitor. Early in the first round Meza was flattened by a left hook. He rose, took some more punches, then rallied in stunning fashion to knock Garza out with seconds left in the round. The message was clear. One punch flush on the jaw, and any champion could lose his crown.

With the music still playing, Billy took off his T-shirt. Victor rubbed baby oil and alcohol on his legs, torso, and arms. Then the T-shirt went back on. Off to the side the WBC championship belt lay folded on the floor. Made of green vinyl and tin, it resembled an oversized cigar band or gaudy trinket from a Times Square novelty store.

At four o'clock referee Tony Perez entered the room. His job in the upcoming bout would be to enforce the rules, and if necessary stop the fight to protect a boxer in trouble. And since fighters seldom listen to a referee's pro forma instructions in the ring immediately before a bout, prudence dictated a visit beforehand to each dressing room.

"Billy, I want a good clean fight," Perez began. "If you score a knockdown, go to the farthest neutral corner. Stay there. Don't come out until I tell you to resume fighting or you'll be hurting yourself. Stay there until I call you. Then you can go for the kill. The three-knockdown rule has been waived. That means if a man is knocked down three times in any round, instead of automatically stopping the fight, I'll use my discretion. The bell can't save you or Mamby from being counted out except for the last round. Any questions?"

"No, sir."

"All right; good luck to you."

Perez left. At 4:10 P.M. the first casette ended, and Jeff put on a recording by Lionel Richie. At 4:18 a commission official came in to announce that it was time for the fighters to tape their hands. Mike went across the hall to Mamby's dressing room to observe the process, and one of Mamby's aides came in to watch Billy in return.

Carefully, as if bandaging a week-old infant, Victor wrapped a roll of gauze around Billy's left wrist and hand; then taped over the gauze as though building a cast. In the background Lionel Richie sounded:

> Well, my friends, the time has come
> To raise the roof and have some fun
> Throw away the work to be done
> Let the music play

At 4:28 P.M. the taping was done. Mamby's aide nodded his approval, and a State Athletic Commission inspector applied a stamp that read "N.Y.S.A.C." over the binding on each hand. Still clad only in shoes, socks, underwear, and a Gerry Cooney T-shirt, Billy stood up and shadow boxed for thirty seconds as a release of nervous energy. Then, alone with his thoughts, he sat back down on the gray folding metal chair. Twenty minutes had passed since he'd last spoken.

At 4:34 P.M. Victor gave Billy three sips of water, then put the bottle in a plastic bucket that would be carried into the ring. During the fight, Victor would be "chief second." Mike and Victor, Jr., would serve as the second and third men in Billy's corner. Under state law they were permitted to bring ice, a taped water bottle, Vaseline, a sponge, Q-tips, towels, adrenalin, and a coagulant (Avitene, Thrombin, Thromboplastin, or Fibroplastin) into the ring. A second bucket for spit, blood, and excess water was also allowed. No other substance to aid the fighter could be used. In the event of a cut, Victor would be responsible for stemming the flow of blood. "It's mostly in the bottle," he would say later. "You got to know pressure points that stop the blood long enough to apply the solution, and sometimes you need a strong stomach. But anyone can be a good cut man if he isn't afraid of blood."

At 4:40 P.M. Billy removed his Gerry Cooney T-shirt for the last time. Victor handed him a black protective cup, and helped lace it over the fighter's hips. Then Billy pulled on his cobalt-blue boxing trunks, and began to bend at the waist, rotating his torso counterclockwise.

4:45 P.M.: Left glove first, Victor laced on Billy's gloves.

4:46 P.M.: The trainer smeared Vaseline on Billy's face and arms.

4:47 P.M.: Mort Sharnik of CBS came into the dressing room to wish Billy well.

4:48 P.M.: Billy began to shadow box again, this time to break a sweat and limber up. On the television monitor, his interview with Tim Ryan of CBS, taped a week earlier at Gleason's Gym, was being broadcast nationwide:

RYAN: For years, Costello has labored in the considerable shadow of his stablemate Gerry Cooney and, after winning the title, Costello's well of resentment bubbled up in an interview with a boxing writer. Costello says the trouble between the two men is over now. But is it?

As Ryan spoke the camera closed in on a photostat of the Michael Marley article, with the now-famous quotation highlighted in yellow: "Hey, let's face it. Gerry was the big man then. He was the white guy, the attraction. Now I'm finally getting my chance. I'm the one who won the fight. And even if I never did anything else, I've done something Gerry has never done. I've won the title."

In the dressing room, Victor and Mike shook their heads. Jeff Boyle broke the silence. "I hope Gerry is getting a drink of water," he said. Then Billy and Ryan were back on screen again.

BILLY: I didn't mean it. At the time, I was really mad. I didn't mean it and I tried to explain to Gerry, but he didn't want to hear it. I'm trying to apologize to the guy and tell him like a man that I'm sorry I said that. I didn't really mean it.

RYAN: Do you get along with him now?

BILLY: Whoa! It's shaky. He's still mad at me, which I can't blame him. But then again, he didn't want to hear my side of the story.

4:51 P.M.: The demonstration taped the day before by Gil Clancy and Sugar Ray Leonard came on the monitor. Billy pulled on his robe. "Remember," Victor told him, "you got to control Mamby's jab. Jab yourself and look to throw the right the first couple of rounds. But the main thing is, control his jab. Do that, and you got the fight won."

4:52 P.M.: A CBS technician opened the door. "Three minutes," he shouted.

Emotions were high. Billy's future was on the line.

"I can't do any more for you," Victor told him. "Now you do it on your own. My heart's in your gloves."

At 4:55 P.M. Billy stood up and pointed to the door. "Let's go," he said. "It's party time." Flanked by Victor and Mike, he left the dressing room and walked to the stage overlooking the arena floor. Then the curtain was drawn aside, and the crowd erupted.

"Billy! Billy!" Again and again, the chant sounted as he walked down the aisle, the Vaseline on his face glistening beneath hot television lights. "Billy! Billy!"

"People were reaching out and touching me," he remembered later. "I didn't want it. I was praying, and staring at the ring, and saying to myself I didn't want to lose. I was trying to bring up the meanness and hunger I'd stored inside."

A commission inspector parted the bottom two ring ropes. Billy climbed the stairs to his corner, stepped between the strands onto the illuminated blue canvas, and the cheers crescendoed to a near-deafening din. Across the ring Saoul Mamby stood waiting, his eyes gleaming, beads of sweat and Vaseline on his forehead. It was an electric moment—two men with one purpose, and only one could win.

A rotund man named Ward Todd, dressed in a black tuxedo and red bow tie, reached for a microphone and moved to the center of the ring: "Ladies and gentlemen, welcome to Kingston, New York. This is the main event. Introducing first, in the red corner, the challenger from the Bronx, New York, the former superlightweight champion, weighing 139¼ pounds, Saoul Mamby. . . . And now, in the blue corner, the current world champion—" The roar grew louder, all but drowning out Todd's words. "—weighing 140 pounds, the pride of Kingston, New York, Billy Costello."

THE BLACK LIGHTS

In the delirium that followed, Tony Perez called the fighters to the center of the ring for last-minute instructions. The two men stared at each other. Then Mamby grinned. "I'm gonna get you, Billy."

Billy said nothing. The fighters returned to their respective corners, and Victor inserted Billy's mouthpiece. "Remember," the trainer told him. "Control his jab. He's gonna try to jab and follow with the right hand. Control the jab, and you win."

The bell rang. Billy Costello and Saoul Mamby were alone, one on one. The fight had begun. Moving to ring center, the two men touched gloves. Mamby led with a jab. Billy advanced. Mamby jabbed again, and followed with a straight right—the first real punch of the fight. Mamby with a righthand lead. Mamby with a double jab. Billy threw a wild left hook, and the challenger ducked under it. Then Billy landed a left hook to the body—his first solid punch. Mamby jabbed, threw a short right behind it, and scored again. The challenger kept jabbing. Billy kept trying to time the jab and land a counter right over the top, but the challenger was an elusive target. Billy's counter was falling short. Again Mamby jabbed, and followed with a right. The round was half over. Seconds were moving slowly. Fractions of an inch seemed like miles. Mamby was still jabbing, with the champion continuing to fall just short with his counter right. Then Billy landed a solid left hook to the body, and Mamby moved into a clinch. Twenty-five seconds were left in the round. Billy was the aggressor. A left jab and straight right backed Mamby up. A left hook grazed the jaw of the challenger. Then round one was over. It had been close, with an edge for the champion because he'd been the aggressor. But someone so inclined could have scored it for Mamby.

Between rounds Mike held an icepack to the back of Billy's neck. Victor wiped the grease from his face with a sponge, and handed his mouthpiece to Victor, Jr., to be rinsed. Then he reapplied Vaseline while giving instructions: "Stay nice and cool. Shorten your punches. Go easy. You got a lot of rounds ahead of you."

Round two. Billy came out with a left hook to the body, missed a wild hook, then landed a short hook and solid right to the challenger's jaw—the best punches of the fight so far. Mamby jabbed. Billy came in underneath, mauling the body, and the challenger held on, forcing the referee to break them apart. Like a steel spring, Billy moved back in. A straight right caught Mamby flush on the cheek, forcing him to hold again. Billy, his left hand free, pumped a hook to the body. Mamby back-pedaled. Billy jabbed, missed an overhand right, and followed with a left hook to the body. A left hook to the jaw moved the challenger back another step. A hard right to the kidneys shook him, and backed him into a corner. Then Mamby came forward. Billy was the aggressor, but the challenger wasn't running. He was forcing the champion to fight, and making him miss as often as he landed. An exchange of right hands saw Billy land first. Then, with thirty seconds left, Mamby landed a left hook flush on Billy's jaw. The champion kept coming. Both men now knew that the challenger lacked the power to stop Billy in his tracks with a single blow. If Mamby were to prevail, it would be over the long haul.

"You're doing good," Victor told his fighter after the round. "But don't get cocky. Each time he jabs, slip inside and hook to the body or throw the right hand over the top."

Round three. Again Billy came out hard, but Mamby fought back, firing a hard right, pumping two jabs that forced Billy back. "Hands up," Victor shouted from the corner. "Keep your hands up." Regaining the initiative with his jab, the champion backed Mamby into a neutral corner. Deftly, the challenger escaped, moving to ring center, surveying his foe. Billy was looser now, punching in combinations, landing more effectively to the body, pressuring his opponent. Mamby's jab was coming more slowly, and he wasn't following it as often with the right. One minute left in the round. . . . Thirty seconds. . . . Billy continued to crowd the challenger, backing him around the ring, landing occasional body shots but not doing much damage. With fifteen seconds left he landed a counter right again over Mamby's jab. It was the champion's round.

"All right," Victor told him during the minute break. "We're gonna change the tactics a little. When this guy jabs, move to the side and punch with the left uppercut. Nice and cool; stay smart; don't get careless."

Round four. Mamby began with a double jab that landed but lacked force. Billy jabbed back, then followed with a hook to the body, a left uppercut, and chopping right to the challenger's head. Stalking his man with animal-like grace, the champion pressed forward. Mamby jabbed, and again Billy landed a counter right over the top. Mamby backed off. Billy missed several hooks, slid to the left, and landed a solid uppercut to the chin off the challenger's jab. Mamby missed a wild left hook in attempted retaliation. The champion landed a hook to the midsection after slipping another jab. A chopping overhand right to the temple forced the challenger to hold. The heavy punches all belonged to Billy Costello. No real damage had been done because Mamby knew how to slip and slide and turn his head a fraction of an inch at the last split-second to absorb a blow, but the champion's assault would take its toll as the bout wore on.

"You're doing well," Victor said again after round four. "Don't get overconfident. Forget the head for a while, and go more to the body."

Round five. Mamby was in retreat; Billy was stalking. A left hook to the body and hook to the chin shook the challenger. A hard right over the jab caught Mamby squarely and snapped his head back. The challenger's jab had been neutralized now. Each time he threw it, he ran the risk of a harder counter right in return. Still, Mamby was game. A solid left hook to the body sent a sting through the champion. Then Mamby jabbed, and with the experience of a professional followed through with his head, risking a clash of brows should Billy throw a righthand in return. "Watch the butt," Victor shouted. Billy fired a double jab, then a hook. Mamby kept jabbing, but he was starting to miss by a lot, which hadn't happened too often in his career. Seconds before the end of the round, the challenger again jabbed and followed with his head. "Watch your head," the referee, Tony Perez, cautioned.

Round six. Once again Billy was off his stool quickly, crowding, pursuing, throwing hooks to the body with the force of a building demolition ball. Thirty-five seconds into the round, Mamby jabbed and again followed with his head down, but this time Billy wasn't countering with the right. Instead he was coming low with a hook to the body, and as momentum brought him up and in, the two men clashed heads, the top of Billy's against Mamby's brow. Then they separated, and a thin slice was visible over the challenger's left eyebrow. For the rest of the round, challenger and champion fought on even terms, but the damage had been done. First blood had been drawn. And if the cut deepened, blood would flow into Mamby's eye, obscuring his vision, making it even harder for him to defend.

The fight was now half over, with Billy Costello in control. He was fresh; Mamby was tired. Not only was the champion ahead on points, he was dominating on a more primitive level of energy and aggression. For the first six rounds he had been beating Saoul Mamby, taking away the tools the challenger needed to win. Now he would take away the tools that Mamby needed to survive.

In the challenger's corner, Bill Prezant worked on the cut above Mamby's eye. The procedure was standard—wipe away the ring grease and grime; swab in Adrenalin; apply pressure until the Adrenalin caused the blood vessels to constrict and small clots to form; reapply Vaseline, stroking away from the eye. One minute was his only grace to perform it all.

Round seven. Billy stepped up the assault, continuing the professional workmanlike brutal job of bringing another professional down. For perhaps ninety seconds the two men battled on even terms. Then a hard righthand lead rocked Mamby. Another right smashed against the challenger's cheek, spinning his head to the side. A left hook, a straight right, and second left hook to the body—all in combination—landed with explosive power. Mamby was hurt, and in the tradition of the trade, he gestured with his hand for more. Billy obliged. An overhand right rocked the challenger, forcing him to hold on. For the first time in the fight, Mamby was starting to take real punishment. The brutalization had begun.

"Stay clever," Victor instructed between rounds. "Watch for the butt. When you're in close, put your head under his chin or on his shoulder."

Round eight. Mamby had been punished in the last round, and he came out determined to be more aggressive. But as the round progressed he began to wear down. Now Billy's jab was landing, with hard rights coming behind. A hook to the body; another jab. A series of overhand rights broke Mamby down a little more. Then a hard straight right split the challenger's lip, and blood began to flow. With the intensity of a panther, the champion stalked his foe. All Mamby had left was guile and courage, but he wouldn't fold. Stepping inside a left hook, he launched a counter blow to the pit of the champion's stomach, and for the first time in the fight, Billy held on as a bolt of pain flashed through his insides. Then the battle resumed, with Mamby tasting his own blood. A left hook to the jaw jolted the challenger. A chopping overhand right caught him leaning in. The two men clinched, and his right hand free, Billy pumped several more blows to the body. An overhand right rocked Mamby again at the bell, and for a brief moment the fighters stood still, searching for something in each other's eyes. Then they touched gloves in a gesture of mutual respect, and returned to their corners. "He takes a good punch," Billy told Victor. "He's tough."

Round nine. Mamby was still throwing punches, but missing by more than before. Almost as soon as the round began, Billy backed him into a corner with a series of jabs and left hooks that landed like shots from a cannon. The challenger's jab was now all but useless. Each time he leaned in, Billy countered over the top with a right hand. When the challenger followed with his head, the champion's uppercut was there. All the heavy punches belonged to Billy. A double left hook to the body; a left hook to the head. Sledgehammer blows. The combinations repeated, bending Mamby's face out of shape, but still he was there. Not only hadn't he quit, he was still trying to win, throwing punches, forcing the champion to work three minutes of every round. "Hook him," Victor shouted from the corner. "Short punches! Hook him, son." A left hook to the body followed by a left hook to the jaw jerked Mamby's head to the side. Again he sought to retaliate, but his strength and relexes were gone. Once more he clinched, and as Perez broke them apart the champion unleashed a left hook to the body followed by a chopping overhand right and another hook that sent Mamby back at the bell.

Round ten. Mamby was traveling on hostile forbidding terrain in a violent storm the likes of which he had never experienced before. He was a beaten fighter, forcing his arms to move faster and punch harder, courageously refusing to accept the inevitable. Two stiff jabs backed Billy against the ropes. Then the challenger scored with a stiff right and left hook to the body. Yet even as the punches landed, Billy seemed to be growing larger and his adversary diminishing in size. Undaunted by the blows, the champion came on. A hard right to the ribs, two jabs, and a left hook to the jaw sent Mamby spinning. A left hook to the body; a right to the head. Then a hard straight right rocked the challenger and sent a spray of perspiration arcing into the crowd. Still, Mamby refused to fall. Unrelenting, Billy continued to press the advantage with savage body blows.

Round eleven. Mamby was desperately behind, hurt, but still trying to win. He jabbed. Billy countered with a straight right, and again spray from the challenger's face filled the air. The champion pursued. Mamby countered, and gathering his resources, pressed forward, backing Billy against the ropes. Then came a sequence frozen in time, a moment that captured everything most courageous and cruel in the world of boxing. Mamby began to throw a left jab—a jab that had been slowed by ten rounds of sledgehammer blows, a jab that even had it landed, wouldn't have done much harm. And as the jab came toward him, Billy Costello countered with a left uppercut fashioned in hell. The blow landed flush on Saoul Mamby's jaw, ripping his teeth through his mouthpiece, tearing them through the skin between his mouth and the cleft of his chin. Mamby's head snapped back. A geyser of blood spurted into the air, splattering the canvas and spectators at ringside. Only the strength of the muscles in his legs kept the challenger from collapsing. And in that moment, two looks flashed across his eyes like the end of a bad dream. The first look was that of a dying animal about to be torn apart by a beast of prey. The second was a snarl of savage hatred and fury. And then, as quickly as they had come, the looks were gone. And methodically, the action resumed, with Billy Costello moving in, picking his punches, taking his time. And Saoul Mamby fought on, blood streaming from his chin, spreading across his body like water from a giant tributary feeding smaller streams. It stained his trunks and splashed onto the ring canvas. And yet, incredibly, for the next two minutes the two men fought on even terms until, with fifteen seconds left in the round, Mamby exacted a measure of revenge. The challenger jabbed; the champion countered. Again their heads collided, and Billy Costello pulled back, knowing that the blood washing across his face was now at least partially his own, flowing from an ugly slice across his right eyelid.

Round twelve. Mamby, his face a red mask, pressed determinedly on. As a professional fighter, he had an ethic; he could not quit. He was required to go as far as body and spirit allowed, regardless of the beating he had endured. No matter how badly battered, he was obligated to keep coming, spitting blood, forcing his arms, legs, lungs, and heart to respect his will. He was required to fight, irrespective of the cost, unless and until someone else said "no more." One minute left. . . . Thirty seconds. . . . The two men traded punches. Then came the final bell, and an embrace between warriors who had earned the right to be proud.

The scoring of the judges was anticlimatic:

> Stuart Kirschenbaum: 119 to 109
> Lou Filippo: 119 to 109
> Spider Bynum: 118 to 110

Each official gave Mamby the last round. Only Bynum had given him another.

After the fight, the champion's dressing room was crowded with wellwishers, commission officials, and reporters. Billy's wife Jane and his brothers Steve, Vinnie, and Tony stood to the side as the others pressed forward. Amid the din, Billy sat on the same folding metal chair he'd gloved up on an hour earlier. Blood was seeping from his right eyelid. Angry welts covered his neck and upper body. As Victor applied disinfectant to the wound, the surrounding reporters fired questions.

"Now that it's over, what do you think of Saoul Mamby?"

"He's slick, a real tough son-of-a-bitch. I hit him about ten good shots that would have knocked most fighters down, and he just kept coming."

"Were you hurt at all during the fight?"

"Not really. He hit me with a couple of hooks to the body that I'll feel tomorrow. And early in the fight I got caught by a hook to the jaw and a straight right. But I hit him more than he hit me."

"How would you compare this with your other fights?"

"This was tougher than Shields or Curry. The way Mamby boxes, lots of times I couldn't do what I wanted. And he's tough. That uppercut I hit him with in the eleventh round, anybody else I've fought would have gone down."

"Were you surprised he was able to stay on his feet?"

"Yeah, I guess so. Lot's of fighters are tough until they get hit, and then they fall apart. When you hit Mamby, he gets tougher. When I hit a guy with my best punch and he don't go nowhere, that tells me, 'Hey, relax, take your time.' "

A commission doctor came into the room with a request for a postfight urine sample. Billy went to the bathroom, then returned to more questions.

"How come you ran for most of the last round?"

"The fight was won. I was cut and the blood was making my vision blurry. I figured why take a chance on making the cut worse."

"What was the key to winning this fight?"

"Everything Mamby does works off his jab. I took away the jab, and then I had him."

"What will you do with all the money?"

"Taxes. The car is broke. I'll put as much as I can in the bank, but Christmas is coming and I got lots of relatives who'll be expecting something."

"Are you satisfied with the way you performed today?"

"Yeah, I won."

Dr. Steven Goodman, a plastic surgeon, came into the room and examined the cut. "You'll need stitches," he told the fighter. "I'll put them in now if you want."

Billy looked toward Victor, who nodded.

"All right, get it over with," the fighter said.

Goodman administered a shot of novacaine to deaden the pain, then began to work. Fifteen stitches. It was the first time in his career that Billy had been seriously cut, and no matter how good a job Goodman did, the scar tissue would never be as strong as normal skin. The eye would be a target for opponents in the future.

Throughout the stitching, Billy sat impassively. Victor watched with a concerned look. Then when the job was done, trainer and fighter embraced. "I'm proud of you, son," Victor said. "You fought a good fight. Keep struggling, don't change. God smiled when he made you."

An hour later, at the Holiday Inn, Billy, Victor, and Mike went separate ways. Billy was exhausted. After several minutes of handshaking he went upstairs to bed. Victor dawdled in the hotel lobby, engaging in post mortems, until a bellhop approached and handed him a pink slip. "Congratulations to everybody," the message read. The signature, taken by the hotel switchboard operator, was Gerry Cooney's. Slowly the trainer read the message through twice, then folded it in half, and slipped it in his pocket. "Maybe this is a new beginning," he said.

Meanwhile Mike had gone to wait outside Peyton Sher's room with Benny Georgino and Jimmy Montoya, while Sher added up the afternoon's gate receipts. When the task was done, the fighters would be paid. In boxing, checks are picked up as soon as possible.

"That's quite a fighter you got," Georgino said. "Billy doesn't just beat people. He beats them up."

Mike nodded. "Billy took everything out of Saoul Mamby but his heart."

A reporter came by with word that Edwin Rosario, the WBC lightweight champ, had been knocked out in the fourth round of his afternoon bout in Puerto Rico. Two fighters, Rosario and Garza, had lost their titles in the course of an hour. In both instances, Don King had options on the new champion.

"We dodged a bullet," Mike said. "Now, with a little luck, Billy will be a top-echelon attraction. People are finally starting to realize how good he is."

Georgino knocked on Sher's door. "Come on, we're hungry."

"A few more minutes," a voice from inside said.

* * *

Room 212 of the Holiday Inn was virtually identical to the others—two double beds, a color television, a bureau, nighttable, two chairs. Saoul Mamby lay on one of the beds surrounded by his wife Yolanda, Carl King, and several friends. It had taken fifteen stitches to close the gash beneath his lower lip. Another twelve had been sewn in place above his eye. Dried blood was visible from another wound on top of his head, and his lower lip was badly split. Now Mamby looked questioningly at the gentle man standing above him—Dr. Edwin Campbell, 65 years old, a "fight doctor" for 30 years.

The fighter's symptoms were not good—vomiting, dizziness, overall weakness, diarrhea, all consistent with a cerebral edema. Working swiftly, Campbell took a pencil-thin flashlight and looked into Mamby's eyes. Both pupils were equal in size, with no sign of constriction or enlargement.

"All right, now follow my finger from side to side."

The fighter did as instructed. Then Campbell put his hands on Mamby's knees, and told him to lift his legs. The fighter complied.

"What's your name?"

"Saoul Mamby."

"When did you first win the WBC title?"

"1980, in Korea."

"Do you recall ever having fought in Thailand?"

Mamby nodded.

"And what did we do together before that?"

"I came to your office for a complete physical."

The answers were clear, with no hint of confusion or personality disorder. Campbell reached down and put two fingers over the radial artery on the fighter's right hand. Mamby's pulse rate was sixty beats per minute, normal for a professional fighter.

"You'll be okay," Campbell told him. "What you're experiencing now is extreme fatigue and the results of dehydration. You can't lose a quart of perspiration like you did this afternoon and put it all back at one time without overloading the gastrointestinal system. There's no indication of more serious damage."

As Campbell was talking, Mike Jones entered the room. Somewhat awkwardly, he came over to the bed, leaned down, and offered Mamby his hand.

"You're a courageous fighter. Billy learned a lot from you this afternoon."

"I gained a lot of respect for Billy," Mamby answered. "He's strong. He's getting better as a fighter." Then Mamby smiled. "This is some way to make a living, isn't it?"

Mike left. The fighter watched him go, then shook his head. "Damn! I saw the openings. I saw mistakes Costello was making in the ring, and I couldn't capitalize on them. My mind told me what things to do, but my reflexes just wouldn't do them."

"You won the last round," someone suggested. "Fifteen rounds, maybe it would have been a different story."

Mamby stared incredulously at the speaker. "Not today," he answered. "Billy beat me. All these years, I never got knocked down—not by Duran, not by Cervantes, and not now by Costello.

But I never went through this before. I've never been hurt like this in the ring."

"You'll be all right," his wife said softly. "And what people will remember is, Saoul Mamby gave Billy Costello a good fight. Saoul Mamby made it rough for an undefeated champion."

Mamby smiled. "Yeah, I guess that's right. People will be calling for me to fill in as an opponent all over the world. I can still beat a lot of guys, but if I can't be champion, what's the use?"

"You've been a world champion. Now you've got to find another goal. You're still a young man."

Mamby smiled again. "I guess so; but it won't be the same. Remember the night I won the title in Korea, with thousands of fans screaming for the other guy? They gave me that big championship trophy, and I had to take it apart to fit it in my suitcase to bring it home. And when we got home, I was exhausted. But before we went to sleep, I stayed up all night putting the damn trophy together again." His voice weakened. "I'll miss it. I love boxing. Everything passed too soon."

* * *

Down in the hotel bar, Mike Jones was on his second beer when Dr. Campbell returned from Mamby's room.

"How is he?" Mike asked.

"He'll be all right. He got beaten pretty badly, but he'll be okay. If not tomorrow, the day after."

One of the locals, who'd had too much to drink, moved to a stool nearby. "I guess that's it for Saoul Mamby," he said with a grin.

Mike ignored him.

"Billy really kicked the shit out of him."

Mike took another sip of beer. "Don't say that. Saoul Mamby put up one of the most courageous fights I've ever seen. He pushed himself beyond what any normal person could do. He wouldn't quit, even when he was being battered and had no chance to win. Saoul Mamby, for your information, is a professional fighter."

Author's Note

The reconstruction of events is often diffi-
cult, and this is particularly true in the world of boxing, where
it's hard to separate fact from fiction and reality from myth.
Still, I'm confident that *The Black Lights* is an honest portrayal
of the sport and business of professional boxing as they exist
today. Where conversations and other statements are included
in quotation marks, they are the result of my own personal observation, verbatim transcripts, or a reconstruction based on the
memory of one or more participants to a particular conversation.
On occasion I have joined separate quotations from the same
speaker to facilitate reporting on a particular topic or event.
I'm confident that in doing so I've done nothing to compromise
the fairness of the book. At various junctures in the manuscript,
unflattering opinions about individuals are expressed. I would
like to caution the reader that these are matters of opinion, not
necessarily fact, and I do not agree with every statement reported. Rather, I have incorporated as many divergent views
as possible in the belief that readers should be allowed to make
their own judgments.

As always, I'm deeply indebted to a wide range of family
members and friends for their support. I also owe special thanks
to the following members of the boxing community, listed alpha-
betically, who have given generously of their time and knowledge: Muhammad Ali, Vito Antuofermo, Ray Arcel, Teddy Atlas,
Ira Becker, Tyrell Biggs, Johnny Bos, John Branca, Mark Breland,

THE BLACK LIGHTS

Teddy Brenner, Mike Burks, Bob Busse, Spider Bynum, Edwin Campbell, Al Certo, Gil Clancy, Mike Cohen, John Condon, Gerry Cooney, Howard Cosell, Steve Crossen, Cus D'Amato, Leroy Diggs, Mickey Duff, Angelo Dundee, Duke Durden, Lou Duva, Steve Farhood, Lou Filippo, Frank Folk, Joe Frazier, Eddie Futch, Bill Gallo, Rich Giachetti, Jimmy Glenn, Murray Goodman, Randy Gordon, Emile Griffith, Marvin Hagler, Leroy Haley, Mustafa Hamsho, Thomas Hearns, Larry Holmes, Evander Holyfield, Bob Iger, Mike Katz, Carl King, Stuart Kirschenbaum, Marvin Kohn, Sugar Ray Leonard, Butch Lewis, Panama Lewis, Steve Lott, Saoul Mamby, Ray Mancini, Jack McCallum, Arthur Mercante, Davey Moore, William Nack, Dave Odem, Terry O'Neil, Randy Neumann, Floyd Patterson, Dave Pearl, Tony Perez, Bill Prezant, Pat Putnam, Sugar Ray Robinson, Edwin Rosario, Mike Rosario, Tim Ryan, Ed Schuyler, Mort Sharnik, Peyton Sher, Manny Siaca, Michael Spinks, Ron Stevens, Emanuel Steward, Bert Sugar, Jose Sulaiman, Pinklon Thomas, Jose Torres, Alex Wallau, Harold Weston, Bruce Williams, Dave Wolf.

This list does not include Billy Costello, Mike Jones, Victor Valle, their friends and members of their families, all of whom have been a source of information, inspiration, and friendship. Also omitted are Don King and Bob Arum who were unwilling to grant me formal interviews. However, during the course of my research I was able to observe and talk with both men on a number of occasions. For example, I was in Don King's office with Mike Jones and Gil Clancy throughout the climactic events of October 29, 1984.

Last, I owe special thanks to three people. Jim Jacobs introduced me to the world of professional boxing. He's one of the most honest, able, unique individuals I've ever known, and it's a privilege to be his friend. Bill Cayton, Jim's partner, is equally special, and has been just as generous in his support. Bruce Sloman has shared my writing and been my friend for years. My thanks to them and to all the others who made this book possible.

Afterword: A Remembrance of Mike Jones—June 28, 1990

I met Mike Jones in 1984. I was researching this book and thought it would be a good idea to interview Gerry Cooney. Mike, who was Cooney's co-manager, set it up; and Cooney turned out to be a less-than-spectacular person. But along the way, something wonderful happened. I got to know Mike, who became my guide through the Byzantine world of professional boxing.

Ultimately, the book focused on Mike, Billy Costello (who was Mike's only world champion), and Billy's trainer, Victor Valle. But by then, Mike wasn't just someone I was writing about. He was my friend. We talked on the phone four times a week for the better part of six years. This past January, he told me he was suffering from multiple myeloma. The disease isn't curable. Some people live with it for a dozen years. The statistical average is two to five.

Mike's doctor told him, "It helps to be lucky." Mike wasn't. Six months after the disease was diagnosed, he died at age fifty-five.

Mike's skill as a manager is a matter of record. In addition to his success with Billy Costello, he guided Howard Davis, Gerry Cooney, Wilford Scypion, and Ronnie Harris to world-title bouts. When he died, he and Jim Fennell were co-managing Glenwood Brown, Alex Stewart, and Jade Scott—all fighters with world-class potential. But what always impressed me most about Mike as a manager was the way he blended skill with compassion. He looked after his fighters, physically and financially. And beyond that, he was concerned for the welfare of everyone in the ring.

Once, Mike refused to use the only sparring partner in Billy Costello's camp because the sparring partner had recently been knocked unconscious. Another time, he dismissed a Gerry Cooney sparring partner because the fighter suffered from impaired vision in one eye. Neither of those acts might seem like much. But in the world of boxing, where sparring partners are treated like dead meat and interruptions in training are avoided at all costs, Mike's decency ran against the grain. And, in the end, even when Cooney turned against him and sought to break their managerial contract, Mike never stopped rooting for him. I was sitting with Mike the night Cooney was knocked out by Michael Spinks. Mike looked like a little boy trying hard not to cry.

After I finished writing about boxing, I went on to other things. Then, in 1988, Muhammad Ali asked if I'd be interested in authoring the definitive Ali biography, and I returned to the sweet science. As might be expected, Ali has kept me busy over the past two years, but Mike and I continued our friendship. Several weeks before he died, reflecting on the fact that my only boxing books were about him and Ali, Mike said with satisfaction, "I guess I'm in pretty good company."

"So is Ali," I told him.

And I meant it.

Mike loved boxing. In a business where most people have only allies, he had friends. His word was good; he never walked out on a deal. Now that he's gone, I feel sorry for his wife Stella, his children, his friends, his fighters, and everyone else who loved and relied upon him. But most of all, I feel sorry for Mike. He led a good life, and it should have been longer. But if there's a better world, I'm sure he's there.